The Zsh Handbook

Practical Solutions for Shell Scripting and Workflow Automation

Richard Johnson

Published by Wang Press

For permissions and other inquiries, write to:
P.O. Box 3132, Framingham, MA 01701, USA

Contents

1 Introduction: Zsh and Shell Scripting   **9**

    1.1   Exploring the Shell Environment   9

    1.2   Getting Started with Zsh   13

    1.3   Understanding Zsh Shell Features   18

    1.4   Basics of Shell Scripting   23

    1.5   Zsh vs Other Shells   28

2 In-depth: Setting Up and Configuring Zsh   **35**

    2.1   Installing Zsh on Different Platforms   35

    2.2   Making Zsh the Default Shell   39

    2.3   Configuring the .zshrc File   43

    2.4   Customizing Zsh Prompt   48

    2.5   Using Oh My Zsh Framework   53

    2.6   Managing Plugins and Themes   58

3 Basic Zsh Commands and Operations   **63**

    3.1   Navigating the File System   63

    3.2   Managing Files and Directories   67

    3.3   File Permissions and Ownership   70

3.4 Handling Text Files 73

3.5 Using Command-Line Editors 77

3.6 Zsh Command History and Shortcuts 81

4 Advanced Zsh Features and Customization   85

4.1 Auto-completion and Auto-suggestions 85

4.2 Globbing and Pattern Matching 89

4.3 Using Aliases and Functions 92

4.4 Scripting with Zsh Arrays 95

4.5 Customizing Key Bindings 98

4.6 Environment Variables Management 101

5 Scripting with Zsh: Control Structures   105

5.1 Using Conditional Statements 105

5.2 Looping with for and while 110

5.3 Case Statements for Pattern Matching 113

5.4 Functions and Script Modularity 118

5.5 Error Handling with Exit Codes 122

5.6 Selective Execution with eval and exec 126

6 Working with Files and Directories in Zsh   131

6.1 Manipulating Files with Zsh 131

6.2 Directory Management Techniques 136

6.3 Working with Hidden Files 140

6.4 Batch Processing of Files 144

6.5 Symlinks and Hardlinks 149

6.6 Zsh and File Compression 154

7 Zsh and Workflow Automation   159

7.1 Automating Tasks with Scripts 159

7.2 Using Cron Jobs for Scheduling 165

7.3 Background and Scheduled Execution 170

7.4 Integrating Zsh with Other Tools 176

7.5 Parameter Expansion for Efficiency 183

7.6 Streamlining Workflows with Functions 188

8 Error Handling and Debugging in Zsh Scripts　　**197**

8.1 Understanding Exit Status and Codes 197

8.2 Debugging Techniques with set Options 203

8.3 Handling Errors Gracefully 209

8.4 Using Traps for Exception Handling 214

8.5 Logging and Output Redirection 221

8.6 Testing and Validation of Scripts 226

9 Enhancing Productivity with Zsh Plugins　　**233**

9.1 Overview of Zsh Plugin Ecosystem 233

9.2 Installing and Managing Plugins with Oh My Zsh . . . 237

9.3 Essential Productivity Plugins 241

9.4 Customizing Plugin Configuration 245

9.5 Creating Your Own Zsh Plugins 249

9.6 Troubleshooting Common Plugin Issues 253

10 Best Practices and Common Pitfalls in Zsh Scripting 259

10.1 Writing Readable and Maintainable Scripts 259

10.2 Optimizing Script Performance 263

10.3 Security Considerations in Scripting 267

10.4 Avoiding Common Scripting Mistakes 271

10.5 Version Control for Scripts 275

10.6 Adhering to Shell Script Standards 280

Introduction

In the world of computing, the command-line interface is an environment that often demands sophisticated operation and efficiency. The Z shell, or Zsh, is one of those robust command-line interfaces that stands out due to its rich feature set, making it a preferred choice for many developers and system administrators. Zsh is not just a shell but a powerful scripting environment that can significantly enhance productivity through automation and customization.

The primary objective of this handbook is to familiarize readers with the practical applications of Zsh, targeting both novice users and those who seek to expand their knowledge. This book has been structured to convey essential concepts and provide illustrative examples that will enable users to effectively harness the potential of Zsh in their daily tasks.

Initially, the text introduces Zsh as an alternative to other popular shells, outlining its advantages and distinct features. The process of setting up and configuring Zsh to suit individual preferences is discussed in detail, allowing users to tailor the shell environment to their specific needs. Furthermore, fundamental Zsh commands and operations are explored, providing readers with a solid foundation in basic shell functionality.

As the reader progresses, the book delves deeper into advanced features and customization options offered by Zsh. This segment is crucial for users wishing to exploit the full capabilities of the shell environment. These advanced topics guide readers in creating efficient scripts through the use of control structures, as well as the management of files and directories within the shell.

The later chapters focus on how Zsh can be utilized for workflow automation, error handling, and debugging, all of which are indispensable skills in software development and system administration. Attention is also given to enhancing productivity through the use of Zsh plugins, offering a glimpse into the extensive plugin ecosystem that can be leveraged to optimize various tasks.

In crafting this book, we've incorporated best practices and commonly encountered challenges in Zsh scripting to equip the reader with knowledge and foresight, ensuring they can produce reliable and effective scripts.

Comprehensively, this handbook is designed not only as an instructional manual but as a resource for continuous learning and improvement in Zsh usage. By concluding with a chapter on best practices, readers are encouraged to adopt a methodical approach to scripting that emphasizes maintainability, security, and performance.

Whether you are embarking on your first venture into shell scripting or seeking to deepen your proficiency, "The Zsh Handbook: Practical Solutions for Shell Scripting and Workflow Automation" aims to be a dependable companion in mastering the art of Zsh.

Chapter 1

Introduction: Zsh and Shell Scripting

Zsh, an extended Unix shell with an array of sophisticated features, serves as a powerful tool for both interactive use and scripting. This chapter guides readers through understanding the shell environment, setting up Zsh, and leveraging its unique functionalities. By focusing on differences between Zsh and other shells such as Bash, it emphasizes the advantages Zsh offers, setting the foundation for employing shell scripting in automating tasks and enhancing user productivity.

1.1 Exploring the Shell Environment

In computer science, the shell serves as a critical component of the operating system. It acts as an interface between the user and the computer, interpreting user commands and initiating the appropriate processes. Understanding the shell environment is essential for users who wish to harness the full potential of their machine. This section provides an in-depth look into what a shell is, its central role in the operating system, and contrasts between various shells like Bash and

Zsh.

Fundamentally, a shell is a command-line interpreter that allows users to convey instructions to the computer in a human-readable format. The process involves accepting user input, processing it, executing commands, and displaying the output. In operating systems like Unix and Unix-like systems (including Linux), the shell provides an interface that is primarily text-based, although graphical shells also exist. By facilitating direct interaction with the operating system's services and utilities, shells are instrumental in executing and automating tasks efficiently.

To better understand the function of a shell, consider its operational environment. The shell environment encapsulates the set of resources and configurations that the shell relies upon to function. This includes environment variables, user profiles, configuration files, and settings that determine command behavior. Environment variables, for instance, provide the shell with critical data such as the system path, user home directory, and other system-wide or session-specific information. These variables can be modified to tailor the shell's behavior to meet the user's specific requirements.

A typical command cycle in the shell environment involves the following stages:

1. **Input:** The user types a command into the shell. This command often consists of a program name, options, and arguments.

2. **Interpretation:** The shell parses the command, separating it into components that it understands. For instance, in a command like ls -l /home, ls is the command, -l is an option, and /home is an argument.

3. **Execution:** The shell locates the program corresponding to the command, either from in-built commands or external binaries, and executes it. For instance, ls might translate to running the list directory utility.

4. **Output:** The shell presents the return value or output to the user, which may include file listings, error messages, or other program-specific information.

Beyond these fundamental operations, shells offer a comprehensive suite of features, including pattern matching, command substitution, and redirection. These features empower users to perform complex tasks through simple command sequences. Pattern matching, or "globbing," is the practice of using wildcards to represent groups of filenames or commands, facilitating batch processing of files. Command substitution allows the output of one command to become the input of another, enhancing scripting capabilities. Redirection guides the input and output of commands to and from files, enabling data to be handled flexibly.

There are numerous types of shells available, each varying in features and intended use cases. Some of the most prominent ones include the Bourne Shell (sh), the Bourne-Again Shell (Bash), the C Shell (csh), the KornShell (ksh), and the Z Shell (Zsh). While each shell executes core functions similarly, they differ in syntax, scripting capabilities, customization options, and user experiences. Notably, the evolution of shells over time has seen them incorporate distinct advanced features to enhance usability and script automation.

The Bourne Shell (sh), developed by Stephen Bourne at Bell Labs, was one of the original Unix shells. It laid the foundation for all subsequent Unix shells and remains an essential part of many Unix systems. Its minimalistic design focuses on fundamental command execution, making it highly compatible across systems. However, it lacks advanced interactive features and scripting enhancements which were subsequently introduced in later shells.

Bash, an acronym for Bourne-Again Shell, emerged as an advancement over the original Bourne shell. It introduces additional functionality including increased scripting capability, command-line editing, command history, and improved error-checking while maintaining POSIX compliance. Bash's popularity stems from its balance between robust scripting features and user-friendly interaction.

On the other hand, Zsh or the Z Shell, is renowned for its extensibility and interactivity. It incorporates features similar to Bash but further enhances them, offering better user configuration, extended pattern matching capabilities, and built-in spelling correction. Zsh is particularly appealing to users seeking a customizable and dynamic shell experience.

11

Coding within the shell environment is predominantly realized via shell scripting. Shell scripts are text files containing a series of commands anticipated to be executed by the shell. They serve as powerful tools to automate complex and repetitive tasks, thereby increasing efficiency. An essential characteristic of shell scripts is that they are executed in a non-interactive shell, which implies they run without user intervention once initiated. This capability is crucial for administrative tasks, such as system monitoring and backups, where automation is vital.

Consider the following example of a simple Bash script designed to back up user directory files. This example demonstrates fundamental shell scripting concepts, illustrating variable usage, command execution, and conditional statements.

```
#!/bin/bash

# Define variables
SOURCE_DIR="/home/user/documents"
BACKUP_DIR="/home/user/documents_backup"
DATE=$(date +%Y%m%d)

# Create backup directory if it doesn't exist
if [ ! -d "$BACKUP_DIR" ]; then
    mkdir -p "$BACKUP_DIR"
    echo "Backup directory created."
fi

# Backup files
cp -r "$SOURCE_DIR"/* "$BACKUP_DIR"
echo "Backup completed on $DATE."
```

This script initiates by defining key variables: the directory to back up, the backup location, and the current date. It checks if the backup directory exists; if not, it is created. The script subsequently copies all files from the source directory to the backup directory, efficiently automating directory backups.

Shell scripting facilitates such automation for various system tasks. It conserves time and effort by reducing manual oversight, proving indispensable for system administrators and developers alike. Moreover, as operating systems evolve, the scope of shell scripting expands, integrating modern programming paradigms such as loops, conditionals, and functions to introduce additional logic and control flow.

A comparison between different shells underscores the distinct functionalities that make each one suitable for particular scenarios. Bash and Zsh, for instance, have garnered substantial followings due to their extensive features and active community support. While Bash is prevalent for its comprehensive documentation and widespread use in many Unix-based systems, Zsh appeals to users who favor more flexibility and an enriched interactive experience.

Zsh's standout features include theme and plugin support via frameworks like Oh My Zsh, advanced globbing mechanisms, and more extensive customization possibilities. While Bash scripts often translate directly to Zsh with minimal modification, Zsh provides nuanced enhancements such as native file completion and default shell options that streamline the user experience.

Given the palpable differences in design philosophy and feature set, the choice between shells impacts the manner in which users interact with their systems and develop scripts. An informed decision requires a detailed understanding of the operating environment, anticipated workflows, and user preferences. Users must assess each shell's toolset, leveraging the most relevant functionalities to optimize efficiency and productivity.

Consequently, a comprehensive study of the shell environment is foundational for adept system navigation and proficient command-line interaction. The knowledge of how different shells interpret commands and scripts not only enhances personal workflow but also fosters a deeper appreciation for the operating system's architectural paradigms. As users evolve in their command-line proficiency, the shell becomes an integral partner in their exploration of computational capabilities. By optimizing shell usage, users harness the computational power available to them, propelling their productivity to new heights.

1.2 Getting Started with Zsh

The Z Shell (Zsh) is a powerful and highly customizable shell that has gained popularity among developers and system administrators for its enhanced user interface and extensive features. Installing and configuring Zsh is a straightforward process that empowers users to take full advantage of its capabilities. This section provides a comprehensive guide to installing Zsh on different platforms and setting it as the default shell, with a focus on providing clear instructions for a seamless transition from other shells.

Zsh is available across common operating systems such as Linux, macOS, and Windows (via the Windows Subsystem for Linux). For users to unlock Zsh's full potential, understanding the installation procedures for each platform is crucial.

Installing Zsh on Linux:

Most modern Linux distributions provide Zsh in their package repositories. Thus, installation can typically be performed using the distribution's package manager. Below are detailed instructions for installing Zsh on various popular Linux distributions:

- **Debian-based systems (e.g., Ubuntu):** Open a terminal window and execute the following commands:

```
sudo apt update
sudo apt install zsh
```

- **Red Hat-based systems (e.g., Fedora, CentOS):** For Fedora, use the command:

```
sudo dnf install zsh
```

  For CentOS, use:

```
sudo yum install zsh
```

- **Arch Linux:** Execute the following command:

```
sudo pacman -S zsh
```

Installing Zsh on macOS:

macOS comes with Zsh pre-installed as of macOS Catalina. However, users might wish to install the latest version for access to the most recent features and improvements. To do this, use Homebrew, a popular package manager for macOS:

```
brew install zsh
```

If Homebrew is not installed, it can be installed by executing the following command in the terminal:

```
/bin/bash -c "$(curl -fsSL https://raw.githubusercontent.com/Homebrew/install/
    HEAD/install.sh)"
```

Installing Zsh on Windows:

On Windows, users can run Zsh through the Windows Subsystem for Linux (WSL). First, set up WSL by enabling it in the Windows features and installing a Linux distribution from the Microsoft Store. Once WSL is configured and a Linux terminal is open, install Zsh through the package manager (as per the chosen Linux distribution's procedures above).

Making Zsh the Default Shell:

Once Zsh is installed, users typically wish to set it as their default shell. This ensures that newly opened terminal sessions default to Zsh. Follow the below steps according to the operating system in use:

- **Linux and macOS:** Change the default shell to Zsh by running the following command in the terminal:

  ```
  chsh -s $(which zsh)
  ```

  Users might need to log out and log back in, or restart their terminal emulator for the change to take effect.

- **Windows (WSL):** To change the default shell to Zsh in WSL, you may need to update the .bashrc or .profile file with the following line:

  ```
  exec zsh
  ```

First-time Zsh Configuration:

Upon running Zsh for the first time, users are greeted with an initial configuration wizard that allows them to configure some basic settings interactively. This provides an excellent starting point for customization.

Users can follow the set of prompts to configure options like history management, prompt settings, and more. While experienced users

15

might prefer to skip this guided setup and manually edit the configuration file, it is beneficial for newcomers.

By default, Zsh loads configurations from the .zshrc file located in the user's home directory. This file governs shell behavior and can be personalized according to user preferences. Typical customizations include setting aliases, environment variables, paths, and loading functions or plugins.

Here's an example of a simple .zshrc file:

```
# Set the prompt theme
PROMPT='%n@%m:%~$ '

# Enable command auto-correction
setopt CORRECT

# Add custom directory to PATH
export PATH="$HOME/bin:$PATH"

# Create aliases
alias ll='ls -la'
alias gs='git status'

# Enable history sharing
setopt SHARE_HISTORY

# Load custom scripts or plugins
source ~/.custom_script.sh
```

In this sample, the prompt is configured to display the username, hostname, and current working directory. Command auto-correction is enabled for convenience, custom paths and aliases are defined, history options are set, and external scripts are sourced.

Enhancing Zsh with Plugins and Themes:

One of Zsh's most distinguishing features is its extensibility through plugins and themes. Frameworks such as Oh My Zsh simplify managing plugins and themes, offering a wide range of bundled features and easy-to-switch themes.

To install Oh My Zsh, first ensure Git is installed, then run:

```
sh -c "$(curl -fsSL https://raw.githubusercontent.com/ohmyzsh/ohmyzsh/master/tools
    /install.sh)"
```

Oh My Zsh can be configured by editing the .zshrc file. Users will find a variety of themes and plugins to enhance productivity and aesthetics.

For example, activating the git plugin and setting the agnoster theme can be done as follows:

```
# Set the theme for Oh My Zsh
ZSH_THEME="agnoster"

# Activate plugins
plugins=(git)

# Source Oh My Zsh
source $ZSH/oh-my-zsh.sh
```

Each plugin and theme introduces unique utilities or changes the shell's appearance, aiding efficiency and user satisfaction.

Apart from Oh My Zsh, other frameworks such as Prezto and Antigen also support Zsh. They provide alternative approaches to extend Zsh's capabilities through different methodologies and design philosophies.

Advanced Customization with Zsh:

Advanced users might delve deeper into Zsh's array of options and settings to tailor it carefully to their workflows. Some advanced features include:

- **Advanced Pattern Matching:** Zsh supports sophisticated pattern matching syntax, allowing fine control over command execution and file manipulation activities. Patterns such as **/*.txt allow for recursive directory matching.

- **Shell Functions:** Users can define shell functions for repeated command sequences, which increases efficiency by replacing cumbersome command pipelines with succinct function calls.

- **Associative Arrays:** Useful in scripts, associative arrays are a collection of key-value pairs, allowing complex data structures to be manipulated with ease.

As users become more comfortable with Zsh, exploring and incorporating these advanced features into their daily tasks unlocks even greater flexibility and control.

The journey of transitioning to and working with Zsh involves exploring its vast potential to achieve optimal productivity. Through straightforward installation, thoughtful customization, and methodical enhancement with plugins and themes, Zsh presents itself as a formidable tool for anyone engaging deeply with the command-line interface. As users grow proficient in leveraging Zsh's capabilities, they enable themselves to interface with their operating system in a way that is both powerful and personal. While the learning curve may seem steep initially, the time investment pays dividends by improving command-line efficiency and task automation beyond what many traditional shells offer. The versatility and potential offered by Zsh make it a prized asset for developers, system administrators, and command-line aficionados alike.

1.3 Understanding Zsh Shell Features

The Z Shell (Zsh) is acclaimed for its comprehensive array of features that significantly enhance the command-line experience. These features distinguish Zsh from other shells, offering users advanced capabilities for both interactive use and scripting. In this section, we examine the key features that make Zsh a preferred choice among shell enthusiasts, delving into their applications and benefits with concrete examples.

Zsh is a highly customizable shell that extends many of the functionalities found in other shells, such as Bash, while introducing several unique features. These enhancements make Zsh a potent tool, thus understanding its features allows users to customize and optimize their workflow effectively.

- **1. Command-Line Editing**

    Zsh provides sophisticated command-line editing capabilities, allowing users to navigate and manipulate commands with ease. It supports both Emacs and Vi modes, enabling users to choose their preferred editing style. By default, Zsh uses Emacs mode, but this can be changed to Vi mode by adding the following line to the .zshrc file:

    ```
    bindkey -v
    ```

18

In Vi mode, users can leverage keybindings similar to the Vi editor to perform operations like navigation, insertion, and deletion directly in the command line.

- **2. Command Completion**

Command completion is a distinguishing feature of Zsh, enhancing user efficiency by predicting and completing commands, options, and file names. Unlike other shells, Zsh supports context-sensitive command completion, adapting completions based on the type of command and the arguments it accepts.

Adding the following to .zshrc enables the robust auto-completion system:

```
autoload -U compinit
compinit
```

For example, when typing a command that requires a filename, Zsh can automatically suggest and complete file paths. This is especially useful when dealing with complex commands or large directories.

- **3. Globbing and Pattern Matching**

Zsh excels at sophisticated pattern matching, referred to as "globbing," allowing users to craft complex file expressions with ease. The extended globbing capabilities in Zsh surpass those available in traditional shells by providing additional flags and qualifiers.

For instance, recursive globbing in directories is facilitated using the pattern '**':

```
# List all .txt files in the current directory and subdirectories
ls **/*.txt
```

Additionally, Zsh supports numeric qualifiers and conditions, allowing users to filter files based on size, modification time, etc.:

```
# List files over 100 kilobytes
ls *(Lk+100)

# List files modified within the last seven days
ls *(m-7)
```

- **4. History Mechanism**

19

Zsh's history mechanism provides advanced features for recalling and manipulating previously executed commands. It supports features like shared history across multiple shell sessions, ensuring command logs are consistent across different terminal instances.

The following options can be set in .zshrc to enhance history capabilities:

```
setopt SHARE_HISTORY
setopt HIST_IGNORE_DUPS
setopt HIST_FIND_NO_DUPS
```

Zsh also allows for incremental search through history using the 'Ctrl + R' keybinding, where typing part of a previous command filters results, making it easier to locate and execute past commands efficiently.

- **5. Prompt Customization**

A significant appeal of Zsh lies in its extensively customizable prompts. Users can personalize their prompts using a wide selection of variables and color codes, providing visual cues and relevant information at a glance.

The prompt can be customized by editing the PS1 variable in the .zshrc file. Here's an example prompt configuration:

```
# Display username, hostname, and current working directory
PS1="%n@%m:%~%# "

# Use colors to distinguish parts of the prompt
PS1="%F{cyan}%n%f@%F{green}%m%f:%F{yellow}%~%f%# "
```

In this configuration, '

- **6. Plugin and Theme Support**

Zsh supports a rich plugin ecosystem, allowing users to extend functionality beyond its core capabilities. Frameworks like Oh My Zsh, Prezto, and Antigen simplify plugin and theme management, enabling easy installation and configuration.

Plugins provide various utilities, such as enhanced completion for specific commands or Git integration. Themes adjust the prompt's aesthetic, making the shell visually appealing and informative.

To activate plugins and themes using Oh My Zsh, users should modify their .zshrc as follows:

```
ZSH_THEME="robbyrussell"
plugins=(git docker)

source $ZSH/oh-my-zsh.sh
```

- **7. Session Control and Job Management**

Zsh offers comprehensive session control and job management utilities. It allows for backgrounding and foregrounding jobs, as well as managing job execution order and priority.

Users can utilize commands like 'bg', 'fg', and 'jobs' to manage current processes and suspend or resume job execution. Here's a simple demonstration:

```
# Start a long-running process in the background
sleep 100 &

# List current jobs
jobs

# Bring job to the foreground
fg %1

# Suspend a foreground job with Ctrl + Z
```

- **8. Associative Arrays and Advanced Scripting Features**

For script developers, Zsh supports associative arrays, offering a data structure to store collections of key-value pairs, augmenting script efficiency.

```
# Define an associative array
typeset -A colors
colors[red]="#FF0000"
colors[green]="#00FF00"

# Access array elements
echo "Red color code is ${colors[red]}"
```

Furthermore, Zsh's extended syntax offers robust constructs for elegantly handling loops, conditionals, and function definitions, promoting cleaner and more maintainable script code.

- **9. Command Correction**

21

A convenient feature for reducing typographical errors is Zsh's command correction. When enabled, Zsh can detect and suggest corrections for mistyped commands before execution, saving time and reducing frustration.

This feature can be activated by adding the following to the .zshrc:

```
setopt CORRECT
```

- **10. Path Expansion and Replacement**

  Zsh allows seamless navigation and manipulation of directory paths with its advanced path expansion and replacement features. It facilitates path substitutions, cutting down on typing effort, and enhancing efficiency.

  For example, users can quickly change directories using shorthand notations or substitute parts of paths in commands:

```
# Short notation to switch to recent directories
cd -

# Substitute directories in paths
echo ~/path/to/file(//home/otheruser)
```

- **11. Parallel Execution**

  Zsh can execute multiple commands in parallel using the 'zargs' command, akin to 'xargs' but with Zsh's extended capabilities. This feature simplifies parallel execution of commands for batch processing tasks.

With its multitude of sophisticated features, Zsh presents a compelling option for users seeking a powerful and customizable command-line experience. Its diverse capabilities range from intuitive interactive features for everyday terminal users to advanced scripting tools for developers and system administrators.

In essence, mastering Zsh involves understanding both its constituent components and how they interrelate to deliver a seamless, productive environment. As one delves deeper into Zsh's myriad features, they discover a shell that not only meets their needs but also evolves with them, supporting increasingly complex requirements through its inherent flexibility and extensibility.

The introduction to these core features serves as a stepping stone into the universe of Zsh, providing users with the foundational knowledge to fully exploit this advanced shell. By continually experimenting and tailoring Zsh to their specific use cases, users can significantly enhance their command-line productivity and streamline their workflow in exciting and innovative ways.

1.4 Basics of Shell Scripting

Shell scripting is a fundamental skill in computer science that allows users to automate repetitive tasks, manage system operations, and compose more complex computational workflows. This section delves into the core concepts of shell scripting, providing a foundation for effectively writing and executing scripts, emphasizing syntax, constructs, and typical usage scenarios.

Shell scripts are text files that contain a sequence of commands intended for execution by the shell. They can range from simple command sequences to sophisticated programs comprising functions, conditionals, loops, and more. By automating mundane tasks, shell scripts enhance system efficiency and user productivity, particularly in Linux and Unix-like environments where command-line interfaces are standard.

1. Shell Script Structure

At its core, a shell script is a series of commands listed in plain text. A shell script typically starts with a shebang (#!) line that indicates the interpreter to be used for executing the script. While the shebang is often followed by /bin/sh (for the Bourne shell) for portability, specifying /bin/zsh or /bin/bash is common when leveraging specific features of Zsh or Bash.

A minimalist shell script looks like the following:

```
#!/bin/zsh

# Display "Hello, World!"
echo "Hello, World!"
```

After the shebang, the script contains shell commands and comments

23

(preceded by #), enhancing readability and maintainability.

2. Variables and Data Types

Variables in shell scripts are used to store and manipulate data. Variable names are usually composed of alphanumeric characters and underscores, and assignment is done without spaces. Shell scripts do not require explicit data type declarations, as variables are treated as strings by default.

Consider the following example:

```
#!/bin/zsh

# Assign values to variables
name="Alice"
age=30

# Display variable values
echo "Name: $name"
echo "Age: $age"
```

Environment variables can be exported across sessions using the export keyword. These variables become available to any subsequent shell or command invoked from the script.

```
export PATH="$PATH:/usr/local/bin"
```

3. User Input

Shell scripts can interact with users by accepting input. The read command is employed to prompt users for input, assigning the input to specified variables:

```
#!/bin/zsh

# Prompt for user input
read -p "Enter your name: " user_name

# Use the input in a greeting message
echo "Hello, $user_name!"
```

This script asks users for their name and then personalizes a greeting message accordingly.

4. Command Substitution and Arithmetic

Command substitution allows the output of a command to be captured and used as a variable's value or part of an expression. This is typically achieved using `command` or $ (command) syntax.

```
#!/bin/zsh

# Capture system date
current_date=$(date +"%Y-%m-%d")

# Display the date
echo "Today's date is $current_date"
```

Arithmetic operations within shell scripts are enabled by command substitution with $(()), allowing basic calculations.

```
#!/bin/zsh

# Calculate the sum of two numbers
sum=$((3 + 5))

# Display the result
echo "The sum is $sum"
```

5. Conditional Statements

Conditional statements direct the flow of execution, allowing scripts to make decisions based on comparisons and evaluations. Commonly used conditional constructs include if, then, else, elif, and fi.

```
#!/bin/zsh

# Compare numbers
num1=5
num2=10

if [ $num1 -lt $num2 ]; then
    echo "$num1 is less than $num2"
else
    echo "$num1 is not less than $num2"
fi
```

Additional operators for testing conditions include -eq, -ne, -gt, -ge, -lt, and -le for numerical comparisons, and =, != for string comparisons.

6. Loops

Loops support the execution of repetitive tasks within a script, iterating over sets of values or ranges. Zsh provides several looping constructs, including for, while, and until, each suited for different scenarios.

- **For Loop:**

  A for loop iterates over a list of predefined elements or generated

25

sets of data.

```
# Loop through a list of colors
for color in red blue green; do
    echo "Color: $color"
done
```

- **While Loop:**

  A while loop executes as long as the specified condition remains true.

```
# Countdown from 5 to 0
count=5
while [ $count -ge 0 ]; do
    echo "Count: $count"
    ((count--))
done
```

- **Until Loop:**

  An until loop is akin to a while loop but runs until a condition becomes true.

```
# Output numbers until reaching 3
num=0
until [ $num -eq 3 ]; do
    echo "Number: $num"
    ((num++))
done
```

7. Functions

Defining functions allows scripts to modularize code for reusability and clarity. Functions abstract execution blocks that can be invoked multiple times with arguments.

```
#!/bin/zsh

# Define a function to calculate square
function square {
    local num=$1
    echo $(( num * num ))
}

# Call the function
result=$(square 4)
echo "The square of 4 is $result"
```

Functions encapsulate logic, isolate functionality, and facilitate code reuse, enhancing script organization.

26

8. Exit Status and Error Handling

Every command and script in Unix-like systems returns an exit status, indicating success (0) or failure (non-zero). Scripts can capture this using the $? variable, enabling error handling and conditional action based on command success.

```zsh
#!/bin/zsh

# Example command
mkdir new_directory

# Check the exit status
if [ $? -eq 0 ]; then
    echo "Directory created successfully."
else
    echo "Failed to create directory."
fi
```

Handling errors and improper command execution proactively within scripts averts unintended consequences and enhances robustness.

9. Redirection and Pipelines

Redirection allows managing command input and output effectively, saving outputs to files or directing inputs from files. Standard output (>) and standard input (<) redirections enable easier data handling.

```zsh
#!/bin/zsh

# Redirect output of ls to a file
ls > file_list.txt

# Redirect input for a command
sort < file_list.txt > sorted_list.txt
```

Pipelines (|) concatenate multiple commands, passing the output of one command as the input to the next, simplifying complex processing sequences.

```zsh
#!/bin/zsh

# Combine commands into a pipeline
cat file.txt | grep "pattern" | sort
```

10. Practical Script Example

Here's a complete example incorporating the concepts discussed above—a script to back up a directory.

```
#!/bin/zsh

# Define source and backup directories
SOURCE_DIR="$HOME/documents"
BACKUP_DIR="$HOME/backup"
DATE=$(date +%Y%m%d)

# Create a dated backup directory
mkdir -p "$BACKUP_DIR/$DATE"

# Function to backup files
backup_files() {
    for file in "$SOURCE_DIR"/*; do
        cp "$file" "$BACKUP_DIR/$DATE"
        if [ $? -ne 0 ]; then
            echo "Failed to back up $file"
        else
            echo "$file backed up successfully."
        fi
    done
}

# Execute the backup function
backup_files

echo "Backup completed on $DATE."
```

This script demonstrates practices such as command substitution for date acquisition, loops for iterating over files, conditional checks for error handling, and user-friendly output.

As this section illustrates, basic shell scripting provides a crucial toolset for automating and streamlining tasks prevalent in computing environments. Mastery over scripting constructs, from basic command execution to advanced logic within functions, enables more efficient and effective system management and operation, diminishing manual effort and mistake potential while yielding consistent outcomes. Such proficiency, reinforced by systematic experimentation and iterative development, empowers users to tailor their computational interactions to their unique requirements, forging a more cohesive and productive digital workspace.

1.5 Zsh vs Other Shells

Zsh, short for Z Shell, stands out in the landscape of Unix shells due to its advanced features and customization options. In this section, we offer a detailed comparison between Zsh and other widely-used Unix shells such as Bash, Csh, and Fish. By evaluating each shell's features, capabilities, and intended use cases, users can make informed decisions about which shell best aligns with their workflow needs and personal preferences.

Unix shells serve as command-line interpreters, providing interfaces for running commands, scripting, and automating tasks. Each shell comes with its set of features, syntax peculiarities, and user experiences. Understanding these differences helps users leverage the strengths of a shell, whether for interactive use or script development.

1. Feature Comparison -

Zsh is renowned for its versatility and extensibility, accomplished through features like robust command-line editing, enhanced completion, globbing, and plugin and theme support. While many shells share basic functionalities, Zsh distinguishes itself with additional capabilities fit for both beginners and power users.

- **Bash (Bourne Again Shell):**

  Bash is arguably the most prevalent shell, featured in many Unix and Unix-like systems as the default shell. Its strength lies in its scripting capabilities and Bourne shell compatibility, making it an excellent fit for scripts standardized across systems.

  Bash excels at:

  1. **Script Portability**: Due to its widespread adoption, scripts written in Bash run reliably on different systems without modification.

  2. **Comprehensive Documentation**: Extensive tutorials and guides are available, facilitating learning and troubleshooting.

  However, Bash falls short compared to Zsh in aspects of interactive use, such as command completion and shortcut customization.

```
#!/bin/bash

# Define a variable
greeting="Hello, World"
```

```
# Display the greeting
echo $greeting
```

- **Csh (C Shell) and Tcsh:**

  Csh, along with its enhanced version Tcsh, offers syntax and interactive features inspired by the C programming language. It is appreciated for its history substitution and job control features.

  Csh is notable for:

  1. **C-Like Syntax**: Appeals to users with proficiency in C programming.
  2. **Interactive Features**: Csh improves user command-line efficiency with history mechanisms.

  However, its scripting syntax is less intuitive compared to alternatives like Bash and Zsh, making script readability and maintainability more challenging.

```
#!/bin/csh

# Set a variable
set greeting = "Hello, World"

# Print the variable
echo $greeting
```

- **Fish (Friendly Interactive Shell):**

  Fish aims to be user-friendly and provides a number of advanced, interactive features out of the box, such as syntax highlighting and autosuggestions.

  Fish's strengths include:

  1. **User-Friendly Defaults**: With syntax highlighting and autosuggestions, Fish reduces the need to customize configurations for everyday use.
  2. **Intuitive Syntax**: Fish syntax simplifies learning and lowers the barrier for creating simple scripts.

  Fish, however, lacks native scripting portability due to its distinct syntax, and its strict adherence to proprietary features can limit broader script compatibility.

30

```
#!/usr/bin/env fish

# Assign a variable
set greeting "Hello, World"

# Display the greeting
echo $greeting
```

2. Command-Line Editing and Completion -

Command-line editing and completion are pivotal for enhancing interactive use. Zsh excels in combining Emacs and Vi mode with programmable completion, offering extensive contextual suggestions.

In Zsh, command-line completion can be fine-tuned using commands to auto-load completions for specific programs or broaden completion contexts.

```
# Enable Zsh completion
autoload -U compinit
compinit

# Program-specific completion
autoload -U bashcompinit
bashcompinit
source /etc/bash_completion
```

3. Customization and Themes -

A defining feature of Zsh lies in its vast customization potential, particularly through plugins and themes. Frameworks like Oh My Zsh and Prezto simplify modifying the shell environment, enabling bespoke interface environments tailored to user requirements.

Themes alter the shell's appearance, improving clarity and distinguishing command segments with visual cues. Themes like 'agnoster' or 'robbyrussell' are popular among users for their aesthetics and utility.

```
ZSH_THEME="agnoster"
```

In contrast, Bash requires manual configuration for comparable customizations, and Csh lacks such an ecosystem, making Zsh favorable for users seeking personalized setups.

4. Scripting Capabilities and Syntax -

Zsh and Bash share similarities in scripting constructs, enabling com-

31

plex structures through parameters, loops, and conditionals. However, Zsh introduces additional elements like associative arrays and user-defined data structures, enabling more elegant code.

```
# Declare associative array
typeset -A colors
colors[blue]="#0000FF"
colors[red]="#FF0000"

# Access array elements
echo ${colors[blue]}
```

In Csh, syntax can be less intuitive for beginners, deterring its effectiveness in scripting for more extensive, modern computing needs.

Meanwhile, Fish's syntax lowers entry barriers for new users, yet its distinct structure limits compatibility with standard shell scripts, hindering widespread adoption in scripting environments beyond personal configuration.

5. Interoperability and Portability -

Bash's ubiquitous implementation guarantees high portability across Unix-like systems. It aligns with POSIX standards, thereby fostering compatibility in system administration and development scenarios.

Zsh, while not default on many systems, often requires minimal setup to operate effectively, thriving where user customization outweighs transportability concerns.

Fish, though fitting for customized personal setups, sacrifices portability for productivity-improving features, thus playing a supportive rather than primary role in multi-device environments.

6. Advanced Features Unique to Zsh -

Zsh incorporates features that outshine its counterparts, particularly in:

1. **Globbing Patterns**: Extended glob qualifiers allow for complex filename matching operations, exceeding standard wildcards in capability.

2. **Spelling Correction**: Zsh suggests corrections for mistyped commands, mitigating everyday user-errors seamlessly.

3. **Path Replacement**: Powerful syntax facilitates rapid direc-

tory navigation and manipulation, increasing command-line efficiency without additional typing.

For instance, Zsh's advanced globbing enables recursive directory searches and file filtering based on metadata conditions, which are elaborated further in:

```
# List all text files edited in the last two days
ls **/*.txt(m-2)
```

Unlike Csh, mandatorily dependent on external utilities to accomplish similar tasks, Zsh integrates features natively, blending functionality with performance.

7. Community and Learning Resources -

Zsh's growing community continuously develops resources, ranging from comprehensive documentation to dynamic community forums. Frameworks such as Oh My Zsh aid beginners and experts alike in exploring Zsh's capacities, making configuration accessible without in-depth shell programming experience.

Conversely, Bash enjoys legacy status with copious guides available, yet innovations appear incrementally, while Fish focuses on simplicity, appealing to users requiring minimal setup and faster initial interaction.

Csh, with diminishing adoption, faces challenges in maintaining modern, sprawling community forums and extensive quality improvements, reinforcing its specialized rather than mainstream applicability.

8. Visual Comparison Table -

For quick reference, a visual matrix below highlights the core strengths and distinguishable differences between Zsh, Bash, Csh, and Fish:

33

Feature	Zsh	Bash	Csh/Tcsh	Fish
Scripting	Rich feature-set with associative arrays, custom data structures	Standard POSIX-compliant syntax	C-like syntax, limited advanced constructs	Simplified syntax, less cross-compatibility
Customization	Extensive plugin and theme support	Requires manual configuration	Limited visual customization	Built-in user-friendly defaults
Command Completion	Superior contextual and programmable completion	Built-in, requires customization for extended use	Basic, interactive history mechanisms	Autosuggestions and highlighting default
Interactivity	Rich customization, spelling correction	Reliable, user-friendly	History substitution features	Intuitive design, fast onboarding
Portability	High, after initial configuration	Ubiquitous	Reduced, legacy usage	Reduced, proprietary syntax

9. Conclusion -

In the ecosystem of Unix shells, Zsh emerges as a frontrunner for interactive and customized shell experiences. Its commendable balance of powerful features and flexibility allows users to mold it per individual or collective needs, contrasting with Bash's widespread compatibility and Fish's user-centric immediacy. Each shell holds its niche yet expands peripherals to suit growing digital and interactive requirements.

Choosing the right shell involves careful deliberation of use case scenarios and the environment in use. Whether scripts need portability, interactive ease, or a combination of the two, each shell offers unique advantages designed to enhance functionality and workflow effectiveness dynamically. For developers, system administrators, and users forging deeper connections with their computing environment, Zsh promises an engaging and richly equipped journey.

Chapter 2

In-depth: Setting Up and Configuring Zsh

This chapter provides a comprehensive guide to installing and configuring Zsh across various operating systems, ensuring it becomes the default shell environment. It details the customization of the .zshrc file, adjustments to the Zsh prompt, and the utilization of the Oh My Zsh framework for enhanced configuration management. Additionally, it covers the management of plugins and themes, equipping users with knowledge to personalize and optimize their Zsh experience effectively.

2.1 Installing Zsh on Different Platforms

Zsh, or Z Shell, is a powerful Unix shell that extends the Bourne Shell (sh) with numerous features and improvements, making it highly popular among power users and developers. The installation process for Zsh can vary significantly depending on the underlying operating system. This section offers a detailed, step-by-step guide on how to install Zsh on various platforms, including Linux, macOS, and Windows, and verifies its installation.

1. Installing Zsh on Linux

Linux distributions are varied, with package managers differing from one to another, making it essential to tailor the installation steps to the specific distribution you are using. Here, we will cover the installation for some of the most widely used Linux distributions: Ubuntu/Debian, Fedora, and Arch Linux.

Ubuntu/Debian Based Systems:

For Debian-based systems, such as Ubuntu, Zsh is readily available in the default package repositories. The installation process is straightforward, relying on the Advanced Package Tool (APT).

```
sudo apt update
sudo apt install zsh
```

After running these commands, verify the installation by checking the version of Zsh installed:

```
zsh --version
```

This should output the version number of Zsh, confirming successful installation.

Fedora Based Systems:

For Fedora or similar RPM-based distributions, the DNF package manager is used. Here's how you can install Zsh:

```
sudo dnf update
sudo dnf install zsh
```

As with Ubuntu, verify the installation using the version check:

```
zsh --version
```

Arch Linux:

In Arch-based systems, the installation utilizes the pacman package manager. Zsh can be found in the official repositories:

```
sudo pacman -Syu
sudo pacman -S zsh
```

Following installation, the version can be checked just like with other distributions:

36

```
zsh --version
```

2. Installing Zsh on macOS

On macOS, Zsh is pre-installed as it is the default shell starting from macOS Catalina (10.15). However, to ensure compatibility with the latest features and updates, users may prefer installing the most recent version independently. Homebrew is a popular package manager on macOS, used here for installation.

First, update Homebrew to ensure you have the latest package information:

```
brew update
```

Then proceed to install Zsh:

```
brew install zsh
```

After installation, confirm by checking the version:

```
zsh --version
```

If you wish to use this newly installed version of Zsh instead of the default macOS version, you may need to change your shell configuration settings.

3. Installing Zsh on Windows

Windows does not natively support Unix shells like Zsh; however, several methods enable the use of Zsh on Windows. The most common approaches involve using Windows Subsystem for Linux (WSL) or Cygwin.

Using Windows Subsystem for Linux (WSL):

WSL allows you to run a Linux distribution directly on Windows. To install Zsh via WSL, follow these steps:

- Install WSL by following Microsoft's official guidelines, ensuring you setup a Linux distribution of your choice.

- Open the WSL terminal.

- Use the package manager specific to your chosen WSL distribu-

37

tion to install Zsh. For instance, on Ubuntu:

```
sudo apt update
sudo apt install zsh
```

- Verify the installation:

```
zsh --version
```

Using Cygwin:

Cygwin provides a large collection of GNU and Open Source tools which provide functionality similar to a Linux distribution on Windows. To install Zsh using Cygwin:

- Download and run the Cygwin setup from the official Cygwin website.

- During the setup, select 'zsh' from the list of packages.

- After completing the installation, open Cygwin terminal.

- Execute the following command to initiate Zsh:

```
zsh
```

- As always, verify the Zsh version:

```
zsh --version
```

These methods enable a Unix-like environment to run Zsh on Windows, enhancing the development experience by offering familiar tools and seamless interoperability with Linux environments.

Considerations for Enterprise and Multi-User Environments

In enterprise and multi-user environments, additional considerations such as user permissions, availability of dependencies, and compliance with organizational policies may influence the installation of Zsh. Administrators might prefer:

- *System-Wide Installation:* This involves installing Zsh at the system level, accessible by all users, often beneficial in a shared computing environment. The process may require elevated privileges and should be executed with caution.

- *Dependency Management:* Ensure all necessary libraries and dependencies are identified and handled during installation, especially on minimalistic Linux distributions or customized environments.

Post-Installation Verification and Configuration

Post-installation, confirming that Zsh is correctly set up involves a few checks and basic configuration. First is the verification through version checking, as previously detailed. Beyond this, certain initial configurations can enhance usability:

- *Default Shell Configuration:* Ensuring Zsh is set as the default shell, which will be covered in subsequent sections.

- *Customization and Scripting:* Creating or modifying the '.zshrc' file to include custom settings, aliases, or scripts should be considered once installation is verified.

Overall, the installation of Zsh across different platforms requires a careful approach, considering the specific nuances and requirements of each operating system. The advantage of Zsh's powerful features, such as improved scripting capabilities and enhanced customization, makes this process worthwhile for users aiming to optimize their command-line interactions.

2.2 Making Zsh the Default Shell

Transitioning to Zsh as the default shell on your operating system can significantly enhance your command-line experience by leveraging its advanced features. This section delves into the methodology for setting Zsh as the default shell across various platforms like Linux, macOS, and Windows, highlighting both the technical steps involved and the rationale behind making Zsh the preferred shell environment.

- **1. Understanding Shells and their Role**

  A shell in Unix-based systems serves as the command-line interface that allows users to communicate with the operating system kernel. The default shell is the shell that is automatically started when a terminal session is initiated. Popular shells include Bash, C Shell, and Zsh, each offering distinct features and capabilities. Opting for Zsh means benefiting from enhanced scripting abilities, customizable prompts, improved history management, advanced auto-completion, and an extensive plugin system.

- **2. Setting Zsh as the Default Shell on Linux**

  The process of changing your default shell to Zsh varies slightly across different Linux distributions. Generally, the 'chsh' (change shell) command-line utility is employed to modify user shell preferences.

  Basic Command Synopsis:

  The 'chsh' command modifies the user's login shell using the following syntax:

```
chsh -s /bin/zsh
```

  In this command:

  - '-s' specifies the shell to be set as default.
  - '/bin/zsh' is the path to Zsh, which might vary depending on your installation path.

  Once executed, the above command prompts for the password, after which your default shell changes to Zsh. To confirm the change, log out and log back into your system, then check the current shell:

```
echo $SHELL
```

  The output should be '/bin/zsh', confirming that Zsh is the default shell.

  Distribution-Specific Considerations:

  Different Linux distributions may have specific configuration files that affect shell management. For instance, Red Hat-based

40

systems might require adjustments in the '/etc/passwd' file, whereas some Linux derivatives might offer graphical user interfaces to adjust user shell settings.

On systems where Zsh is not installed at a standard path, verify the location of Zsh using:

```
which zsh
```

Ensure that the output from this command matches the path provided to the 'chsh' command.

- **3. Setting Zsh as the Default Shell on macOS**

Beginning with macOS Catalina, Zsh is the default login shell. However, for users migrating from older macOS versions or wishing to use a custom version of Zsh installed via Homebrew, manually changing the shell might be necessary.

Modifying Shell Settings via Terminal:

The 'chsh' utility is also available on macOS to streamline this process. Execute the command:

```
chsh -s /usr/local/bin/zsh
```

This sets '/usr/local/bin/zsh' as the default shell. Adjust the path as necessary depending on your installation.

To verify that Zsh has been set as the default shell:

```
echo $SHELL
```

The output should indicate Zsh's installation path. macOS also provides a graphical method to change the shell in the System Preferences under Users & Groups. Unlock the settings, then right-click your user account and modify the shell under "Advanced Options."

Persisting Changes Across Updates:

It is crucial to ensure that the shell configuration persists across macOS updates, which could potentially revert the default shell. Creating a backup of configuration files or setting version control systems on critical files can be effective strategies to safeguard your customized shell environment.

41

- **4. Using Zsh as Default on Windows**

Windows does not natively support setting Zsh as the default shell due to its Windows Command Prompt and PowerShell environment. However, users employing the Windows Subsystem for Linux (WSL) can emulate a Unix-like interface where Zsh can indeed function as the default shell.

Setting Zsh as Default in WSL:

Assuming WSL is installed and Zsh is available, the default login shell can be changed through the profile configuration:

1. Launch WSL and edit the '.bashrc' file located in your home directory to include a switch command to Zsh. Append the following lines:

```
if [ -t 1 ]; then
    exec zsh
fi
```

The condition '[-t 1]' checks if the shell is being run interactively, causing a switch to Zsh only in interactive sessions.

2. Reload the Bash configuration:

```
source ~/.bashrc
```

3. Upon next login or terminal launch within WSL, Zsh should automatically start.

Cygwin Configuration:

For users utilizing Cygwin, navigate to the Cygwin terminal and use Cygwin's 'chsh' equivalent or edit the user profile scripts to embed Zsh initiation.

Persistent Configuration:

Ensure that changes in configuration files, such as '.bashrc', are preserved and version-controlled, particularly when system updates or reconfigurations occur. Employing software like Git to manage snapshots of these configuration files can provide assurance that preferences and scripts remain intact.

- **5. The Importance of Shell Customization and Management**

Adopting Zsh as a default shell inherently encourages further customization, offering an opportunity to tailor the command-line interface to individual workflows, simply through automated scripts and plugins. Advanced users may script custom commands to streamline repetitive tasks, capitalize on robust auto-completion scripts to improve shell efficiency, or integrate version control systems directly into the shell interface for ongoing project management.

Consequently, making Zsh the default shell not only improves usability but also fosters a development environment conducive to productive and innovative work. The integration capabilities of Zsh can vastly improve daily automation processes and task management, influencing both personal productivity and broader organizational workflows.

Understanding these steps and applying precise configurations ensures that users can exploit Zsh not only as a default login shell but as a powerful command-line ally that enhances interactive computing experiences. Given Zsh's versatility and robustness, it has evolved into an essential tool in the toolbox of modern software developers and system administrators alike. Embracing Zsh as the default shell is a meaningful stride towards mastering the art of command-line operations and scripting.

2.3 Configuring the .zshrc File

The '.zshrc' file plays a crucial role in the configuration and personalization of the Z Shell (Zsh) environment. This file is loaded every time a new interactive shell session starts, allowing users to customize their shell experience significantly. This section explores the potential and utility of the '.zshrc' file, guiding through essential configurations, advanced settings, and techniques to optimize shell performance and usability.

1. Understanding the Role of the .zshrc File

The '.zshrc' file is a shell script that contains commands to set shell parameters, initialize shell features, and configure the user's environment. It functions similarly to the '.bashrc' file in Bash, serving as a default framework on which users can build their individualized shell settings.

Primarily, the '.zshrc' file is utilized to:

- Customize the command prompt.

- Set environment variables.

- Define aliases and functions.

- Enable or disable shell options.

- Integrate plugins and themes.

- Script automated tasks that enhance workflow efficiency.

These customizations enhance the user experience, aligning the shell's functionality with specific preferences and project requirements, making the shell not only a tool but a tailored environment conducive to productivity and innovation.

2. Basic Configuration of .zshrc

The initial configuration of '.zshrc' often involves the setup of environment variables and basic settings essential for day-to-day tasks.

Defining Environment Variables:

Environment variables in '.zshrc' are defined in the format 'VARIABLE=value', and they are instrumental in setting paths, configuring language settings, and managing user-specific data.

Example of setting a 'PATH' environment variable:

```
export PATH="$HOME/bin:/usr/local/bin:$PATH"
```

This line appends custom directories to the existing 'PATH', ensuring the shell can locate executables in these directories.

Prompt Customization:

Customizing the command prompt can enhance the visual interface, providing relevant information such as the current directory or the git branch. Zsh's 'PROMPT' variable is used for this purpose.

Example of a simple custom prompt reflecting the username and current directory:

```
PROMPT='%n@%m:%~%# '
```

- '%n' - the current username.

- '%m' - the hostname.

- '% ' - the current working directory.

- '%#' - the prompt character ('#' for root, '$' for others).

Changing these prompt parameters can significantly improve the utility and aesthetics of the shell interface.

3. Advanced Configuration Techniques

Moving beyond basic configurations, '.zshrc' supports more advanced techniques, including alias creation, functions, and integration with external scripts or commands.

Creating Aliases:

Aliases provide shortcuts for lengthy commands, reducing errors, and increasing command efficiency.

Example of setting aliases:

```
alias ll='ls -lh'
alias gs='git status'
alias rm='rm -i'
```

These examples:

- Replace 'll' with an extended list command for easier directory navigation.

- Shortcut 'gs' runs 'git status', streamlining git operations.

45

- Enable interactive confirmation with 'rm', reducing the risk of accidental deletions.

By judiciously using aliases, users can create a nimble command-line interface that suits their precise workflow needs.

Defining Functions:

Functions in '.zshrc' allow the encapsulation of complex command sequences which are reusable across sessions.

Example of defining a function to search for files:

```
findfile() {
  find . -name "$1" 2>/dev/null
}
```

This function invokes the 'find' command with enhanced usability, enabling streamlined searches within directories for files matching specified patterns.

Sourcing External Scripts:

Incorporating external scripts extends '.zshrc' capabilities by modularizing configuration or executing extensive commands without cluttering the file.

To source an external script, the following syntax is used within '.zshrc':

```
source $HOME/scripts/custom-config.sh
```

This command loads 'custom-config.sh', executing the script content within the current shell context, thereby expanding functional scope.

4. Utilizing Plugins and Themes

Zsh's flexibility is further evident in its support for plugins and themes, providing powerful tools for automating tasks and customizing the visual presentation of the shell interface.

Oh My Zsh Framework:

Oh My Zsh is a popular open-source framework that simplifies management of Zsh configurations, offering a vast array of plugins and themes.

To integrate Oh My Zsh, begin by modifying '.zshrc' to set the framework's configuration path, and select desired plugins:

```
ZSH_THEME="agnoster"
plugins=(git zsh-autosuggestions)
source $ZSH/oh-my-zsh.sh
```

A detailed selection of themes and plugins enhances both functional capabilities and aesthetic qualities of the terminal, adapting to a wide range of user requirements.

Developing Custom Plugins:

Advanced users may develop their own plugins to encapsulate specific functionalities or enhance automated processes unique to their workflow.

A simple custom plugin might be structured as follows, placed within a dedicated plugins directory:

```
# File: myplugin.plugin.zsh
echo "My Plugin loaded"
my_command () {
    echo "Executing my custom command"
}
```

This custom plugin loads with the shell, providing bespoke commands and enhancing personalized functionality.

5. Performance and Optimization Considerations

Efficient '.zshrc' configurations ensure optimal shell performance, allowing for rapid execution of scripts and minimizing start-up delays.

Reducing Shell Load Time:

To reduce '.zshrc' load time, consider:

- Minimizing the use of complex functions within '.zshrc'. Offload extensive computations to external scripts loaded only when necessary.

- Avoiding excessive plugin usage which may impact performance. Profile plugin effects and limit their use to essential functionality.

Using the 'zprof' command, profile shell initialization to identify performance bottlenecks:

```
zmodload zsh/zprof
<.zshrc contents>
zprof
```

Output from 'zprof' displays time consumed by each element of '.zshrc', offering key insights for performance tuning.

6. Version Control and Management of .zshrc

To efficiently manage '.zshrc' changes and ensure they align with evolving work environments, version control is crucial. Git provides robust solutions to track modifications, branch configurations, and rollback changes when required.

To initiate version control, navigate to the '.zshrc' directory and execute:

```
git init
git add .zshrc
git commit -m "Initial commit"
```

Adapt '.gitignore' to exclude unnecessary files, ensuring a streamlined version control setup focused on vital configuration scripts.

Combining intelligent '.zshrc' configurations with best practices for customization, performance optimization, and version management equips users with a sophisticated shell environment tailored to specific needs and preferences. As Zsh users gain expertise and refine their configurations, they harness increased control over their computing environments, promoting productivity and innovation within command-line interactions.

2.4   Customizing Zsh Prompt

Customizing the Zsh prompt is an essential step for users seeking to optimize their command-line environment for both aesthetics and functionality. By tailoring the prompt, users can enhance their interactions with the shell, making information readily accessible and improving workflow efficiency. This section explores the intricacies of prompt

48

customization, delving into syntax, examples, and advanced configurations to achieve a personalized shell experience.

1. Understanding the Zsh Prompt

The Zsh prompt, displayed at the beginning of each command line, serves as both a visual cue and a functional element of the shell. It can be configured extensively to display contextually relevant information, such as the current working directory, user identity, host information, and the status of the last command. Zsh prompts are highly customizable through the 'PROMPT' variable, often abbreviated as 'PS1', which defines the primary shell prompt displayed before each command.

The basic elements in customizing a prompt involve various placeholders and escape sequences represented within the 'PROMPT' variable, allowing users to create unique and informative prompts.

2. Basic Prompt Customization

Prompt Variables and Escape Sequences:

Zsh leverages specific escape sequences that denote dynamic information, providing opportunities for significant customization. Each escape sequence within Zsh begins with a percent ('%') symbol, followed by one or more characters that specify the desired information to be included in the prompt.

Common escape sequences include:

- %n - Expands to the username of the current user.

- %m - Expands to the hostname of the system without domain.

- %M - Expands to the full hostname.

- % - Expands to the current working directory, relative to the home directory.

- %# - Displays '#' if the effective UID is zero (root), otherwise '$'.

- %? - Displays the exit status of the last command executed.

Example of a basic Zsh prompt customization:

```
PROMPT="%n@%m:%~ %b%?>
$ "
```

This configuration results in a prompt displaying the username, hostname, and current directory followed by the exit status of the last command.

Prompt Functionality and Style:

Beyond basic functionality, users can style prompts for improved readability and aesthetic appeal using text formatting. Zsh supports various visual effects, including color changes and text formatting, applied through escape sequences. Colors are typically introduced via termcap codes (%F{color} for foreground and %K{color} for background) or ANSI escape codes.

Example demonstrating a colored prompt:

```
PROMPT="%F{green}%n@%m%f:%F{blue}%~%f %# "
```

In this sequence, %F{green} begins coloring the username in green, %f resets the foreground color, and %F{blue} colors the directory path in blue.

3. Incorporating Advanced Contextual Information

Including Git Branch Information:

When working within a Git-managed repository, reflecting branch and status information on the prompt helps streamline version control tasks.

For Git integration, a common approach involves adding a function within the '.zshrc' to extract relevant details:

```
parse_git_branch() {
  git branch --no-color 2> /dev/null | sed -e '/^[^*]/d' -e 's/* //'
}
PROMPT='%n@%m:%~ $(parse_git_branch) %# '
```

This setup will append the current Git branch to the prompt whenever the working directory is within a repository.

Displaying Command Execution Time:

Including the execution time of commands in the prompt can be invaluable when optimizing scripts or commands. Incorporate RETRN and SECONDS variables to achieve this:

```
precmd() { RETRN=$?; }
PROMPT='[%T] %n@%m:%~ %? %4v %# '
```

50

With this, the prompt displays the time stamps, enabling users to monitor the efficiency and completion time of executed commands.

4. Using Prompt Theme Frameworks

Zsh supports robust frameworks aimed at simplifying prompt customization through themes. Popular among these is the Oh My Zsh theme framework, offering a variety of pre-configured themes and an infrastructure for developing custom ones.

Employing Oh My Zsh Themes:

When using Oh My Zsh, setting a prompt theme is as straightforward as specifying it in the '.zshrc' file:

```
ZSH_THEME="agnoster"
PROMPT='%n@%m:%~ %# '
```

By sourcing the framework's infrastructure, working with themes enhances functionality without requiring detailed manual prompt coding, although customization remains supported.

Developing Custom Themes:

For users desiring unique aesthetics, creating custom themes is possible. Themes are encapsulated as scripts housed within the themes directory specified by Oh My Zsh.

Example of a minimal theme starting template:

```
local user_host='%F{yellow}%n@%m%f'
local current_dir='%F{cyan}%~%f'
local git_branch='$(parse_git_branch)'

PROMPT="${user_host}:${current_dir} ${git_branch} %# "
```

This script can be augmented with additional functionality or styles, offering an opportunity for customized command-line branding.

5. Optimizing Prompt Performance

Prompts, if overly complex, might introduce delays in shell responsiveness, especially when executing intensive commands like Git status checks on large repos. Minimizing prompt load involves refining prompt scripts and using caching strategies.

Asynchronous Commands:

Implementing asynchronous command execution can mitigate prompt lag. This involves backgrounding computationally intensive functions, updating the prompt asynchronously upon completion.

Example with asynchronous Git prompt:

```
update_git_prompt_info() {
  (parse_git_branch &)
}
add-zsh-hook precmd update_git_prompt_info
```

This structure ensures prompt updates without blocking terminal input during processing.

6. Managing Prompt Configurations with Version Control

Maintaining version-controlled records of prompt configurations ensures experiments, iterations, or theme creations are well-organized and reversible. Git serves this methodology well, offering rapid branching, rollback capabilities, and collaboration facilities.

To initialize version control for prompt configurations:

```
cd ~/.oh-my-zsh/themes
git init
git add custom-theme.zsh-theme
git commit -m "Initial theme design"
```

Organizing theme developments in a version-controlled repository clarifies modifications, and structures cooperation, solidifying customization work and fostering sustained improvements.

Customizing Zsh prompts elevates shell interaction beyond simple command execution into a dynamic, aesthetically pleasing, and informative experience. With precise configuration, extended functionality, and performance optimization, any user can craft a truly personalized command-line interface that resonates with their workflow and productivity objectives. By contributing to deeper engagement, prompt customization aids in transforming the Zsh environment into an integral component of daily computational tasks.

2.5 Using Oh My Zsh Framework

Oh My Zsh is a popular open-source framework that facilitates managing and customizing Zsh configurations. It significantly enhances the user's command-line experience through a plethora of plugins and themes designed to boost productivity and personalization. This section provides a detailed exploration of the Oh My Zsh framework, covering installation steps, configuration options, and ways to leverage its extensive features to optimize shell environments.

Introduction to Oh My Zsh

Oh My Zsh is designed as a robust tool to streamline the management of Zsh shell settings, particularly appealing due to its modular plugin architecture and vibrant theme collection. Its modularity helps individuals and large teams enhance their shell functionality with ease. By simplifying complex customization tasks, Oh My Zsh empowers users to tailor their terminal experiences to fit particular workflows and preferences seamlessly.

Installation and Initial Setup

Prerequisites:

Before installing Oh My Zsh, ensure Zsh is installed and set as the default shell. Refer back to earlier sections for detailed instructions on installing Zsh across different platforms.

Installation Instructions:

The recommended method to install Oh My Zsh is via a Git clone from its GitHub repository directly into the home directory. For most Unix-like systems, the following command initiates the installation:

```
sh -c "$(curl -fsSL https://raw.githubusercontent.com/ohmyzsh/ohmyzsh/master/tools
    /install.sh)"
```

Alternatively, using 'wget' if 'curl' is unavailable:

```
sh -c "$(wget https://raw.githubusercontent.com/ohmyzsh/ohmyzsh/master/tools/
    install.sh -O -)"
```

Upon successful installation, Oh My Zsh sets the '.zshrc' file accordingly, establishing a base configuration that is ready to expand through plugins and themes.

Post-Installation Verification:

Examine the '.zshrc' file to confirm the installation. It should include:

```
export ZSH="$HOME/.oh-my-zsh"
ZSH_THEME="robbyrussell"
plugins=(git)
source $ZSH/oh-my-zsh.sh
```

This reflects the basic structure, indicating the default theme and examples of included plugins.

Themes in Oh My Zsh

Themes in Oh My Zsh allow users to modify the aesthetic qualities and informational content of the command prompt. With hundreds of customizable themes provided, users can experiment to find a prompt that fits their needs or create their own.

Setting a Theme:

Switching themes is straightforward—modify the ZSH_THEME value in the '.zshrc' file:

```
ZSH_THEME="agnoster"
```

Once set, apply changes by restarting the terminal or sourcing the configuration:

```
source ~/.zshrc
```

Creating Custom Themes:

For users pursuing personalized themes, the Oh My Zsh framework allows theme creation. Custom themes are defined in '.zsh-theme' files within the custom themes directory:

```
# File: mytheme.zsh-theme
PROMPT='%F{green}%n%f@%F{cyan}%m%f:%F{yellow}%~%f %# '
RPROMPT='%F{red}%T%f'
```

Save this file under ' /.oh-my-zsh/custom/themes/' and apply it in '.zshrc':

```
ZSH_THEME="mytheme"
```

Plugins and Their Usage

Plugins are key to leveraging Oh My Zsh's functionality, with a vast repository available to integrate various tools and commands, greatly enhancing productivity. Whether managing version control systems, optimizing command search, or enhancing directory navigation, plugins provide invaluable aids to the command-line suite.

Activating Plugins:

Oh My Zsh plugins are activated by listing them in the '.zshrc' file, plugins array:

```
plugins=(git zsh-autosuggestions zsh-syntax-highlighting)
```

Once added, source the '.zshrc' to effect the updates:

```
source ~/.zshrc
```

Popular Plugin Overview:

- git: Offers alias shortcuts for common Git operations enhancing efficiency in version control tasks.

- zsh-autosuggestions: Displays suggestions for commands based on history and typed commands, streamlining repeat command entry.

- zsh-syntax-highlighting: Highlights command syntax, visually distinguishing correct, incorrect, and unexecuted commands for better command-line accuracy.

- npm: Provides useful aliases and functions for interacting with Node Package Manager, simplifying command interactions.

Building Custom Plugins:

Custom plugins can be developed to fit specific needs, adding tailored functionality or integrating particular tools within the Zsh environment.

Example of a simple custom plugin script, 'myscript.plugin.zsh':

```
# Directory of custom Oh My Zsh plugins
echo "Custom plugin loaded!"
alias myupdate="sudo apt-get update && sudo apt-get upgrade"
```

55

Add this plugin within the custom plugins directory and append it to the '.zshrc' plugins array to activate it.

Configuration Management in Oh My Zsh

Managing '.zshrc' configurations becomes increasingly complex as new plugins and themes integrate into the system. Employing a structured approach to manage this complexity ensures a seamless and intuitive shell experience.

Organizing Configuration:

Adopt modular configuration practices by externalizing complex setups into separate files or scripts:

```
# .zshrc
source $HOME/.zshrc.d/aliases.zsh
source $HOME/.zshrc.d/environment.zsh
```

This facilitates compartmentalized control over individual settings, streamlining adjustments, and reducing potential errors introduced by manual configuration errors.

Version Control for Configuration Files:

Git provides robust principles and tools to maintain '.zshrc' settings. By initializing a Git repository within configuration directories, iteration and rollback processes are simplified:

```
cd ~/.oh-my-zsh/custom
git init
git add .
git commit -m "Initial commit with customized shell configurations"
```

Branching and merging features provide collaborative extensions, ensuring all changes are trackable and reversible, suitable for both solo and team environments.

Troubleshooting and Best Practices

While using Oh My Zsh, users might encounter issues ranging from plugin conflicts to theme rendering problems. Understanding troubleshooting methods proves vital for maintaining a stable and reliable shell environment.

Debugging Common Issues:

To systematically resolve issues, employ the following strategies:

- Check for syntax errors in '.zshrc' and associated script files using the 'zsh' command in verbose or debug mode:

```
zsh -xv
```

- Disable recently added plugins incrementally to identify potential conflicts.

- Ensure all installed plugins and themes are updated. Use package managers as applicable to fetch and apply updates.

Adopting Best Practices:

- Regularly clean and review '.zshrc' settings to remove obsolete or inefficient entries.

- Leverage external configurations and small scripts to maintain a clean and readable primary configuration file.

- Document custom modifications and new plugin integrations, creating a living document that aids future troubleshooting and customization endeavors.

- Stay engaged with Oh My Zsh community forums and repositories to remain aware of maintenance updates, user-contributed plugins, and tips on maximizing the tool's capabilities.

Oh My Zsh transforms the command-line interface from a functional necessity into a customizable powerhouse. Its intuitive framework and rich ecosystem of plugins and themes present users with opportunities for both personalization and enhanced productivity. By mastering Oh My Zsh's installation, configuration management, plugin usage, and troubleshooting, users can tailor their terminal environments to their precise specifications and requirements, significantly improving their overall command-line experience.

2.6   Managing Plugins and Themes

The management of plugins and themes in Zsh is fundamental to tailoring the shell environment to individual needs and maximizing its functional capabilities. Oh My Zsh, as a comprehensive framework, presents a vast collection of plugins and themes that enhance productivity, ensure smoother workflow, and optimize visual aesthetics. This section meticulously details the processes and methodologies required to efficiently manage plugins and themes within the Zsh environment, encapsulating installation, customization, conflict resolution, and performance optimization strategies.

Understanding the Role of Plugins and Themes

Plugins in Zsh extend the shell's functionality by embedding useful tools and shortcuts tailored to specific applications, programming languages, or workflows. They encapsulate repetitive commands, augment command-line capabilities, and facilitate interactions with complex systems like version control or package management tools.

Themes, contrastingly, focus on the visual and informational aspects of the terminal. They define prompt layout and styling, encapsulating elements like colors, icons, and data integrations (e.g., version control status) to provide critical information at a glance.

The intelligent selection and configuration of plugins and themes not only enhance efficiency and appearance but can also positively impact time management and user satisfaction, inducing a structured and coherent workspace within the command-line interface.

Installing and Activating Plugins

Basic Plugin Activation:

Oh My Zsh simplifies plugin management through a centralized 'plugins' array within the '.zshrc' configuration file. To activate plugins, simply edit this array to include desired plugin names:

```
plugins=(git docker zsh-autosuggestions zsh-syntax-highlighting)
```

This snippet activates plugins for Git shortcuts, Docker management, command autosuggestions, and syntax highlighting, enhancing both user interaction and task execution.

Upon modifying the '.zshrc', to apply changes, source the file:

```
source ~/.zshrc
```

Installing Additional Plugins:

If a desired plugin isn't included by default within Oh My Zsh, manually installing it involves cloning the plugin repository into the custom plugins directory:

```
git clone https://github.com/zsh-users/zsh-completions ${ZSH_CUSTOM:=~/.oh-my-
    zsh/custom}/plugins/zsh-completions
```

Add 'zsh-completions' to the 'plugins' array in '.zshrc' to activate it.

Configuring and Customizing Plugins

Plugin Configuration:

Many plugins offer customizable settings, allowing users to tailor functionality precisely. For example, the 'gitfast' plugin, intended to speed up common Git operations, can be configured by defining specific aliases within '.zshrc' beyond its defaults:

```
# Custom git alias example
alias gst='git status -sb'
```

Ensure associations are declared before sourcing the primary Oh My Zsh script to apply these during shell initialization.

Creating Custom Plugins:

Crafting custom plugins enables users to bundle commands, functions, or environment configurations as reusable packages. Plugin scripts, structured as '.zsh' shell scripts, reside within the custom plugin directory of Oh My Zsh, providing encapsulation and modularity.

Example:

```
# File: custom-tool.plugin.zsh
echo "Custom Tool Plugin Loaded"
alias hello="echo Hello, World!"
```

Add 'custom-tool' to the plugins array to activate it, ensuring all personalized commands and enhancements remain compartmentalized.

Managing Themes for Maximum Impact

Selecting and Applying Themes:

Themes in Oh My Zsh change aesthetic elements by adjusting prompt visualizations. To select a theme, modify the 'ZSH_THEME' variable in the '.zshrc' file:

```
ZSH_THEME="agnoster"
```

This choice can be sourced to apply instantaneously:

```
source ~/.zshrc
```

Over 150 themes are available, appealing to different styles, information inclusion preferences, and visual clarity. Experimentation or user input often determines the most suitable theme for situational needs.

Designing Custom Themes:

Custom themes can be developed to complement branding demands or workflow enhancements. Themes involve defining 'PROMPT' and 'RPROMPT' structures utilizing escape sequences for data integration:

```
# File: mytheme.zsh-theme
PROMPT='%F{green}%n%f@%F{cyan}%m%f:%F{yellow}%~%f %# '
RPROMPT='%F{red}%*%f'
```

Store under ' /.oh-my-zsh/custom/themes/', referencing in '.zshrc' to activate as needed:

```
ZSH_THEME="mytheme"
```

Conflict Resolution and Performance Optimization

Handling Plugin Conflicts:

Installation and usage of conflicting plugins may deplete shell performance or cause operational inconsistencies. Detect issues through error logs and command execution monitoring, systematically deactivating plugins as needed until the source is identified.

```
# Temporarily disable conflicting plugin in .zshrc:
# plugins=(docker zsh-autosuggestions)
```

Employ Oh My Zsh's community forums or GitHub issues as resources to resolve recurrent compatibility concerns or acquire guidance on debugging specific plugins.

Optimizing Theme and Plugin Load Times:

Excessive or complicated themes may slow prompt output. To prevent this, streamline themes by simplifying prompt constructs, removing non-essential information, or utilizing asynchronous updates:

```
autoload -Uz promptinit; promptinit
prompt oliver
```

This example employs the 'prompt' command to load a theme optimized for speed without excess functionality overhead, prioritizing prompt responsiveness.

Leveraging Community Resources and Version Control

Oh My Zsh enjoys an active developer and user community contributing plugins, themes, and insights. Engaging with this community ensures exposure to best practices, novel developments, and troubleshooting techniques enhancing Zsh environments.

Participating in the Community:

Join mailing lists, GitHub discussions, and forums to remain current with new releases, bug fixes, and feature requests. Engage in code contribution opportunities, fostering shared learning and collaboration.

Version Controlling Customizations:

Employ Git to administer and track customization changes, securing work against accidental loss while promoting efficient branching and experimentation:

```
cd ~/.oh-my-zsh
git init
git add custom
git commit -m "Initial installation with custom plugin and theme arrangements."
```

This setup allows for streamlined collaboration, whether across individual projects or within larger development teams, ensuring changes remain transparent and properly documented.

Effectively managing plugins and themes in Zsh, via trialing new setups, utilizing community inputs, and adhering to version control best practices, ensures that the shell environment remains a powerful, efficient, and personalized tool. By continually refining these aspects to better suit evolving needs and technological advancements, users maximize the utility and enjoyment derived from their command-line interactions.

Chapter 3

Basic Zsh Commands and Operations

This chapter focuses on essential commands and operations that form the backbone of using Zsh effectively. It covers navigating the file system, managing files and directories, and understanding file permissions and ownership. Readers are introduced to handling text files, leveraging command-line text editors, and utilizing command history and shortcuts. Mastery of these basic operations is crucial for efficient daily use of the Zsh shell.

3.1 Navigating the File System

The file system is the backbone of any operating system, serving as the structure through which users access and manage files and directories. In Unix-like systems, including Zsh, navigation through the file system is accomplished through a series of commands that allow for the exploration and manipulation of directories. The primary commands for navigating the file system include cd (change directory), ls (list), and pwd (print working directory). These commands form the basis of file system navigation, and understanding their usage is crucial for efficient interaction with the shell.

The cd command is used to move between directories. When issued without any arguments, it typically returns the user to their home directory, represented by the tilde (). To change to a specific directory, the absolute or relative path must be provided. An absolute path begins from the root directory and details each subsequent directory down to the destination. A relative path specifies the directory in relation to the current directory, often utilizing the dot (.) and double dot (..) to reference the current directory and parent directory, respectively. For instance, the command cd .. takes the user up one level in the directory hierarchy.

```
cd Desktop/Projects/2023
cd ../
cd /home/user/Documents
```

The above example demonstrates changing directories with both relative and absolute paths. Moving into a sub-directory requires specifying the sub-directory name, while using double dots navigates up the directory structure. Additionally, switching between directories can be made more efficient using an undocumented feature of cd, called *directory stack*, allowing users to quickly toggle back to previously visited directories.

The ls command is crucial for listing files and directories within the current directory. This command supports a wide array of options that enhance its functionality. By default, ls lists entries in columns, presenting filenames without additional details. However, options such as -l (long format), -a (all files, including hidden), and -R (recursive) provide extended views.

```
ls -l
ls -a
ls -R
```

The ls -l option displays detailed information including permissions, number of links, owner, group, size, and modification date of each file or directory. The ls -a command is valuable for revealing hidden files, those starting with a period, which are typically configuration files. ls -R is particularly useful for visualizing an entire directory tree, displaying all contents recursively.

Understanding the output of ls -l requires familiarity with Unix-based permission schemes, a topic covered in more detail in later sections of this chapter. However, briefly, file permissions are composed of three groups: user (owner), group, and others, each with associated read (r), write (w), and execute (x) permissions.

The pwd command is perhaps the simplest yet most informative command, outputting the full pathname of the current directory. This command is essential when working within deeply nested directory structures, ensuring users maintain orientation and avoid confusion. While pwd is simple, it highlights the hierarchical nature of the file system.

Combining cd, ls, and pwd allows for efficient navigation. Consider the integrated use of these commands in a workflow:

```
pwd
cd ~/Documents
ls -l
cd Projects
pwd
```

This workflow begins by confirming the current directory, navigating to the Documents directory, listing its contents, moving into Projects, and again confirming the current path. This sequence exemplifies fundamental operations within the file system, showcasing how these commands work in concert.

Another vital aspect of navigation involves navigating special directories. Unix-like systems include directories that hold significant operational importance. The root directory (/) is the top-level directory from which all other directories stem. /home contains user-specific directories, while /etc holds system configuration files. Understanding these special directories aids navigation, especially when system-level changes are required.

Effective file system navigation entails understanding shell features such as tab completion and shortcut keys, as these enhance efficiency. Tab completion automatically completes partially typed directory names, reducing typing requirements and minimizing error likelihood. For instance, typing cd Doc and pressing Tab might auto-complete to cd Documents, assuming no other similarly named entries exist in the current directory.

Shortcut keys also contribute to navigation efficiency. The use of Ctrl +

R facilitates the search of recent commands, expediting repeated navigation tasks. Additionally, employing Ctrl + L to clear the terminal window comes in handy during extended navigation sessions, maintaining a clear and organized terminal workspace.

A deeper understanding of cd is rooted in the consideration of shell environment variables, pivotal in navigating frequently accessed directories. Two notable variables include $HOME and $OLDPWD. $HOME holds the path of the home directory and is invoked with cd $HOME or simply cd, returning the user to the home directory. $OLDPWD contains the previous working directory, accessible via cd -, which switches the user back to the last directory visited.

The integration of respectful directory structures and naming conventions cannot be overlooked. Adhering to naming strategies that utilize consistent, logical naming schemes assists navigation. Prefer lowercase letters, separate words with underscores, and avoid spaces or special characters in directory names to strengthen navigation proficiency and script robustness.

An advanced navigation strategy includes the creation and utilization of symbolic links. These serve as shortcuts or references to other files or directories, beneficial when directories are frequently accessed from multiple locations. Creating a symbolic link involves the ln command with the -s option:

```
ln -s /path/to/original /path/to/link
```

This command results in the link acting like the original target, effectively reducing navigation time by not requiring repeated manual path traversals.

Navigating the file system in the Zsh shell combines command execution with an understanding of the system's structure and efficient use of built-in features. Mastery of commands like cd, ls, and pwd, enhanced by practical conventions and utilities such as environment variables and symbolic links, lays the groundwork for proficient system navigation.

3.2 Managing Files and Directories

Effectively managing files and directories is fundamental to the efficient use of any Unix-like operating system. When operating within the Zsh shell, this involves mastering commands that facilitate the creation, modification, and deletion of files and directories, allowing users to organize and control their digital workspace. The primary commands in this process include touch, cp, mv, and rm, among others. These commands provide granular control over file system contents, enabling users to perform complex operations simply and effectively.

The foundational command for file creation is touch. Primarily, touch is used to update the access and modification timestamps of existing files without altering their content. However, a secondary use case is the creation of empty files. Executing touch followed by a filename results in the creation of an empty file if it does not already exist.

```
touch example.txt
```

The above command, touch example.txt, creates a new file named example.txt in the current directory if it does not exist, or updates its timestamp if it does. The creation of files serves as the first step in file management, enabling additional operations such as editing and data insertion.

Duplicating files and directories is achieved through the cp command. This command facilitates the copying of files or directories, preserving their original form while creating replicas. The syntax cp source destination encompasses both a single file copy and directory copy, depending on options used. The -r option is required for recursive copying of directories.

```
cp file1.txt file2.txt
cp -r dir1 dir2
```

The command cp file1.txt file2.txt copies the contents of file1.txt to file2.txt, creating file2.txt if it does not exist. For directories, cp -r dir1 dir2 clones dir1 into dir2, preserving the directory structure. An awareness of file and directory permissions is crucial here, as insufficient permissions result in command failure.

Moving and renaming files and directories utilize the mv command.

Much like cp, mv follows the syntax mv source destination, but instead of duplicating, it relocates. Additionally, renaming is inherently part of this functionality, as moving a file to a new name within the same directory effectively renames it.

```
mv oldname.txt newname.txt
mv file.txt /new/directory/
```

In the first example, mv oldname.txt newname.txt, oldname.txt is renamed to newname.txt, maintaining its content and location. In the second case, mv file.txt /new/directory/ moves file.txt into /new/directory/, removing it from its original location. This capability is central to organizing files, allowing users to restructure their directories dynamically.

Removal of files and directories, an equally important task, is carried out using the rm command. For files, the syntax is straightforward, rm file, whereas directory removal requires the -r option, rm -r directory, to accommodate recursive deletion. The addition of -f (force) circumvents prompts and warnings, although caution is advisable due to irreversible actions.

```
rm unnecessary.txt
rm -r old_directory
rm -rf critical_directory
```

The command rm unnecessary.txt deletes a file straightforwardly, while rm -r old_directory removes a directory and all its contents. The combination rm -rf critical_directory forcefully deletes without confirmation, an option that demands careful consideration due to its potential data loss consequences.

When discussing directory management, we must also consider the creation and manipulation of directories. The command mkdir stands for making directories, allowing for organizational structuring through inception of new folders.

```
mkdir new_folder
mkdir -p /nested/directory/structure
```

The simple command mkdir new_folder generates new_folder in the current directory, while mkdir -p /nested/directory/structure constructs /nested/directory/structure, creating any non-existent parent directories in the process. This sequence of actions supports the hierarchical organization of data, reflecting logical project or data dependencies.

The reverse operation, directory removal, was touched upon with rm -r; however, for empty directories, rmdir offers another method without the need for recursive deletion.

```
rmdir empty_directory
```

Here, rmdir empty_directory deletes empty_directory assuming it is vacant. Attempting to use rmdir on a populated directory results in an error unless forcefully removed using rm -r.

Advanced file and directory management operations often involve manipulation of file attributes and metadata, achievable through additional Zsh shell tools. For instance, stat provides complete insights into file and directory details, encompassing size, permissions, and timestamps, complementing basic management tasks by supplying necessary information for decision-making.

```
stat example.txt
```

Executing stat example.txt outputs comprehensive details about example.txt, crucial for verifying attributes before undertaking significant file management actions.

Beyond executing singular commands, efficient file management within Zsh often leverages scripting and automation. By creating scripts that string together multiple commands, repetitive tasks can be expedited, reducing manual input and minimizing error risks. For example, creating a backup script using cp can automate periodic duplications of essential files.

```
#!/bin/zsh
mkdir -p ~/backup
cp -r ~/important_documents ~/backup
echo "Backup completed on $(date)" >> ~/backup/backup.log
```

This script ensures the creation of a backup directory, copies essential documents, and logs the operation, cementing reliability and traceability in management operations.

Furthermore, integrating these command-line strategies within the broader context of system administration can augment proficiency. For instance, the knowledge of using wildcards with file management commands increases flexibility and efficiency. Using the asterisk (*) or question mark (?) to match multiple filenames simplifies tasks like batch renaming or deleting specific file types.

```
mv *.docx /docs/backups/
rm temp_??
```

The command mv *.docx /docs/backups/ transfers all files with a .docx extension to a backup directory, while rm temp_?? removes files with names starting with temp_ followed by exactly two characters. This pattern matching is invaluable for file system tidying and organization.

Managing files and directories via Zsh commands is paramount for effective system use. Mastering commands such as touch, cp, mv, and rm empowers users to create, replicate, organize, and delete data responsively. Expanded with scripting capabilities, attributes manipulation, and pattern matching techniques, these operations provide a comprehensive toolset for navigating and structuring digital environments.

3.3   File Permissions and Ownership

Understanding file permissions and ownership is crucial in maintaining the security and integrity of a Unix-like operating system. In Zsh, as in other shell environments, every file and directory is associated with a set of permissions and ownership attributes that control access and modification rights. These aspects ensure that files and directories remain secure and prevent unauthorized access or changes. Key commands for managing file permissions and ownership include chmod and chown.

Permissions in Unix are assigned to three categories: the file owner (user), the group, and others (everyone else). Each of these categories can have read (r), write (w), and execute (x) permissions. File permissions are displayed using a sequence of ten characters when using ls -l. These characters include the file type character (- for files, d for directories) followed by the user, group, and other permissions.

For example, consider the output:

```
-rwxr-xr--
```

The first character is a dash (-), indicating a regular file. The next three characters (rwx) represent the owner's permissions: read, write, and execute. The subsequent r-x represents the group's permissions: read and execute but not write. The final r– indicates that others have only read permission.

Modifying these permissions is achieved using the chmod command. This command supports modifying permissions either symbolically or through octal notation. Symbolic mode involves specifying the category (user u, group g, others o, or all a) followed by an operation (+ to grant, - to revoke, or =) and the permission to change.

```
chmod u+x example.sh
chmod g-w report.txt
chmod o=r report.txt
```

The first command, chmod u+x example.sh, adds execute permission for the file's owner. The second command, chmod g-w report.txt, revokes write permission for the group. The third command, chmod o=r report.txt, sets others' permissions to read-only. Each operation prescribes a targeted change to the permission set, ensuring granular control over access and executability.

Alternatively, octal notation assigns permissions using three digits, each ranging from 0 to 7, representing the cumulative permissions for user, group, and others. Each permission type is represented by a bit: 4 for read, 2 for write, and 1 for execute. The sum of these bits determines the digit.

For example:

```
chmod 755 script.sh
```

Here, 755 is translated to rwxr-xr-x: the owner has full permissions (7: read, write, execute), the group has read and execute permissions (5: read and execute, no write), and others also have read and execute permissions (5). This concise mathematical representation in octal format is often utilized for setting permissions quickly, especially in scripts.

Ownership of a file is defined by two attributes: the owner (user) and the group. Changing these attributes is crucial when redistributing files across users or organizing group access. The command chown facilitates these alterations, utilizing the syntax chown user:group file.

Examples include:

```
chown james:developers project.txt
chown :staff /var/www/html
chown tomson: document.pdf
```

The command chown james:developers project.txt assigns james as the owner and developers as the group for project.txt. The expression chown :staff /var/www/html changes only the group to staff without altering the file owner. Conversely, chown tomson: document.pdf modifies only the file owner to tomson, leaving the group unchanged.

Understanding the setuid, setgid, and sticky bits supplements basic permissions, providing additional security and operational flexibility. The setuid bit, when set on an executable file, allows users to execute the file with the file owner's privileges. This capability, often used in administrative scripts, mitigates unnecessary broad permission distributions.

For instance, the command chmod u+s program sets the setuid bit, permitting the executable program to run with owner privileges.

The setgid bit, similarly, applies to directories and files. When set on a directory, it enforces that newly created files inherit the parent directory's group, streamlining permissions management in collaborative environments.

```
chmod g+s /shared/folder/
```

This command sets the setgid bit on /shared/folder/, ensuring that all files created within it belong to the directory's group, fostering cohesive file management in team settings.

The sticky bit, however, governs write permissions in shared directories. When applied, it restricts file deletion or renaming within the directory to the file's owner, the directory's owner, or the superuser, counteracting accidental deletions in directories like /tmp.

```
chmod +t /var/shared/
```

In this command, chmod +t /var/shared/ sets the sticky bit on /var/shared/, ensuring secure collaborative use.

A deeper exploration into file permissions involves Access Control Lists (ACLs), which offer more fine-grained file permissions beyond the traditional owner-group-others model. ACLs allow specific permissions to be set for multiple users or groups, fueling intricate permission schemes needed in complex systems.

Setting and viewing ACLs can be accomplished with the setfacl and getfacl commands, respectively. Example usage includes:

```
setfacl -m u:anna:rw- document.txt
getfacl document.txt
```

The command setfacl -m u:anna:rw- document.txt grants anna read and write permissions on document.txt, independent of her membership in the file's group. getfacl document.txt illustrates the current ACL settings, complementing permission auditing and tuning.

Collectively, managing permissions and ownership secures files against unauthorized alterations and helps enforce organizational policy compliance. Efficiently leveraging commands like chmod and chown, including advanced concepts such as setuid, setgid, and sticky bits, equips administrators and users with the tools to navigate and secure elaborate file systems adeptly.

3.4 Handling Text Files

Text files represent one of the most fundamental data types within computer systems, and Unix-like operating systems, including environments like Zsh, provide a rich suite of tools for handling them. Managing text files efficiently involves a range of operations, from simple viewing and concatenation to more advanced text processing. Familiarity with commands such as cat, less, more, head, and tail is essential for effective text file manipulation and analysis.

The cat (concatenate) command is a versatile tool, primarily used to display the entirety of a text file's contents. Beyond displaying files, cat can concatenate and create text files through redirection. A typical use case for cat is simply outputting a file to the terminal:

```
cat file1.txt
```

73

This command outputs the complete contents of file1.txt directly to the terminal, suitable for small files where complete visibility is manageable. When handling larger files, the output may become overwhelming, necessitating the use of pagination utilities like less or more.

For creating or concatenating files, cat can be employed with output redirection. Consider the scenario of merging multiple files:

```
cat file1.txt file2.txt > combined.txt
```

Here, the contents of file1.txt and file2.txt are merged, and the resulting output is stored in combined.txt. While efficient for merging text files, it's crucial to understand that cat will overwrite the target file when using the single greater-than symbol (>).

To avoid overwriting while appending output, using double greater-than symbols (») ensures that new content is appended:

```
cat additional.txt >> combined.txt
```

This command appends additional.txt to combined.txt, preserving its existing content. This separation between overwriting and appending illustrates the flexible power of cat in text manipulation tasks.

For file viewing with pagination, less provides an interactive method to browse content, fitting for files too large to assess with a single command. less not only displays contents but also supports powerful navigation commands:

```
less largefile.txt
```

Upon launching less, users can navigate through largefile.txt using arrow keys, Page Up, and Page Down. Notably, less supports backward movement across contents, distinguishing it from the more rudimentary more.

Basic less navigation includes keypresses such as:

- G - Go to the end of the file.
- g - Return to the start of the file.
- /pattern - Search forward for pattern.
- ?pattern - Search backward for pattern.

- n - Repeat search in the current direction.

- N - Repeat search in the opposite direction.

The seamless search capability within less supports efficient text location tasks within larger documents, bolstering productivity.

Alternatively, more provides simpler pagination, suitable for users needing basic file visibility without extensive navigation controls:

```
more simplelist.txt
```

Unlike less, more primarily supports forward navigation using Enter to scroll line-by-line or the space bar for page-by-page advancement. While its utility remains limited compared to less, more maintains a role in scenarios demanding minimal control.

For users interested in examining specific sections of text files, head and tail commands extract lines from either the start or end, respectively. By default, both commands output the first or last 10 lines of a file, although their versatility permits specification of line count.

```
head file1.txt
tail file1.txt
head -n 20 file2.txt
tail -n 15 file2.txt
```

In this example, head file1.txt displays the initial 10 lines of file1.txt, while tail file1.txt outputs the last 10 lines. For greater control, head -n 20 file2.txt extracts the first 20 lines of file2.txt. Conversely, tail -n 15 file2.txt gathers the final 15 lines, offering granular access to file segments.

Furthermore, tail includes the -f option, particularly advantageous for real-time monitoring of file growth, such as scrutinizing log files during program execution.

```
tail -f logfile.log
```

This command, tail -f logfile.log, streams new log entries from logfile.log in real-time, a crucial capability for debugging and performance monitoring in dynamic environments.

In addition to direct commands for viewing text files, Unix-like systems boast an array of text-processing utilities that augment the manipulation and analysis of file data. Tools such as sort, uniq, grep, awk, and sed enable complex operations on file contents.

sort orders lines alphabetically or numerically, providing structured views of file data. Consider sorting a list of usernames:

```
sort userlist.txt
```

The command outputs userlist.txt in alphabetical order, presenting an organized perspective. Additional options, such as -r for reverse order, enrich sort's flexibility.

Conversely, uniq filters out duplicate lines from sorted files, essential in deduplication workflows:

```
sort userlist.txt | uniq
```

Here, the combination of sort and uniq results in a unique listing of user names, expunging repetitions. The pipeline pattern demonstrates directive chaining, a hallmark of Unix text processing.

Among the most potent search tools, grep locates patterns within files, supporting options for count (-c), case-insensitive searching (-i), and recursive operation (-r):

```
grep 'pattern' file.txt
grep -i -r 'error' /var/log
```

The initial command, grep 'pattern' file.txt, searches for pattern occurrences within file.txt. In the second example, grep -i -r 'error' /var/log performs a case-insensitive search for error throughout /var/log, returning all instances across existing log files. grep emerges as a versatile search companion, pivotal in data mining and auditing.

For advanced text pattern and field processing, UNIX veterans frequently employ awk, which excels in scanning text line-by-line, splitting into fields and operating per instruction script. A typical awk invocation looks like this:

```
awk '{ print $1 }' data.txt
```

Command awk ' print $1 ' data.txt extracts and outputs the first field from every line in data.txt. This dynamic approach interprets structured data efficiently, suitable for reports or data extraction.

Similarly, sed (stream editor) adapts for per-line text transformation based on regular expressions, useful for substitution, insertion, and formatted transformations:

```
sed 's/old/new/g' input.txt > output.txt
```

Through sed 's/old/new/g' input.txt > output.txt, every occurrence of old in input.txt is replaced with new and saved to output.txt. The global nature of the operation ensures comprehensive transformation, illustrating sed's potency in automation and scripting.

Handling text files extends beyond rudimentary viewing, demanding multifaceted tools to accommodate diverse manipulation needs within Zsh. Mastering core utilities, supplemented by robust text processing techniques, equips users with the necessary expertise to wield text files efficiently, leveraging Zsh shell's capabilities for technical precision and operational mastery.

3.5 Using Command-Line Editors

Command-line text editors are indispensable tools in a developer's toolkit, particularly within Unix-like environments where operations often occur within the terminal. These editors empower users to create, modify, and manage text files directly from the command line interface, offering diverse features tailored to different editing needs. The most popular command-line editors available in Zsh include nano, vim, and emacs, each offering unique advantages and workflows. Mastery of these editors enhances productivity, especially in environments where graphical interfaces are unavailable or impractical.

Nano serves as one of the most user-friendly command-line editors. It offers a straightforward, accessible interface with visible commands at the screen's bottom, making it ideal for beginners or those requiring quick editor access. Open a file in nano simply by typing:

```
nano filename.txt
```

Upon execution, nano opens filename.txt, allowing immediate editing. The command overlay at the bottom provides shortcuts for file operations, enhancing user interaction. For instance, Ô (Ctrl + O) functions as the "WriteOut" command, allowing users to save changes, whereas X (Ctrl + X) exits the editor, prompting for unsaved content.

Key features of nano include:

- K - Cuts the current line, functioning similarly to a clipboard cut command.

- Û - Pastes the last cut text, facilitating block text management.

- Ŵ - Initiates the search function, navigating through the file to locate specific text.

- Ĉ - Displays the current cursor position, useful for navigation in larger files.

While nano's simplicity is its strength for quick edits, its minimalistic approach lacks the depth of features crucial for extensive programming or complex text editing tasks.

On the other hand, vim (Vi IMproved) excels with its modal editing capabilities, extensive scripting support, and a sizable learning curve that yields efficiency gains for experienced users. Vim operates in several fundamental modes, including Normal, Insert, Visual, and Command-line modes. Invoking vim is straightforward:

```
vim example.txt
```

Opening example.txt in vim defaults to Normal mode, from which users can navigate the file with commands like j, k, h, and l representing down, up, left, and right movement, respectively. Transition to Insert mode by pressing i, allowing standard text entry at the cursor location.

Key vim operations include:

- :w - Saves the file in Command-line mode.

- :q - Quits the editor; append ! as in :q! to exit without saving.

- dd - Deletes the entire line where the cursor resides, storing it in a buffer for reuse.

- yy - Copies a line, rendering it ready for pasting with p or P.

- /pattern - Searches for pattern, highlighting occurrences for quick review and navigation.

- v - Initiates Visual mode, allowing text selection for operations like delete or yank.

Vim's strengths lie in its powerful features like macros, which allow users to record and replay a sequence of commands, and its rich plugin ecosystem that extends functionality far beyond text editing. Plugins enhance syntax highlighting, autocomplete functions, and provide refactoring tools, akin to features in integrated development environments (IDEs).

Meanwhile, Emacs offers a feature-rich alternative with a comprehensive programming environment, high customizability through Emacs Lisp, and numerous extensions. Opening files in emacs follows similar initial usage patterns:

```
emacs document.txt
```

Upon entering emacs, users are presented with a buffer where document.txt can be viewed and edited. Emacs uses key bindings defined as sequences often initiated with C- (Ctrl) or M- (Meta, typically the Alt key).

Fundamental emacs functions include:

- C-x C-s - Saves the current buffer.

- C-x C-c - Exits Emacs, prompting to save any unsaved buffers.

- C-x k - Kills the current buffer, closing it within Emacs.

- C-s - Searches incrementally within the buffer, highlighting matches immediately.

- M-w - Copies selected text (known as a "region") to the clipboard.

- C-y - Pastes the clipboard contents, referred to within emacs as the "kill ring."

Emacs' extensibility is its hallmark, enabling customization through Emacs Lisp scripts. This allows users to tailor emacs to very specific

79

work patterns or integrate complex task automations directly into the editor environment. Modes in emacs support syntax highlighting and functionality for numerous programming languages and markup formats, providing an adaptive interface for developers and writers alike.

Regardless of the chosen editor, proficiency requires regular practice and familiarity with command paradigms inherent in the UNIX editing landscape. This adeptness leads to fluency in text navigation and editing directly from the terminal, thus accelerating task completion without transitioning to external programs. Deepening knowledge with these command-line editors can turn them into powerful allies for code development, log file analysis, and system management.

All three editors, nano, vim, and emacs, support user configuration through various configuration files such as .nanorc, .vimrc, and .emacs. These files store custom settings, keybindings, and environment configurations, optimizing the editor's behavior to meet user preferences. Establishing a bespoke environment enhances productivity and accommodates unique user workflows, encouraging consistent and efficient interaction.

Exploring integrated version control features can further mesh command-line editors with modern development practices. For example, plugins in vim and emacs integrate with Git, providing inline access to version control commands, visually marking changes, and simplifying diff viewing directly from the editor. This deep integration transforms them into full-fledged software development environments, providing seamless access to essential tools without leaving the terminal.

In essence, command-line editors provide potent capabilities that, when mastered, facilitate comprehensive text file management and programming tasks. Whether through nano's simplicity, vim's efficiency, or emacs' extensibility, command-line editors remain essential to operating effectively within headless, remote, or resource-constrained environments, ensuring continuous control over text-based operations.

3.6 Zsh Command History and Shortcuts

Efficient command-line use is vital in any shell environment, and Zsh provides a robust feature set that enhances productivity through command history and shortcuts. These functionalities enable users to recall, modify, and execute previous commands quickly, significantly reducing the need to retype frequent or complex command sequences. Understanding and leveraging Zsh's command history and shortcuts is essential for experienced users aiming to streamline their workflows and improve efficiency.

At the heart of Zsh's efficiency is its command history feature. Zsh automatically records each entered command, storing them in a history list accessible for recall and execution. This history persists across sessions, maintained in the .zsh_history file, enabling continuity and ease of access to prior commands.

Basic history navigation utilizes keyboard shortcuts to move through the history list. The up (↑) and down (↓) arrow keys are typically used to navigate backward and forward, respectively, through the list of previously executed commands.

```
# Navigate through command history
# Use ↑to review older commands
# Use ↓to review newer commands
```

Beyond simple navigation, more advanced users harness the power of Zsh's incremental history search feature, accessible through keyboard shortcuts Ctrl + R for a reverse search and Ctrl + S for a forward search, although the latter may be disabled by default due to terminal flow control conflict.

Incremental search provides real-time interactiveness by filtering the command history based on input patterns.

```
# Initiate reverse search
Ctrl + R
# Continue typing to match specific commands
# Use Ctrl + R repeatedly to cycle through matches
```

For users preferring command-based history navigation, the history command displays the history list. Executing history returns a numbered list of stored commands, aiding in quick identification and recall.

```
history
# Output might include:
# 12 ls -al
# 13 cd ~/Documents
# 14 grep -i 'error' logfile
```

Each command's number can be referenced for direct execution by pre-fixing with an exclamation mark (!). For instance, running !13 imme-diately re-executes command number 13 (cd /Documents).

To refine history usage further, Zsh allows for sophisticated event des-ignators, providing means to reference commands based on contextual aspects aside from their numeric history ID. For instance, the double exclamation mark (!!) re-executes the most recent command, while !grep re-runs the latest command starting with grep.

```
!!
# Repeats the last command

!grep
# Executes the most recent 'grep' command
```

Flexible history manipulation supports edits to commands before exe-cution. Modifying previous commands involves more complex history expansions using ^old^new syntax for substitution within the last com-mand, replacing old with new.

```
ls -al /home/user/old_folder
^old_folder^new_folder
# Modifies and executes as:
# ls -al /home/user/new_folder
```

Zsh goes beyond simple navigation and recall by allowing history list manipulation and tailorings, such as configuring how many commands are stored or defining command exclusion from history. The environ-ment variable HISTSIZE regulates the number of remembered com-mands, while HISTFILESIZE sets the storage limit of history entries on disk.

```
export HISTSIZE=1000
export HISTFILESIZE=2000
```

By setting these variables, users can define how extensive the com-mand history is, maintaining a balance between historical depth and resource constraints.

For privacy concerns or reducing clutter, certain commands can be omitted from history via the HISTIGNORE variable:

```
export HISTIGNORE="ls:bg:fg:exit"
```

In this configuration, simple navigation, suspend, and exit commands (ls, bg, fg, exit) are excluded from being stored, streamlining history for more critical entries.

Zsh also supports the management of complex workflows through aliases and keyboard shortcuts, enhancing repetitive task execution efficiency. Aliases create shorthand for longer command sequences, simplifying frequent tasks by reducing keystrokes.

```
alias ll="ls -alF"
alias gs="git status"
```

Here, typing ll executes ls -alF, offering detailed directory contents, while gs activates git status, a common command in software development.

For dynamic command execution, Zsh functions transcend static aliases with parameter inclusion capabilities, facilitating more intricate command constructs.

```
function mkcd {
    mkdir -p "$1"
    cd "$1"
}
```

This mkcd function combines directory creation and navigation, illustrating the advantage of customizable functions to streamline complex command sequences.

Meanwhile, keyboard shortcuts extend Zsh's efficiency without command creation, emulating text editor conveniences within the shell. Common shortcuts like Ctrl + U to erase the command line before the cursor or Ctrl + K to delete from the cursor to line's end enhance responsive command line interaction.

Lastly, embracing alternative keybindings and setup options through configuration files such as .zshrc allows profound personalization of the command-line environment, embedding user-specific preferences directly into Zsh's operation:

```
# Inside .zshrc
bindkey "^[[3~" delete-char
```

This customization binds compatible keys to specific actions, in this case, binding the delete key alternative on some keyboards to delete character action.

Zsh's history and shortcut capabilities empower users with command agility and effectiveness, minimizing manual entry, emphasizing expediency, and fostering tailored solutions for routine and complex command-line tasks alike. By mastering these techniques, users optimize their interaction with the Zsh environment, enhancing productivity through thoughtful integration of history and shortcuts.

Chapter 4

Advanced Zsh Features and Customization

This chapter delves into advanced capabilities of Zsh, focusing on features that enhance both functionality and user experience. Topics include auto-completion, pattern matching, and the creation of aliases and functions. It also explores utilizing arrays in scripts, customizing key bindings, and effectively managing environment variables. These advanced features enable users to tailor Zsh to their specific workflows, maximizing efficiency and productivity.

4.1 Auto-completion and Auto-suggestions

Auto-completion and auto-suggestions are essential features in modern command-line environments that enhance user productivity. In Zsh, these features are implemented with an array of customizable options and configurations, enabling users to streamline their workflows through efficient command input. Zsh's auto-completion system is notably more powerful and flexible than those found in other shells, facilitating a more intuitive interaction with the command line.

The auto-completion feature in Zsh allows users to enter commands more quickly by suggesting possible command completions. It aids in reducing typographical errors and enhancing user efficiency. Zsh attempts to predict what the user is typing based on the current input and any available information, providing the user with a list of potential completions.

To enable auto-completion in Zsh, the first step is to ensure that the completion system is activated. This is typically done by adding the following commands to the .zshrc file:

```
autoload -Uz compinit
compinit
```

The command autoload -Uz compinit tells Zsh to load the compinit script, which sets up the completion system. The compinit command initializes the system, making all its features available during the shell session.

Once the completion system is enabled, Zsh provides numerous options for customizing its behavior. One of the fundamental elements of this system is the use of completion functions, which are predefined logic scripts that dictate how completions are generated for different commands. Users can also write their own completion functions to further tune the shell's behavior to their needs.

For enhanced user experience, Zsh supports dynamic completion lists, where the possible completions update as the user types. This is particularly useful for long commands or paths within complex directory structures. Zsh accomplishes this through a combination of traditional completion and what is known as context-aware completion—distinguishing between different types of arguments and offering suggestions accordingly.

An integral part of auto-completion configuration is the zstyle command, which allows users to customize various aspects of completion behavior, including styling, matching criteria, and presentation of the completion list. For example, to ensure that all file completions are case-insensitive, the user can add the following line to their .zshrc file:

```
zstyle ':completion:*' matcher-list 'm:{a-zA-Z}={A-Za-z}'
```

Here, the zstyle command is used to specify a matching rule that treats upper and lower case characters as equivalent when completing filenames.

In addition to simple completion utilities, Zsh offers a sophisticated framework for enhancing suggestions through understanding complex user intentions, often employing a context-aware approach. For instance, after enabling the completion system, users may want to expand their terminal's capabilities by customizing auto-suggestions based on personal workflows. This can be incredibly beneficial in environments where repetitive commands are frequent, reducing the input required and minimizing errors.

One comprehensive plugin for auto-suggestions in Zsh is the zsh-autosuggestions plugin. This plugin provides suggestions based on the user's command history and displays them just before the cursor in a light grey text, which can be accepted by pressing the right arrow key. To install and use this plugin, follow these steps:

1. Clone the zsh-autosuggestions repository:

```
git clone https://github.com/zsh-users/zsh-autosuggestions ~/.zsh/zsh-
    autosuggestions
```

2. Source this plugin's zsh file in your .zshrc:

```
source ~/.zsh/zsh-autosuggestions/zsh-autosuggestions.zsh
```

3. Restart your shell to observe the auto-suggestions feature.

By default, this plugin leverages the existing command history to provide inline suggestions as you type. This is especially useful as common commands can quickly be retrieved without remembering their exact format or parameters.

The addition of zsh-syntax-highlighting can improve readability and decrease errors by highlighting valid commands differently from invalid ones, thereby operating in tandem with auto-completion. To utilize this plugin, add it to your configuration as follows:

1. Clone the zsh-syntax-highlighting repository:

87

```
git clone https://github.com/zsh-users/zsh-syntax-highlighting.git ~/.zsh/zsh-
    syntax-highlighting
```

2. Source this plugin's zsh file in your .zshrc:

```
source ~/.zsh/zsh-syntax-highlighting/zsh-syntax-highlighting.zsh
```

Customization can be extended further by leveraging conditions and constraints associated with auto-completions or auto-suggestions. For instance, suppose you wish to disable auto-suggestion for certain commands such as sensitive scripts or private management tools that are not needed to appear in the suggestion list. In this scenario, one could employ zstyle or adjustments within plugin-specific configuration files, if available, to filter out these commands contextually.

An effective utilization of Zsh's capabilities concerning auto-completion and auto-suggestions involves organizing and curating user-created scripts and configuring Zsh to offer a streamlined experience. By deliberately designing command namespaces and labels, users can ensure that commands are sensible and do not cause unnecessary clutter or confusion. This is especially important in project directories or environments such as version control system directories, where there might be scripts associated with different project branches.

Exploring completion scripts also contributes significantly to maximizing utilities. A completion script can be written for less common commands by taking advantage of Zsh's programmable completion feature, allowing customized logic and additional rules. A fundamental knowledge of writing completion functions can enable users to create these on their own.

An example structure for a completion function script might look like this:

```
#compdef _mycommand mycommand

_mycommand() {
    local -a options
    options=(
        '--help: show help message'
        '--version: show version information'
    )
```

```
   _describe -t options 'mycommand options' options
}

compdef _mycommand mycommand
```

This snippet establishes a completion function _mycommand for the hypothetical mycommand. It defines an array of options with descriptions and uses the _describe command to present these options dynamically during completion.

Mastering Zsh's auto-completion and auto-suggestion features requires an understanding of its innate capabilities, coupled with the integration of community-driven plugins. Additional scripts and configurations can further enhance the interactive experience, fostering a productive environment by minimizing manual input and encouraging efficient command usage. The intricate customization provides flexibility that accommodates both novice and experienced users, ensuring that terminal operations remain optimally concise and accessible.

4.2 Globbing and Pattern Matching

Globbing and pattern matching in Zsh provide powerful mechanisms for specifying sets of filenames with patterns, executed directly from the command line. These capabilities offer significant enhancements over traditional shell scripting, allowing for complex file manipulations and refined command management without repetitive sequences. Zsh extends the typical pattern matching capabilities significantly beyond those found in more conventional shell environments, making it an invaluable tool for users dealing with extensive file systems or intricate workflows.

In most shells, globbing refers to the process of expanding wildcard patterns in file and directory names. Zsh enhances this definition with a wider variety of wildcard operators and control structures, enabling more sophisticated pattern evaluations. When a user types a command that includes a pattern, globbing allows Zsh to identify anything in the file system that matches this pattern and passes them as arguments to the command being executed.

89

The basic set of wildcards common across shell environments includes:

- The asterisk *, which matches zero or more characters, providing an inclusive selection scope.

- The question mark ?, which matches exactly one character.

- Square brackets [...], containing a series of characters, denote that any single character within the brackets can match.

- Curly braces {...}, used to create alternations between multiple strings separated by commas.

For example, the pattern *.txt matches any file ending with .txt, while file?.txt matches files that have one character substituting the question mark—in this case, filea.txt, file1.txt, etc.

Zsh introduces additional pattern matching syntax that permits exponential increases in specificity and customization, including:

- **/: Matches directories recursively. For instance, **/*.txt matches any .txt file at any directory level.

- <x-y>: Matches a numeric range expanded into any matching numbers within the range. For example, file<1-5>.txt would match file1.txt through file5.txt.

- ~ (tilde-negation): Excludes patterns from matches, allowing selection through subtraction mechanics.

- (foo|bar): Matches either foo or bar, often combined with other operators for complex patterns.

- #, ##: Indicate one or more repetitions of the preceding character class or wildcard. As such, a#b matches ab, aab, aaab, etc.

Consider a practical application of using **/ for selecting log files under a directory structure divided by years and months:

```
grep 'ERROR' logs/**/2023/*.log
```

Here, Zsh's globbing provides a succinct means to search for error entries across all logs in subdirectories under logs for the year 2023. This file selection expedites data evaluations across nested structures without relying on explicit recursion or manually managing directory hierarchy.

Another powerful feature is the approximation of pattern matches, which is often necessary when dealing with large datasets where inconsistencies in input formats exist. Zsh supports this through its approximate matching capability which can be activated using the % operator within a pattern. By default, it permits one mistake in the pattern's match, but users may specify other tolerances as needed.

Moreover, glob qualifiers in Zsh expand on the pattern matching capabilities by focusing on attributes beyond just names, such as timestamps or file type. For instance, to find all files within a directory that were modified within the last day, one could leverage the pattern:

```
ls *(mm-1)
```

Here, the glob qualifier (mm-1) plays a crucial role. The "mm" qualifier stands for file modification time, and "-1" indicates precisely one day relative to the current time, providing explicit control over file group selection based on property specifications.

Nested and conditional glob expressions allow for even more refined selection criteria, where condition checks in patterns direct the matching logic based on runtime evaluation conditions. Complex conditions can involve combinations of these expressions, often linked with unions or intersections when conceptualized as set operations.

```
echo *(^/).(mp4|mkv)(U)
```

In this arrangement, ^/ matches non-directories, .(mp4|mkv) ensures a limited media format match, and U ensures the results are only the latest accessed files, demonstrating a full-bodied manipulation of command targeting.

When combined with Zsh's powerful array management and scripting capabilities, globbing and pattern matching enable the construction of advanced scripts capable of dynamically responding to variable file arrangements. Mastery over these features significantly amplifies how Zsh operates as a versatile facilitator for automation and scripting across diverse project environments.

Additional customization may be attained by adjusting the interactive shell options concerning pattern behavior. Configuration at this level influences how the shell interprets ambiguous glob commands, aligns pattern priorities, and may augment plug-in responsibilities for broader input scenarios.

Zsh's enhancements to globbing and pattern matching offer sophisticated tools to manage files through precise and flexible expressions. Leveraging these capabilities effectively can streamline operations, particularly when dealing with complex file structures or when building robust command-line applications. By allowing more sophisticated pattern definitions and control over matched entities through qualifiers and conditions, Zsh empowers users to transcend simple shell interaction to a domain where user intent and execution are harmonized efficiently.

4.3   Using Aliases and Functions

In Zsh, aliases and functions are essential tools for optimizing command-line workflows. They allow users to reduce repetitive typing, encapsulate complex command sequences into simple and memorable shortcuts, and significantly increase efficiency when interacting with the shell. While aliases provide a straightforward means to bind a complex command to a simpler keyword, functions extend this capability by supporting argument passing and more intricate logic execution.

Aliases serve as shortcuts for longer command strings. They are especially useful for frequently used commands with long or complex options. An alias is declared using the 'alias' command followed by a name and the desired command:

```
alias ll='ls -lh'
alias gs='git status'
alias rm='rm -i'
```

These examples demonstrate common scenarios where aliases can modify behavior ('rm' to 'rm -i' for interactive deletion confirmation) and provide quicker access ('ll' for a detailed file list, 'gs' for checking git status).

Aliases are typically defined in the .zshrc file to ensure they are available in every session. Their simplicity, however, limits some flexibility. Aliases cannot accept parameters; thus, they accomplish only direct, static substitutions.

Zsh functions, on the other hand, provide a broader scope of functionalities. A function is a block of code grouped under a single executing unit which can receive arguments, maintain local variables, and leverage robust control structures like conditionals and loops.

A basic function syntax looks like this:

```
function greet() {
  echo "Hello, $1!"
}

greet "Zsh"
```

Here, the function 'greet' prints a greeting to any given name. $1 represents the first argument passed to the function, showcasing functions' capacity to intake and operate based on passed data.

Unlike aliases, functions can be as simple or complex as necessary, operating as complete scripts on their own. Nesting commands and even conditional executions come naturally within functions, exemplified below:

```
function deploy_project() {
  if [ -z "$1" ]; then
    echo "Please specify a project directory."
    return 1
  fi

  cd $1 || { echo "Failed to change directory."; return 1; }
  echo "Deploying project in $1..."
  git pull origin main
  npm install
  npm run build
  echo "Deployment complete!"
}
```

In this scenario, the 'deploy_project' function automates deploying a project by pulling the latest changes from a git repository and building it using npm, given a directory path. It incorporates error checking and supportive messaging, skills absent in simple aliases.

Functions are stored and initialized during shell session start-up in .zshrc, alongside or after aliases. To structure larger collections of func-

93

tions, users can keep them in separate files and source these files from .zshrc.

To illustrate further, shell functions can employ more abstract logic like loops and multiple conditions. Consider the function 'backup_files':

```
function backup_files() {
  if [ "$#" -lt 2 ]; then
    echo "Usage: backup_files <source> <destination> [files...]"
    return 1
  fi

  local source="$1"
  local destination="$2"
  local file
  shift 2

  for file in "$@"; do
    if [ -e "$source/$file" ]; then
      cp "$source/$file" "$destination/"
      echo "Backed up $file to $destination."
    else
      echo "Warning: $file does not exist in $source."
    fi
  done
}
```

This command encapsulates the action of copying specified files from a source to a destination directory, with individual verification of file existence before proceeding, thus reducing operational errors.

Linking functions and aliases, it is often advantageous to create simple-to-recall aliases that invoke functions with predefined parameters, marrying alias rapidity with a function's versatility.

A practical demonstration could involve combining utility commands. If the goal is frequent scanning for large files, an alias could simplify invocation of a more involved function:

```
function find_large_files() {
  local dir="${1:-.}"
  local size_threshold="${2:-100M}"
  echo "Finding files larger than $size_threshold in $dir..."
  find "$dir" -type f -size +$size_threshold -exec ls -lh {} \;
}

alias flf="find_large_files"
```

This setup allows users to type 'flf' for a default search in the current directory or 'flf /path/to/dir 200M' for specifics, showcasing how aliases augment parameters and logic encapsulated in functions.

Moreover, Zsh's advanced scripting capability features modules like 'zmodload', permitting users to enhance functions. While this extends functions into more full-fledged scripts capable of modularity, typical user interaction focuses on direct and indirect invocation for daily task efficiencies, echoing effective shell practice.

Zsh aliases and functions are robust tools that significantly augment the shell's command-line interface, offering customized, efficient interactions tailored to user workflows. By integrating flexible functions with straightforward aliases, users can streamline their command usage, reducing redundancies, and fostering productivity. Thoughtful alias and function designs enable users to easily master sophisticated shell tasks, ensuring they derive maximum functionality from Zsh's versatile environment.

4.4 Scripting with Zsh Arrays

Arrays are a fundamental data structure in scripting, enabling the management of collections of variables under a single identifier. The robust array handling in Zsh grants users and script developers powerful tools for managing collections of data—be it file paths, user inputs, or command outputs—efficiently and with elegance.

In Zsh, arrays may be indexed or associative, allowing versatility in organizing data. Indexed arrays involve integer keys, while associative arrays use named keys (strings). Understanding and utilizing these arrays effectively can render scripts far more dynamic, readable, and maintainable than treating data as standalone variables.

To declare an indexed array, simple assignment syntax suffices. Here is the declaration of an indexed array and subsequent access:

```
friends=(Alice Bob Charlie)
echo "Second friend: ${friends[1]}"
```

Note Zsh's zero-based indexing where 'Alice' is at index 0. Access to individual elements is achieved using the '$array[index]' notation. To refer to all elements, use '$array[@]' or '$array[*]'; the former is generally preferred due to a difference in delimitations during expansions in certain contexts.

95

To modify arrays, element assignments can be performed directly:

```
friends[0]="Alex" # Update first element
friends[3]="Diane" # Append new element
```

Array operations extend beyond individual access, encompassing manipulations like slicing, length determination, and concatenation. For
example, the length of an array is easily determined using '#', as
demonstrated here:

```
echo "Number of friends: ${#friends[@]}"
```

Slicing extracts subarrays, relying on starting indices and lengths:

```
sub_friends=("${friends[@]:1:2}") # Extracts two elements starting from index 1
echo "Sublist: ${sub_friends[@]}"
```

Associative arrays function through explicit declaration, using the
'typeset -A' command to distinguish the map-like structuring:

```
typeset -A capitals
capitals=([France]="Paris" [Japan]="Tokyo" [Australia]="Canberra")
echo "Capital of Japan: ${capitals[Japan]}"
```

In associative arrays, key uniqueness is maintained by default; reas-
signment alters the existing mapped value rather than appending. Iterating over associative arrays involves accessing both keys and values,
typically executed using loops:

```
for country in "${!capitals[@]}"; do
  echo "The capital of $country is ${capitals[$country]}."
done
```

Array manipulation dovetails with numerous built-in functions, enhancing their interaction with system commands. This is crucial when
handling file system data or command outputs that are inherently
suited to list processing. For instance, consider the manipulation of
outputs from commands:

```
files=(*.txt)
echo "Found ${#files[@]} text files."
```

Here, globbing gathers all '.txt' files into an array, whose size is subsequently computed. Utility functions such as 'mapfile' or parsing command output via '$(...)' construction routinely yield arrays.

Zsh arrays accept operations typically suited for list comprehension, including in-place transformations and filtering through pattern matching or extended attribute qualifiers:

```
# Convert filenames to lowercase
lowercased_files=("${files[@],,*.txt}")
echo "Lowercased filenames: ${lowercased_files[@]}"
```

Additional array capabilities capitalize on Zsh's ability to splice and enumerate efficiently, injecting iterative control and modularity into scripts. This aptitude is crucial when scripts grow beyond basic administrative tasks to accommodate sizable datasets requiring structured yet flexible handling.

Advanced script implementations usually involve arrays in contexts where configuration management or data consolidation are paramount. Let's integrate complex array handling through a script managing server hosts:

```
typeset -A servers
servers=(
  [web]='web01.example.com'
  [db]='db01.example.com'
  [cache]='cache01.example.com'
)

# Command function to check connectivity
function check_connectivity() {
  local server_name=$1
  ping -c 1 "${servers[$server_name]}" > /dev/null 2>&1

  if [ $? -eq 0 ]; then
    echo "$server_name server is reachable."
  else
    echo "$server_name server is down."
  fi
}

# Iterate over all servers
for server in "${!servers[@]}"; do
  check_connectivity $server
done
```

This snippet demonstrates associative arrays used to map server roles to hostnames, with a function to validate connectivity encapsulating repeated logic. Iteration over associative array keys invokes checks succinctly, reducing room for redundancy or error.

Arrays in Zsh transcend a mere data collection role, representing piv-

97

otal instruments in intelligent script compositions. They underpin essential loop and conditional operations that transform necessary logics into reusable and dynamic structures, ensuring scripts can address varied input sizes and complexities.

Mastering Zsh's array capabilities endows script developers with a potent arsenal for data-centric command-line tasks. By accommodating both indexed and associative paradigms, Zsh enables efficient organizing, processing, and retrieving of data, optimizing performance and reliability in script automation. Thorough comprehension of array operations further ensures flexibility in adjusting to diverse requirements, making Zsh scripting a powerful and adaptive programming environment.

4.5   Customizing Key Bindings

Zsh's extensive customization options extend beyond scripting capabilities and aliases or functions to the configuration of key bindings. Key bindings in Zsh facilitate user interaction with the shell by assigning specific commands or scripts to key sequences, allowing for efficient and personalized command-line navigation. Customizing key bindings can significantly improve productivity by creating a keyboard layout that aligns with individual workflows and preferences.

In Zsh, key bindings are managed primarily through two command-line editing modes: 'emacs' and 'vi'. These modes cater to users familiar with the corresponding text editors and offer an array of keyboard shortcuts corresponding to their editor counterparts. By default, Zsh is configured to use the 'emacs' mode, but users can switch to 'vi' mode with the command:

```
bindkey -v
```

Alternatively, for users more comfortable with 'emacs' commands, the default behavior is sufficient or can explicitly be set with:

```
bindkey -e
```

At the heart of key binding customization in Zsh lies the 'bindkey' command. This command allows users to assign, view, and modify key mappings. To understand the current key bindings and explore potential modifications, the command:

```
bindkey
```

can output a list of all current bindings, offering insights into how keypresses are interpreted by Zsh.

Customizing key bindings often begins with on-the-fly command adjustments or creating shortcuts for cumbersome sequences of operations. For example, binding 'Control+l' to a command that clears the screen:

```
bindkey "^l" clear-screen
```

Here, 'l' denotes 'Control+l', a notation shared across UNIX systems. The 'clear-screen' command, bound to this action, is built into the command-line editing framework within Zsh to standardize views.

Users can define new custom key bindings which call arbitrary functions or execute specific scripts. Consider an everyday scenario where one might want to switch directly to the top-level directory of the current git repository, a frequent operation in software development workflows:

```
# Define a function to switch to the git root directory
function cd_git_root() {
  local root_dir
  root_dir=$(git rev-parse --show-toplevel) || return
  cd "$root_dir" || echo "Could not switch to the git root directory"
}

# Bind the function to a key sequence
zle -N cd-git-root cd_git_root
bindkey "^g" cd-git-root
```

In this script, 'zle -N cd-git-root cd_git_root' makes the function 'cd_-git_root' available to the Zsh Line Editor (ZLE), allowing it to be invoked by key bindings. The 'bindkey "^g" cd-git-root' line associates this function with 'Control+g', enabling execution through the assigned key sequence.

For users familiar with 'vi' or 'emacs', replicating behaviors from their editors, such as mapping key sequences that move the cursor by word or line, can bridge the gap between text editing and shell interaction, providing a smoother transition between contexts. Users can achieve this by exploring and customizing key sequence commands like 'vi-forward-word' or 'emacs-forward-word'.

A common configuration scenario might involve extending these bindings to integrate system utilities or bespoke scripts, such as launching specific applications or scripts with a single keystroke rather than typing out the commands each time.

To implement a binding that launches a preferred editor, assuming it is Vim, the user might add:

```
bindkey "^e" vi-start-edit
alias vi-start-edit='vim $(fzf)'
```

The 'fzf' command provides a fuzzy file selector which integrates with this binding to quickly open any file, based on user navigation, using Vim.

For effective key binding customization, users should also acquaint themselves with 'zsh' options that enable complex behaviors or adjust 'ZLE' settings. The '.zshrc' file facilitates persistent key binding customizations, ensuring these settings are applied every session. Advanced users might further manipulate key sequences via raw key codes, often derived from utility functions or libraries that extend 'ZLE' capabilities with new interactive commands or behaviors.

To unbind keys, ensuring effective cleanup and optimization when designing personal configurations, employ the sequence:

```
bindkey -r "^r"
```

This command removes any binding for 'Control+r', a default history search command, where users might want to replace it with a more comprehensive alternative or defer to another integration strategy.

For a productive shell environment tuned to personal preferences, custom key bindings should reflect commonly utilized commands and custom scripts, optimizing entry and feedback cycles susceptible to frequent iterations. Imagining workflows with modulated key shortcuts should capture typical operations, boosting productivity through tailored, intuitive command executions.

Zsh's ability to customize key bindings represents a potent personalization attribute, fostering an efficient and comfortable command-line interaction. Through deft utilization of 'bindkey', users can map custom scripts, streamline routine shell operations, and embrace a natural extension of their favorite editing tools' environment. This facility significantly upgrades not only productivity but also promotes an enjoyable computing experience tailored exclusively to the user's needs.

4.6 Environment Variables Management

Environment variables play a pivotal role in a computer system, acting as dynamic placeholders for storing data that can influence the behavior of running processes or the shell environment itself. They are often used to configure system paths, provide user information, and manage system-wide settings. In Zsh, as in other shells, effective management of environment variables is crucial for robust script development and an optimized user environment.

Environment variables can be categorized into two types: session variables and persistent variables. The former exist only during the session in which they are defined, while the latter are loaded at the start of every session, typically set in configuration files like '.zshrc', '.profile', or '.zprofile'.

Defining environment variables in Zsh follows a straightforward syntax. For example, to set a temporary variable, use:

```
export MY_VAR="Hello World"
echo $MY_VAR
```

The export command marks MY_VAR so that it is available to any subprocess or script invoked from that shell session. Querying the value of a variable is done using the $ symbol, as shown above.

Much of the system's functionality depends on specific environment variables that dictate how commands are executed and where programs are searched. Some commonly used environment variables include:

- PATH: A crucial environment variable specifying a colon-delimited list of directories for executable files. It enables users to run commands without typing the full path to their executable files.

- HOME: Points to the current user's home directory and is especially useful for managing user-specific configurations and paths.

- USER: Contains the username of the currently logged-in user.

- SHELL: Indicates the path to the user's default shell executable.

- LANG: Sets the language and character encoding, influencing how software presents and processes text.

Configuring the PATH variable is often one of the first tasks in environment setup, ensuring smooth operation of frequently used programs and scripts:

```
export PATH="/usr/local/bin:/usr/bin:/bin:$HOME/bin:$PATH"
```

This command prepends custom program directories to the existing PATH, ensuring that locally-stored executables in $HOME/bin are prioritized.

Environment variable persistence is achieved through entries in files that load on initial shell start-up. Place your variable declarations in /.zshrc to ensure their availability in every Zsh session:

```
# .zshrc
export PATH="$HOME/bin:$PATH"
export EDITOR="vim"
```

Here, setting EDITOR to vim indicates a preference for it in scenarios where text editing operations are initiated by scripts or system utilities.

Environment variables can dramatically dictate script behavior and enable customization beyond mere static scripting. For instance, scripts may adapt based on user roles or presence of specific configurations, utilizing condition checks on environment variables:

```
if [[ $HOSTNAME == "production-server" ]]; then
  echo "Running in production mode"
  export LOG_LEVEL="ERROR"
else
  echo "Running in development mode"
  export LOG_LEVEL="DEBUG"
fi
```

In this example, script execution differs depending on whether it detects the environment to be a production server—a decision influenced by the HOSTNAME variable, with log verbosity controlled accordingly.

To encapsulate environment configurations for specific applications, environment variables are vital for initializing application states or setting resource paths. Consider a Python application requiring a virtual environment and specific library paths:

```
export PYTHONPATH="/path/to/lib:$PYTHONPATH"
source /path/to/venv/bin/activate
```

Management of environment variables can thus extend to application lifecycle control and dependency management, underscoring their importance in development workflows.

Lastly, accessing environment variables within scripts often requires refinement in cases where defaults or absence management are preferred. The use of parameter expansion provides sophisticated handling:

```
MY_CONFIG="${MY_CONFIG:-default_value}"
```

This syntax assigns default_value to MY_CONFIG only if it is unset, allowing scripts to carry forth safe execution even under varying environments.

Environment variables are a powerful mechanism available in Zsh for managing configuration and executing automation scripts. Mastery over their usage entails an understanding of declaration, scope, persistence, and procedural control. By leveraging these variables smartly, users can construct highly dynamic and contextual shell environments, providing both stability and flexibility across various computing tasks. Properly managed environment variables are therefore instrumental in beginning complex operations, exploring expansive datasets, or transitioning seamlessly across diverse computing settings.

Chapter 5

Scripting with Zsh: Control Structures

This chapter addresses the essential control structures in Zsh scripting, such as conditional statements, loops, and case constructs, which are fundamental for creating dynamic and responsive scripts. It provides insight into using functions for modular script design and covers best practices for error handling with exit codes. The chapter emphasizes strategies for optimizing script logic and execution flow, equipping users with the tools needed for effective automation and script development.

5.1 Using Conditional Statements

In Zsh scripting, conditional statements are a pivotal construct used to control the flow and behavior of scripts based on varying criteria. They allow the execution of particular code segments when specific conditions are true, offering the flexibility to manage different program states effectively. The primary conditional constructs available in Zsh are if, else, and elif. Understanding these constructs is essential for any script that needs to make decisions or check conditions dynamically.

105

The if statement forms the foundational structure of conditional logic in Zsh scripts. It evaluates a given expression and, if the expression is true, executes the code within its block. The syntactic form of a basic if statement is as follows:

```
if expression; then
    # code to execute if expression is true
fi
```

The expression used in the if statement usually involves string comparisons, file checks, or numeric evaluations, determined by the specific requirements of the script. It is critical that these expressions are properly formed and that the evaluation criteria are precisely defined to avoid potential logical errors.

To expand the decision-making capabilities, Zsh integrates the else clause. This clause provides an alternative pathway when the initial if condition evaluates to false. Integrating the else clause enhances the control flow by covering additional scenarios that were not met initially:

```
if expression; then
    # code if expression is true
else
    # code if expression is false
fi
```

The elif construct, short for else if, is used to handle multiple conditions sequentially. This construct is particularly useful when several conditions need to be checked in series, allowing for a tiered decision-making process:

```
if expression1; then
    # code if expression1 is true
elif expression2; then
    # code if expression2 is true
else
    # code if neither expression1 nor expression2 is true
fi
```

This hierarchical approach can be vital when writing scripts that require detailed conditional checks, providing substantial flexibility in logical structuring.

Consider a Zsh script that checks user input to determine a course of action. Suppose the script reads a user's choice and executes different commands based on whether the input is "start", "stop", or "exit". The implementation using if, else, and elif would be:

```
echo "Enter a command (start/stop/exit):"
read user_input

if [[ $user_input == "start" ]]; then
    echo "Starting the process..."
    # command to start the process
elif [[ $user_input == "stop" ]]; then
    echo "Stopping the process..."
    # command to stop the process
elif [[ $user_input == "exit" ]]; then
    echo "Exiting the script."
    exit 0
else
    echo "Invalid command: $user_input"
fi
```

In this example, the script handles user input efficiently by evaluating each condition successively. The use of double square brackets [[ ]] for expression evaluation allows for a more robust pattern matching and string handling unique to Zsh.

Besides checking equality, Zsh's conditional logic also supports operators for greater nuances such as numeric comparison, file tests, and logical operators. For instance:

- -eq, -ne, -lt, -le, -gt, and -ge for numeric comparison.

- -f (file exists and is a regular file), -d (file exists and is a directory), -s (file exists and is not empty) for file operations.

- Logical operators like && (and), || (or), and ! (not) for combining conditions.

A more complex script might check several criteria using these operators:

```
if [[ -f /tmp/example.txt && -s /tmp/example.txt ]]; then
    echo "Example.txt exists and is not empty."
else
    echo "Example.txt does not exist or is empty."
fi
```

In this code, the script checks if the file /tmp/example.txt exists and is not empty, providing a safeguard against attempting to process non-existing or empty files.

Moreover, Zsh provides built-in test commands and syntax alternatives for improved precision and readability. A classic alternative to the if block is using the test or [ ] command, synonymous in functionality but allowing for clearer readability and simpler syntax:

```
if [ -f "/etc/passwd" ]; then
    echo "The passwd file exists."
else
    echo "The passwd file is missing."
fi
```

An important aspect of conditional logic implementation is ensuring both performance and clarity. The usage of brackets for test commands can help in this regard, but one must choose based on script context. Understanding different syntactic instances and when to apply them can finely tune script efficiency.

Combining if conditional constructs with loop constructs such as for or while can lead to even more sophisticated script behavior. For example, iterating over a list of values and performing actions conditionally based on their content:

```
for i in {1..10}; do
    if (( i \% 2 == 0 )); then
        echo "$i is even."
    else
        echo "$i is odd."
    fi
done
```

In the given loop, the script checks each number from 1 to 10, prints an appropriate message based on its parity, showcasing how conditional statements and looping constructs can be merged for more dynamic script functionalities.

Equally important is handling user inputs with numerical comparisons; scripts benefit from the concise arithmetic evaluation feature Zsh supports:

```
echo "Enter a number:"
read num

if (( num > 0 )); then
    echo "$num is positive."
elif (( num < 0 )); then
    echo "$num is negative."
else
    echo "$num is zero."
```

```
fi
```

This illustrates the arithmetic comparison capability Zsh possesses directly within the if statements, promoting minimal syntax and leveraging arithmetic expressions efficiently.

Zsh also supports compound conditions using logical operators, useful for more intricate scenarios requiring multiple condition checks. Logical AND && and OR || let scripts address complex criteria in fewer lines with heightened clarity:

```
if [[ $var1 -gt 10 && $var2 -lt 20 ]]; then
    echo "Both conditions are true."
else
    echo "One or both conditions are false."
fi
```

In this scenario, the script checks two conditions concurrently, illustrating compound evaluation application and empowering scripts to process multi-faceted checks elegantly.

Combining conditionals with built-in shell states or system variables becomes useful when a script should adapt dynamically to the environment in which it is executed. For instance, a script could behave differently based on the operating system:

```
if [[ "$(uname)" == "Linux" ]]; then
    echo "Running on Linux."
elif [[ "$(uname)" == "Darwin" ]]; then
    echo "Running on macOS."
else
    echo "Unknown operating system."
fi
```

Mastering conditional statements in Zsh requires understanding the nuances of expression evaluation, leveraging operators correctly, combining condition checks logically, and structuring scripts for scalability. Ensuring reliable conditions and optimizing error handling contribute substantially to robust, flexible, and efficient script design. This mastery becomes indispensable as scripts grow in complexity and require adaptive behavior under diverse conditions.

5.2   Looping with for and while

Loop constructs are fundamental in programming, allowing for tasks to be repeated efficiently without redundancy. In Zsh scripting, the primary loop constructs are for and while loops. Each serves unique purposes, offering solutions to different iteration requirements, and using them effectively can substantially enhance the productivity and capabilities of your scripts.

The for loop in Zsh executes a sequence of commands repeatedly for a specified range or list of elements, iterating over each item systematically. A basic for loop structure is as follows:

```
for variable in list; do
    # commands to execute
done
```

Here, list can be an explicitly defined list of values, a range, or results from a command. The variable is successively assigned the value of each element in the list, iterating over the set and executing the enclosed commands for each item.

Consider a simple usage example where the for loop iterates over a predefined list of numbers:

```
for num in 1 2 3 4 5; do
    echo "Number: $num"
done
```

In this instance, the script prints each number from the list, demonstrating how repeat tasks can be managed efficiently with minimal code.

The versatility of the for loop is further exemplified when iterating over command outputs. By integrating command substitution, the loop can dynamically process lists generated during script execution. For instance, listing files in a directory:

```
for file in $(ls /path/to/directory); do
    echo "File: $file"
done
```

This construction iterates over the files in the specified directory, presenting each filename as it proceeds through the list. It highlights how for loops can easily integrate with other shell commands to handle more complex scenarios.

Additionally, Zsh introduces a more concise for loop syntax when working with ranges directly:

```
for i in {1..5}; do
    echo "Count: $i"
done
```

This syntax automatically generates a sequence from 1 to 5, simplifying the loop setup and reducing opportunities for syntax errors.

Contrastingly, the while loop in Zsh executes as long as a condition remains true. It checks the condition before every iteration, ensuring robust control over the loop execution based on predefined criteria. The basic structure is:

```
while condition; do
    # commands to execute
done
```

The while loop is particularly adept at scenarios where the termination condition is not known in advance, unlike the fixed iteration count of the for loop.

For example, consider a script where a counter is incremented until it exceeds a specific value:

```
counter=1
while [[ $counter -le 5 ]]; do
    echo "Counter: $counter"
    ((counter++))
done
```

In this loop, the script continues iterating, incrementing the counter variable by 1 each time, until it surpasses 5. This showcases the loop's suitability for condition-based repetitions.

Zsh also supports the break and continue commands within loops, offering fine-grained control over iteration behavior. The break command exits the loop prematurely, while continue skips the remainder of the current iteration, moving directly to the condition check or the next iteration of a for loop.

An example of using break follows:

111

```
for i in {1..10}; do
    if [[ $i -eq 6 ]]; then
        echo "Breaking at $i"
        break
    fi
    echo "Number: $i"
done
```

Here, the loop terminates when it reaches the value 6. This capability is particularly useful for stopping execution under specific conditions without evaluating the full loop range.

Similarly, utilizing continue is useful to bypass certain conditions:

```
for i in {1..5}; do
    if [[ $i -eq 3 ]]; then
        continue
    fi
    echo "Current number: $i"
done
```

In this script, the number 3 is intentionally omitted, illustrating precise control within the loop without full termination.

Combining loops with conditional checks unlocks powerful patterns for complex automation tasks. Consider a script that checks a list of URLs, identifying those that are currently accessible:

```
urls=("http://example.com" "http://nonexistent.xyz" "http://anotherexample.com")

for url in "${urls[@]}"; do
    if curl -s --head --request GET $url | grep "200 OK" > /dev/null; then
        echo "$url is accessible"
    else
        echo "$url is not accessible"
    fi
done
```

Here, the script iterates over a list of URLs, using curl to verify each URL's accessibility and reporting the result, demonstrating an integration of for loops with networking commands.

The while loop, incorporating file handling, databases, or dynamic data sources, is similarly advantageous. Imagine processing a file line by line until EOF is reached. By redirecting file content to a while loop:

```
while IFS= read -r line; do
    echo "Line: $line"
done < /path/to/file.txt
```

Here, each line is processed individually, which is optimal for text processing or batch operations that depend on sequential data handling.

Nested looping—loops within loops—can incrementally refine control structures in Zsh. This is vital in multidimensional data processing or multi-tiered automation processes:

```
for i in {1..3}; do
    echo "Outer loop iteration: $i"
    for j in {1..2}; do
        echo " Inner loop iteration: $j"
    done
done
```

With this structure, an outer loop dictates overall cycles, while inner loops operate within each outer cycle, enabling tiered data transformations, task automation, or configuration setups.

Moreover, Zsh extends loop constructs with specific features, such as associative arrays or process substitutions, further enriching loop functionalities. Understanding these Zsh-specific advancements allows automated solutions paradigms to leverage shell scripting's full potential.

In all, loop constructs in Zsh are cornerstones of efficient scripting, offering broad functionalities and integrating seamlessly with other programming constructs. Their strategic application can simplify repetitive tasks, optimize script performance, and streamline complex processes, making Zsh an invaluable tool for dynamic scripting needs. Success in mastering these constructs hinges upon an intricate understanding of their syntax, capabilities, and operational contexts. As scripts evolve in complexity and scope, these constructs will inevitably become indispensable assets in automating and controlling repetitive operations within the shell.

5.3 Case Statements for Pattern Matching

In Zsh scripting, the case statement is an invaluable construct for managing multiple conditions, particularly when dealing with pattern matching. This control structure provides a clean and efficient method to dispatch variable conditions, streamlining the decision-making process by allowing scripts to branch based on matching patterns instead of evaluating multiple if conditions. The case statement is akin to a switch-case construct in other programming languages, designed for handling situations where a variable should be checked against various patterns and execute corresponding code blocks.

The general syntax for a case statement in Zsh scripting is as follows:

```
case expression in
    pattern1)
        # commands to execute if expression matches pattern1
        ;;
    pattern2)
        # commands to execute if expression matches pattern2
        ;;
    *)
        # default commands if no pattern matches
        ;;
esac
```

The expression can be any given variable or command output. The script tests the expression against each pattern specified sequentially. When a match is found, the commands associated with that pattern's block are executed, after which the case statement is terminated by esac.

Consider a practical example where a script reads a user input and performs an action based on specific string patterns:

```
echo "Enter a fruit (apple, banana, cherry):"
read fruit

case $fruit in
    apple)
        echo "Apples are red or green."
        ;;
    banana)
        echo "Bananas are yellow."
        ;;
    cherry)
        echo "Cherries are small and red."
        ;;
    *)
        echo "Unknown fruit: $fruit"
        ;;
esac
```

This script waits for user input, matches it against specified fruit types, and outputs a corresponding description. If the input doesn't match any predefined fruit patterns, it triggers the default clause *, which acts

114

as a catch-all.

The efficiencies of using case statements are highlighted in scenarios demanding structured, complex condition management. Unlike multiple if statements, the case structure avoids the extensive conditional checks, compartmentalizing potential conditions neatly and understandably. This not only enhances readability but also boosts script performance by terminating evaluations once a match is identified.

Importantly, patterns within the case statement can utilize shell pattern matching (globbing) as well, enabling sophisticated pattern recognition. For instance, wildcards and character classes expand the potential use cases extensively:

- * matches any sequence of characters.

- ? matches any single character.

- [a-z] defines a range, matching any single character within a specified set.

Leveraging these capabilities, scripts can adapt to various input conditions more flexibly. Consider a scenario involving user input starting with a specific letter:

```
echo "Enter your choice (start with a letter):"
read choice

case $choice in
    a*)
        echo "Your choice starts with 'a': $choice"
        ;;
    [bB]*)
        echo "Your choice starts with 'b' or 'B': $choice"
        ;;
    c?d)
        echo "Your choice matches the pattern 'c?d': $choice"
        ;;
    *)
        echo "Your choice does not match any known patterns: $choice"
        ;;
esac
```

This application checks for specific starting letters or patterns, utilizing wildcard and character class matching. Incorporating such techniques helps handle broader input data variability efficiently.

Combining case statements with commands analyzing or transforming inputs allows for advanced decision-making structures. Consider a scenario of managing file types from a directory extraction:

```
for file in *; do
    case $file in
        *.txt)
            echo "$file is a text file."
            ;;
        *.jpg | *.jpeg)
            echo "$file is a JPEG image."
            ;;
        *.png)
            echo "$file is a PNG image."
            ;;
        *.sh)
            echo "$file is a script file."
            ;;
        *)
            echo "$file is of an unknown type."
            ;;
    esac
done
```

In this script, file names are matched against predetermined extensions, employing pattern matching for identifying file types. The use of vertical bars (|) allows multiple extensions to be treated under single pattern-check conditions. Hence, .jpg and .jpeg extensions both map to the same code block, representing JPEG images.

Though powerful and versatile, executing a case statement effectively requires caution with pattern specificity and ordering. Patterns should be strategically defined and sequenced such that more specific conditions precede general ones—ensuring precise matches receive appropriate response priority.

Furthermore, case statements can integrate with functions, enhancing modularity and reuse within scripts. This is particularly consequential for complex logic branching that may be necessary across various sections of a script or multiple scripts. Consider an example with a function responding to system states:

```
check_system_state() {
    local state=$1
    case $state in
        running)
            echo "System is running smoothly."
            ;;
        stopped)
            echo "System has been stopped."
```

```
            ;;
      error)
            echo "System error detected."
            ;;
      *)
            echo "Unknown system state: $state"
            ;;
   esac
}

state=$(get_system_state_command)
check_system_state $state
```

In this illustration, the function check_system_state encapsulates the case logic, centralizing condition response handling for different system states. Functions like this promote code reuse and maintainability, especially beneficial in large-scale scripts where complex condition handling is requisite.

In addition to expressiveness in pattern handling, case statements can be combined with other control structures to enhance functionality. This can involve using loops to iterate over multiple items or employing conditional checks within the case blocks for nested decision-making:

```
for user in $(cat users.txt); do
    user_status=$(get_user_status $user)
    case $user_status in
        active)
            echo "$user is active."
            ;;
        inactive)
            echo "$user is inactive."
            ;;
        *)
            if [[ $user_status == warning* ]]; then
                echo "$user has a warning: ${user_status#warning}"
            else
                echo "Unknown status for $user: $user_status"
            fi
            ;;
    esac
done
```

This script iterates over a list of users, evaluates their status using a hypothetical command, and processes each status condition, showcasing nested checks within a case block for tailored responses based on substrings.

The case statement's robust mechanism, capable of handling specific patterns while maintaining clarity, plays a crucial role in Zsh scripting.

Its pattern matching efficiency and readability make it an essential feature for anyone looking to develop organized, efficient scripts capable of handling extensive conditional logic. By integrating these pattern matching techniques into scripts effectively, script authors can anticipate and manage the wide spectrum of input conditions they may encounter, empowering scripts with enhanced operational resilience and adaptability. Mastery of the case statement contributes notably to a sophisticated toolbox of scripting techniques, essential for the development of advanced automation and management solutions in a shell environment.

5.4 Functions and Script Modularity

Functions represent an essential concept in programming, permitting the encapsulation of blocks of code that perform specific tasks into single callable entities. In Zsh scripting, functions serve as powerful tools for enhancing the modularity and reusability of scripts. By organizing scripts into functions, we achieve clarity in code structure, facilitate maintenance, and simplify enhancements without disrupting the overall logic of the script.

A function in Zsh is defined using the following basic syntax:

```
function_name() {
    # commands to execute
}
```

Once defined, a function can be invoked simply by using its name, leading to the execution of the enclosed commands. Functions encapsulate repeated operations or logically related commands into a single block, reducing redundancy and promoting code reuse.

Consider a simple example demonstrating a function that prints a greeting message:

```
greet_user() {
    echo "Hello, User!"
}

greet_user
```

Here, the function greet_user is defined to encapsulate a greeting mes-

118

sage, making it reusable within the script without duplicating the echo command.

Functions can also accept parameters, providing flexibility to perform operations across diverse data without altering the function's logic. Parameters are passed by specifying them after the function name, accessible within the function block using positional parameters ($1, $2, ...):

```
greet() {
    echo "Hello, $1!"
}

greet "Alice"
greet "Bob"
```

In this illustration, the same function greet adapts to greet different users by accepting the name as a parameter, emphasizing how functions enhance adaptability and reusability.

Moreover, functions support returning values, essential for scripts where derived data needs to be passed back to the calling entity. While Zsh functions do not directly support returning values like some high-level languages, return values can be communicated using echo statements or through global variables.

To retrieve output from a function, command substitution can be employed:

```
add_numbers() {
    echo $(($1 + $2))
}

result=$(add_numbers 5 10)
echo "The sum is $result"
```

Here, add_numbers computes the sum of two numbers, returning the result through echo, with the output captured using command substitution.

In more sophisticated scripts, organizing functionality into multiple cohesive functions enables script modularity—breaking large scripts into manageable sections. This modular approach allows individual components to be independently developed and tested, fostering maintainability:

```
initialize_setup() {
    echo "Setting up environment..."
```

```
    # setup code
}

process_data() {
    echo "Processing data..."
    # data processing code
}

cleanup() {
    echo "Cleaning up..."
    # cleanup code
}

initialize_setup
process_data
cleanup
```

This script example structures operations into descriptive functions, clearly separating concerns and enhancing readability. Calling these functions in sequence mirrors a high-level plan or logic flow, assisting both in the understanding and debugging process.

Furthermore, functions can call other functions, enabling complex operations to be broken down hierarchically. This nested function structure ensures that each component focuses on a single responsibility, aligning with sound software engineering principles:

```
calculate_average() {
    sum=$(add $1 $2)
    echo $(($sum / 2))
}

add() {
    result=$(($1 + $2))
    echo $result
}

average=$(calculate_average 10 20)
echo "The average is: $average"
```

Within this example, a function calculate_average calls another function add to delegate the sum calculation task. This division of responsibilities eliminates code duplication and encapsulates arithmetic operations, enhancing modularity.

Error handling is another domain where functions augment script modularity and robustness. Incorporating dedicated functions to check the success or failure of operations can streamline error management across scripts:

```
check_directory() {
    if [[ -d $1 ]]; then
        echo "Directory $1 exists."
    else
        echo "Directory $1 does not exist."
        return 1
    fi
}

handle_error() {
    echo "An error occurred: $1"
    exit 1
}

directory="/path/to/check"
check_directory $directory || handle_error "Failed to find directory $directory"
```

Here, check_directory verifies the existence of a directory, and should an error occur, handle_error manages the error message and script termination. This methodology separates error handling from primary logic, leading to cleaner and more understandable scripts.

Zsh functions support local variables, allowing variables to be confined to the scope of the function, preventing side effects and unintentional interactions with the script's global state. Defining a variable as local within the function:

```
increment_counter() {
    local count=$1
    ((count++))
    echo $count
}

global_counter=100
updated_counter=$(increment_counter $global_counter)
echo "Incremented counter: $updated_counter"
echo "Global counter: $global_counter"
```

The example demonstrates the utility of the local keyword, isolating count within increment_counter. This ensures the global variable global_counter remains unaffected by operations within the function, a crucial aspect of avoiding conflicts in larger scripts.

Advanced use of functions includes options and attributes, such as autoload and trap, for dynamic loading and signal handling, respectively. These attributes control the function's behavior, optimizing execution:

- autoload enables lazy loading of functions, where functions are defined in separate files and sourced on-demand.

121

- trap manages the function's response to signals, enhancing control over unexpected terminations or interruptions.

Integration of these attributes can profoundly influence script efficiency and resilience, particularly in intricate automation scripts.

```
autoload -U check_status
# Assuming check_status function is sourced when first called

trap 'cleanup' EXIT

cleanup() {
    echo "Performing cleanup..."
}
```

This snippet signifies how autoload defers function definition, importing only when needed, while trap binds the cleanup function to trigger on script exit, ensuring proper resource management.

By thoughtfully integrating functions into scripts, Zsh script developers harness a wide array of organizational and performance benefits. Functions reinforce modularity by clustering related operations, leading to scalable, maintainable scripts. The advantages of reduced redundancy, improved clarity, and simplified testing significantly compound over time, emphasizing the pivotal role of functions in sophisticated script development. Ultimately, mastering the function construct and script modularization empowers developers to create comprehensive and flexible solutions, aiding in harnessing the full capabilities of Zsh.

5.5   Error Handling with Exit Codes

Error handling is a critical part of script development in any programming or scripting language. In Zsh scripting, exit codes serve as indispensable tools for managing and responding to errors. An exit code, sometimes referred to as a return code or exit status, is a number returned by a command after execution. By convention, an exit code of 0 indicates successful execution, whereas a non-zero exit code signifies an error or exception. Leveraging exit codes for error handling ensures scripts behave predictably and robustly, especially in dynamic environments where error conditions can vary.

In Zsh, every command executed is associated with an exit code stored

in the special variable $?. This variable can be accessed immediately
following a command's execution to determine success or failure:

```
mkdir /tmp/example_directory
if [[ $? -eq 0 ]]; then
    echo "Directory created successfully."
else
    echo "Failed to create directory."
fi
```

In this example, the script attempts to create a directory and checks
the exit code using $?. The logic evaluates whether the operation was
successful, executing the appropriate response. Such straightforward
handling is essential for managing individual command results effectively.

For improved readability and maintainability, scripting best practices
recommend the use of logical flow constructs rather than checking $?
directly. Utilizing conditionals can simplify these checks, enhancing
script legibility:

```
if mkdir /tmp/example_directory; then
    echo "Directory created successfully."
else
    echo "Failed to create directory."
fi
```

This idiom uses command attribution within the if statement, implic-
itly checking the command's exit code. A successful command executes
the then branch, and an unsuccessful one triggers the else branch, encapsulating error handling with minimal syntax.

A core component of robust error management involves anticipating
and mitigating potential error conditions before they affect script execution. Scripts should include predefined responses to expected errors,
utilizing exit codes to trigger these responses:

```
file_to_create="/tmp/example_file.txt"

if touch $file_to_create; then
    echo "File created: $file_to_create"
else
    exit 1
fi
```

In this manner, the script can gracefully terminate if an operation critical to its functioning fails, using exit 1 to signify an error state globally.

123

The exit command provides a controlled shutdown, communicating an explicit error code to any processes that might have invoked the script.

Exit codes, when standardized across scripts and functions, facilitate scalable error handling. Tracking exit codes through a uniform convention aids in diagnosing issues and integrating scripts within broader systems. Common conventions include:

- Exit code 0: success

- Exit code 1: general errors

- Exit code 2: misuse of shell built-ins

- Other exit codes above 127 usually reflect system or signal-related errors

By employing clearly delineated exit codes, scripts can be integrated into larger scripts or applications, where specific codes map to defined corrective actions, logging, or alerts.

Moreover, functions within scripts can employ exit codes to communicate their outcomes, providing interfaces for invoking code to respond accordingly. Consider a network connectivity check function:

```
check_connectivity() {
    local url=$1
    curl --head --silent --fail $url > /dev/null
    if [[ $? -ne 0 ]]; then
        echo "Failed to reach $url"
        return 1
    fi
}

check_connectivity "http://example.com" || echo "Network check failed."
```

Here, check_connectivity attempts to connect to a URL, propagating its success or failure via an exit code return 1 to denote when connectivity could not be established. These encapsulated checks extend a function's operational utility by allowing caller-specific error responses, maintaining clean functional interfaces.

For scripts demanding more complex error management, trap statements can catch and process signals, ensuring resources are managed even if a script encounters unexpected errors or interruptions:

```
trap 'clean_up; exit 1;' INT TERM

clean_up() {
    echo "Performing cleanup tasks."
    # Include resource cleanup logic here
}

# Main script logic
```

In this example, the trap command binds signals INT and TERM, ensuring that the clean_up function is executed, maintaining system stability and consistent resource management even when scripts terminate abruptly.

Combining traps with exit status permits the handling of cross-script dependencies, where a script's effectiveness depends on the outcomes of subprocesses or invocations. The exit status can reinforce operation flow control in complex automated workflows:

```
echo "Running dependency script..."
dependency_script && echo "Dependency succeeded." || { echo "Dependency failed.";
    exit 1; }
```

Here, using && and || operators in combination with exit codes strengthens logical dependencies, dictating subsequent action strictly upon preceding results. This construct is particularly valuable in CI/CD pipelines and orchestration scripts where stepwise validation is paramount.

Nevertheless, an essential aspect of using exit codes involves informative error handling, facilitating troubleshooting and debugging. When a script exits due to an error, clear, actionable log messages should accompany the exit, aiding in prompt identification and rectification:

```
copy_file() {
    local source=$1
    local destination=$2
    if ! cp $source $destination; then
        echo "Error: Failed to copy $source to $destination." >&2
        exit 2
    fi
}

copy_file "source.txt" "/nonexistent/path/destination.txt"
```

By directing error messages to standard error (>&2), the script separates error outputs from regular outputs. This separation ensures logging systems and human users can distinguish errors promptly, optimizing the monitoring and intervention process.

Moreover, with Zsh's enhanced error trapping and management capabilities, combining traditional exit code checks with autoloaded or asynchronicity-enabled functions widened tools offer sophisticated diagnostics and recovery options. By aligning error handlers with specific offenders, Zsh scripts maximize reliability and resilience throughout varied execution environments.

Error handling using exit codes forms the bedrock of stable, predictable Zsh scripting practices. As scripts mature in complexity and integration, they must reliably interpret and respond to error states, supporting user expectations with grace and insight. Mastering these techniques enables developers to weave error resilience into every script, elevating success rates, minimizing unexpected behaviors, and effectively exploiting Zsh's robust feature set for meaningful automation and innovation.

5.6 Selective Execution with eval and exec

In Zsh scripting, the constructs eval and exec offer advanced capabilities for executing commands under selective conditions. These constructs diverge from typical command execution by enabling dynamic command evaluation and process replacement, providing powerful tools for script optimization and control flow management. Understanding and leveraging these commands can enhance scripts' sophistication, allowing for both dynamic flexibility and resource efficiency.

The eval command in Zsh evaluates arguments as a single concatenated command, executing them as a fresh command. This is particularly valuable when building commands dynamically or when command composition requires the execution of strings as commands. The general syntax for utilizing eval is:

```
eval [arguments...]
```

The power of eval lies in its ability to process variables or strings constructed during script execution, which represents commands to be executed. Consider a scenario involving dynamic variable construction and execution:

```
command="ls -l"
eval $command
```

Here, the eval function interprets the string stored in command as an executable command. This usage illustrates eval's ability to execute dynamically constructed strings, elevating command flexibility in various scripting contexts.

A more complex example involves constructing command options conditionally, showcasing eval's role in building and running composite command strings:

```
base_command="grep"

if [[ $case_sensitive == "no" ]]; then
    base_command+=" -i"
fi

base_command+=" pattern file.txt"
eval $base_command
```

In this snippet, the script conditionally builds a grep command with the potential inclusion of the -i flag for case insensitivity and executes it with eval. This approach allows script authors to dynamically tailor command attributes frameworked by runtime logic without requiring explicit enumeration of all command variations.

Care must be exercised when leveraging eval due to its capability to execute arbitrary code upon evaluating unsafe strings. This poses potential security risks if untrusted inputs are involved. Thus, usage should be deliberate, especially in contexts such as input parsing or file content evaluation where external influence might present vulnerabilities.

On the other hand, the exec command provides means to replace the current shell process with a specified command, effectively terminating the preceding script environment. This differs fundamentally from typical command execution, as no return control exists following an exec invocation—the replaced process inherits the open file descriptors and shell environment without forking a new process:

```
exec command [arguments...]
```

A simple utilitarian example where exec can be advantageous involves redirecting a script's environment entirely to a new program, such as executing a shell:

```
exec /bin/sh
```

After invocation, this script line replaces the executing Zsh shell with the Bourne shell. No further script commands are processed past the exec point, as the environment reflects the new shell context.

One practical application of exec is in cases where scripts launch daemons or persistent services and do not necessitate post-execution cleanup or continuation of the script's original shell environment. By utilizing exec, scripts conserve system resources, substituting themselves with the desired executable:

```
exec my_daemon
```

Once executed, my_daemon inherits the shell's process ID, minimizing resource consumption by eliminating the superfluous shell wrapper typical to service launches.

When combined strategically, eval and exec can enhance shell scripts' dynamism and efficiency, particularly in cases where both command flexibility and process efficiency are required. Consider a script that reads configurations dynamically to determine and launch the appropriate service setup:

```
config_line=""

if [[ -f "service.conf" ]]; then
    config_line=$(grep 'start_command' service.conf)
fi

if [[ -n $config_line ]]; then
    eval $config_line
else
    exec default_service
fi
```

This script reads a configuration file for a specific service command using eval for its execution, falling back on a default service launched with exec if none is specified. The blend of command evaluation and efficient execution replacement conveys the potency of these constructs in controlled environments.

128

While eval and exec provide incredible functionalities, understanding their affordances and implications remains crucial to harnessing their power effectively and safely. By mastering these constructs, Zsh script developers can design highly flexible, efficient scripts, adapting dynamically to variable requirements or execution contexts with substantive control over command execution. This adaptive capacity is invaluable where scripts intersect with diverse and evolving environments, ensuring they maintain capability without sacrificing clarity or engagement—a core attribute to advanced shell scripting mastery.

Chapter 6

Working with Files and Directories in Zsh

This chapter provides a comprehensive overview of file and directory manipulation in Zsh. It covers essential commands for managing files, directories, and hidden files, along with techniques for batch processing and handling symbolic and hard links. Additionally, it explores file compression and decompression methods, equipping users with the skills to efficiently manage data and streamline file-related tasks within the Zsh environment.

6.1 Manipulating Files with Zsh

The Z shell, commonly known as Zsh, is a powerful command-line interpreter that expands the capabilities of the standard Bourne Shell (sh) by incorporating modern features from other shells. It stands out for its user-friendly operations, particularly with file manipulation. Mastering Zsh's file manipulation commands empowers users to efficiently create, move, copy, and delete files, thus streamlining their workflows in Unix-like environments. Understanding these commands also lays the foundation for more complex scripting and automation tasks in Zsh.

Creating Files

Creating files in Zsh is a fundamental operation, useful in numerous contexts like initializing a project structure, generating temporary files for data processing, or simply organizing notes. The primary command for file creation in Zsh, inherited from Unix standards, is touch. The touch command can be used in its simplest form as follows:

```
touch filename.txt
```

The above command creates a new file named filename.txt in the current working directory. If the file already exists, touch does not alter its content but updates its access and modification timestamps to the current date and time. This feature can be particularly useful for scripts that rely on file timeliness.

Zsh also allows the use of redirection to create files:

```
echo "Initial text" > newfile.txt
```

This command creates newfile.txt and inserts "Initial text" into it. Should newfile.txt exist, this operation will overwrite it, an important aspect to consider when scripting to avoid unintentional data loss.

Moving Files

Moving files is an essential operation for organizing and structuring directories. The mv command is employed for this purpose in Zsh. It can be used to move a file to a different directory or rename the file within the same directory, as shown below:

```
mv oldfile.txt newfolder/
```

Executing this command will transfer oldfile.txt to newfolder. Alternatively, to rename oldfile.txt to newfile.txt within the same directory, the usage would be:

```
mv oldfile.txt newfile.txt
```

For cases involving wildcard characters, Zsh offers enhanced expansion capabilities. Suppose there are multiple text files that need to be relocated to another directory:

```
mv *.txt newfolder/
```

This command moves all files in the current directory with a .txt extension to newfolder. Beware that when moving files with mv, the original files are deleted from the source directory upon successful completion.

Copying Files

The cp command is analogous to mv, but instead of moving, it duplicates files from one location to another. Here is a basic example:

```
cp myfile.txt ../backup/
```

This command copies myfile.txt into the backup directory positioned one level up in the hierarchy. When copying a directory and all of its contents, it's crucial to use the recursive option:

```
cp -r mydirectory/ ../backup/
```

This will copy mydirectory and every file and subdirectory it contains to backup. It's imperative to specify the -r flag; otherwise, the operation will fail if the target is a directory.

Zsh's syntax also supports using brace expansion to copy multiple similar files simultaneously:

```
cp {file1,file2,file3}.txt ../backup/
```

The above command copies file1.txt, file2.txt, and file3.txt to backup. This feature can save time when dealing with multiple files that share common prefixes or suffixes.

Deleting Files

Zsh incorporates the robust rm command for file deletion, which eliminates files and directories from the filesystem. An example of a straightforward file removal is:

```
rm unwantedfile.txt
```

This operation immediately deletes unwantedfile.txt from the current directory. If multiple deletions are required at once, wildcard expansion can be invaluable:

```
rm *.tmp
```

This command removes all files ending with the .tmp extension in the current directory. When deleting directories, the recursive flag -r is mandatory:

```
rm -r olddirectory/
```

This deletes olddirectory and all its subdirectories and files. Due to the potentially destructive nature of rm, it's advised to use the interactive flag -i during deletions:

```
rm -i importantfile.txt
```

This cautious approach prompts for confirmation before each delete, minimizing accidental data loss.

Linking Files

Beyond the fundamental operations of creating, moving, copying, and deleting files, Zsh also allows users to create links, either symbolic (soft) or hard. Symbolic links, created with the ln -s command, are pointers to the file:

```
ln -s /path/to/original/file symlink
```

This creates a symbolic link called symlink pointing to /path/to/original/file. Symbolic links are particularly useful in situations where files need to be accessed from multiple directories without duplicating their contents.

Hard links, created without the -s option, are another type of link that point directly to the file's inode on the filesystem, rather than the file path:

```
ln /path/to/original/file hardlink
```

Executing this command creates a hard link named hardlink to /path/-to/original/file. Unlike symbolic links, hard links are less flexible since they must reside within the same filesystem as the target file and cannot point to directories.

Special Features in Zsh

When managing files using Zsh, users can capitalize on several notable features to enhance their shell experience and automate tasks. Among these are filename expansion and globbing, which are more advanced in Zsh compared to other shells.

Zsh permits several types of expansions to navigate directories effectively. One powerful feature is the extended globbing capability which utilizes patterns that represent sets of filenames. Consider the following example:

```
mv ^(*.jpg|*.png) images/
```

Here, the command moves all files except those ending in .jpg or .png to the images directory. The caret symbol indicates negation, and the parentheses group multiple patterns, while the pipe symbol | functions as a logical OR between them.

Another efficient use of Zsh's unique features is the integration of conditional execution within loops for batch file processing, altering file properties predictively:

```
for f in **/*.log(.); do
  mv "$f" logs_archive/
done
```

This code iterates over all log files nested within any subdirectory and moves them to the logs_archive directory. The (.) at the end of the pattern signifies that only regular files are included, avoiding directories or other special types of files.

The plethora of built-in functions for manipulating files within Zsh expands one's ability to interact with the filesystem in a programmable, customizable manner, especially when combined with scripts. With these capabilities, users can tailor their shell environment to fit personal workflows or systemic needs effortlessly.

Having delved into the nuts and bolts of file manipulation using Zsh, users can leverage this knowledge to not only execute routine tasks with greater efficacy but also integrate such operations into scripts for more advanced applications and automations. Zsh's blend of traditional Unix command syntax, bolstered by enhancements and unique features, provides a fertile ground for optimizing file-related operations in computational environments.

6.2   Directory Management Techniques

Effectively managing directories is vital for maintaining a well-organized file system, which is especially true in complex computing environments or development projects.   Zsh, with its precedence rooted in Unix-like systems, offers a suite of powerful commands for directory management.   Understanding and leveraging these commands, including mkdir, rmdir, and cd, enables users to navigate, organize, and manipulate directory structures with proficiency and ease.

Creating Directories

The fundamental operation when organizing data is directory creation, typically performed using the mkdir command. The basic syntax is straightforward:

```
mkdir foldername
```

This command creates a directory named foldername in the current working directory. A noteworthy option associated with mkdir is -p, which allows creating nested directories in a single command:

```
mkdir -p parent/child/grandchild
```

Here, mkdir constructs a hierarchy consisting of parent, child, and grandchild directories. If any intermediate directories (parent or child) do not currently exist, the -p flag ensures their creation along the path. This feature is particularly useful in scripting and automation, where directory structures might need dynamic creation without human intervention.

In scenarios where directory names follow a sequential pattern, brace expansion in Zsh can simplify creation processes:

```
mkdir project_{A,B,C}
```

Executing this command results in the creation of three directories: project_A, project_B, and project_C. This method of batch creation reduces redundancy and potential for error in manual naming sequences.

Navigating Directories

The cd command lies at the heart of directory navigation within Zsh, fundamentally altering the shell's working directory context. A basic usage example follows:

```
cd /path/to/directory
```

With this, the user navigates into /path/to/directory, setting it as the new current working directory. The command cd without an argument defaults to the user's home directory, offering a quick return to this familiar location:

```
cd
```

Zsh enhances traditional navigation through its introduction of directory stacks, manipulated via pushd, popd, and dirs. Using these, users can maintain a list of directories to which they wish to return, navigating more effectively between deep or unrelated parts of the file system.

```
pushd /path/to/first/directory
pushd /path/to/second/directory
dirs
```

dirs will display a stack of directories navigated using pushd. popd removes the top directory from this stack, returning the user to the previous directory state.

Removing Directories

Directory removal in Zsh is executed via rmdir and rm -r, with each serving specific purposes. rmdir deletes empty directories:

```
rmdir emptyfolder
```

Attempting rmdir on non-empty directories results in an error, underscoring its specificity for handling only vacuous directory deletions.

Conversely, rm -r (a recursive remove) is necessary for direct removal of non-empty directories:

```
rm -r fullfolder/
```

For critical operations that entail significant deletions, especially in nested directories, inclusion of the interactive flag -i is recommended to prompt confirmation before each action, a safeguard against costly errors:

137

```
rm -ri crucialfolder/
```

Including the -i flag ensures deliberate decision-making at each deletion step, which is apt during maintenance of valuable directory architectures.

Advanced Directory Manipulations

Zsh's directory manipulation capabilities are not confined to these fundamental operations; they extend into advanced features that optimize
everyday usage through a blend of aliasing, shortcutting, and environment customizations.

Alias Creation and Path Shortcuts

Users frequently navigate the same directories, and typing lengthy
paths repeatedly can be time-consuming. Zsh permits path aliasing
via the alias command, simplifying navigation:

```
alias proj='cd /path/to/projectfolder'
```

With this alias defined, executing proj seamlessly transports users into
projectfolder. Alias commands can be included in a user's .zshrc file,
ensuring persistent availability across sessions. Furthermore, managing many aliases becomes feasible through automated or pre-defined
scripts that append or source these settings.

Environmental Variables and Directory Shortcuts

Certain environmental variables also facilitate efficient directory management, the foremost being CDPATH. This variable specifies a list of
base directories for cd to search, easing navigation beyond common
locations:

```
export CDPATH=.:~:/var/www:/usr/local
cd somedir
```

The example above appends multiple directories to CDPATH, allowing
straightforward cd operations to somedir if it exists relative to any directory listed within CDPATH. This functionality enhances productivity
in development environments with standardized, repetitive directory
structures.

Integrating Directory Change with Other Commands

138

Zsh integrations permit concatenation of logical operations post-directory change, streamlining workflows. Combined commands permit auto-execution of tasks immediately upon changing directories.

For example:

```
cd project_directory && git status
```

This command moves into project_directory and subsequently executes git status, providing the immediate status of a Git repository after entering its directory, a routine operation for developers.

Batch Operations on Large Directory Structures

When handling extensive directory hierarchies, manual operations become cumbersome. Zsh features allow the automation of directory management through loops and script-driven processes, such as batch directory renaming or creation:

```
for dir in old_prefix_*; do
    mv "$dir" "${dir/old_prefix_/new_prefix_}"
done
```

This loop iterates over directories prefixed with old_prefix_ and substitutes it with new_prefix_, an action illustrative of automated directory renaming. Such patterns are invaluable during migrations or reorganization of directory structures initiated in changed project specifications.

Where creation of systematic directories across varied contexts is necessary, scripts also lend themselves to simplicity and reproducibility:

```
for year in 2020 2021; do
    for month in {01..12}; do
        mkdir -p "archive/$year/$month"
    done
done
```

This command comprehensively constructs a directory framework reflecting monthly archives over the specified years, crucial for structured data storage, archival processes, or versioned logging systems.

Directory management in Zsh encompasses a rich suite of commands and techniques that can be wielded to great effect for organizing, maintaining, and interacting with large volumes of structured file data. By employing these techniques, users cultivate an efficient workflow that is adaptable, scalable, and robust, aligning with diverse operational demands typical in both personal computing and extensive enterprise environments. The considered use of scripting and automation within Zsh not only enhances routine directory management but lays the groundwork for sophisticated, programmatically driven file system architecture adjustments reflecting advancing technological landscapes.

6.3   Working with Hidden Files

Hidden files are an integral component of Unix-like operating systems, including systems using the Z shell (Zsh). These files, which are not immediately visible in standard directory listings, often store configuration settings and system information. Effective management and manipulation of hidden files are key skills for users who wish to fully control their environment or engage in advanced system configurations.

In Unix systems, a hidden file is designated by a name that begins with a period (e.g., .hiddenfile). Such files are typically used for user preferences, application settings, and system configurations, residing quietly to prevent clutter in day-to-day operations. The ability to manipulate these files with ease is essential for users aiming to customize or troubleshoot their computing setup.

Viewing Hidden Files

By default, the ls command does not display hidden files. However, several options can override this behavior to make hidden files visible. The most straightforward way is using the -a (or –all) option:

```
ls -a
```

This command lists all files in the current directory, inclusive of those that begin with a period. For a more readable, columnar output, the -l option can be combined with -a:

```
ls -la
```

The resulting output provides detailed information about each file, including permissions, number of links, owner, group, size, and timestamp, facilitating a comprehensive overview.

For users interested in filtering just the hidden files, the ls command benefits from the use of wildcard globbing patterns within Zsh:

```
ls -d .*
```

This command outputs entries beginning with a period (.) in the current directory. Note that, by default, this includes the special entries "." and ".." which denote the current directory and parent directory, respectively. Excluding these can be accomplished with the explicit use of pattern negation:

```
ls -d .[^.]* .??*
```

This approach excludes . and .. by defining patterns that require at least two characters following the period.

Creating Hidden Files

Hidden files can be generated using the same commands as regular files, simply prefixing the filename with a period. For instance, using touch:

```
touch .myhiddenfile
```

This command creates an empty hidden file named .myhiddenfile in the current directory. Similarly, redirecting output can both create and populate a hidden file:

```
echo "Configuration data" > .myconfig
```

This command writes "Configuration data" into .myconfig, useful for initializing configuration files.

When creating multiple hidden files, brace expansion serves as a beneficial shortcut in Zsh:

```
touch .{config1,config2,config3}
```

Here, three hidden files, .config1, .config2, and .config3, are created with a concise command.

Editing Hidden Files

Editing hidden files follows the same process as any other file type.

141

Text editors like nano, vim, or emacs are common tools for modifying these files. Using vim, a prevalent choice among seasoned users:

```
vim .bashrc
```

This command opens the hidden .bashrc configuration file in the vim editor, allowing modifications to the user's shell behavior. Given the impact hidden configuration files can have, users should exercise caution and ensure backups are made prior to significant changes.

Moving and Renaming Hidden Files

The mv command is employed for moving or renaming hidden files. Here is an example of renaming:

```
mv .oldname .newname
```

This command simply renames .oldname to .newname within the same directory.

Moving hidden files to a different directory while maintaining their hidden status requires direct specification of their names:

```
mv .myhiddenfile /new/directory/
```

This action relocates .myhiddenfile to /new/directory/ without altering its hidden status.

Deleting Hidden Files

Deletion of hidden files utilizes the rm command, mirroring the procedures for visible files. It's vital to specify hidden files explicitly, as the implicit protection from accidental deletion due to their initial period in typical operations:

```
rm .myhiddenfile
```

Longer validation steps such as listing files before removal or using interactive prompts can help prevent accidental deletions, especially important given hidden files often contain critical configuration data.

For batch deletion, wildcards are helpful, yet caution is duly exercised to avoid mistargeting:

```
rm .myconfig*
```

This command will attempt to delete all files beginning with .myconfig, a broad approach that requires confidence in the listing of file candidates before execution.

Why Hidden Files Matter

The importance of hidden files stems from their roles predominantly in configurations and system operations, granted their inconspicuous nature by default. Key among their functions are:

- **Customization and Configuration:** Hidden files such as .bashrc, .zshrc, or .gitconfig contain user-specific configurations that personalize and optimize user interaction with systems.

- **Application Settings:** Many applications leverage hidden files to preserve states and preferences, enabling seamless user experiences across sessions. Control over these files equates to direct influence over application behavior and personalization settings.

- **Environment and Security:** Hidden files often store sensitive paths, credentials, or tokens, depending on their application. Their hidden nature minimizes exposure, lending an additional layer of security through obscurity.

Scripting with Hidden Files

Scripting, a powerful productivity enhancer, can encompass operations with hidden files. Automating the creation, editing, and archiving of these files speeds up workflows.

Consider this shell script snippet that adds a line to .bashrc if it doesn't exist:

```
if ! grep -q "export PATH=\$PATH:/new/path" ~/.bashrc; then
  echo "export PATH=\$PATH:/new/path" >> ~/.bashrc
fi
```

This script checks for the presence of a particular export PATH line in .bashrc and appends it only if missing, thus preventing redundant entries.

Another script example might archive old configurations:

```
for config_file in .*rc; do
  if [ -f "$config_file" ]; then
```

143

```
    cp "$config_file" backup_directory/
  fi
done
```

This script copies all files ending with rc into backup_directory, a useful operation before large system updates or migrations.

Working with hidden files in Zsh—akin to an art form—requires deliberate attention and respect for the operational and configuration integrity that they provide. Through understanding their roles and developing strategies to manipulate them effectively, users enrich their capacity to customize and control their computing environments fully.

Whether creating, navigating, manipulating, or scripting hidden files, the insights afforded by Zsh's capabilities equip users to harness the full potential residing in these obscured files. From configuring shells to customizing applications and maintaining system security, hidden files embody both the flexibility and intricacy of Unix-like systems. Developing a proficient command over these files empowers users to transcend ordinary limitations, mastering an interface that is as personal as it is powerful.

6.4   Batch Processing of Files

Batch processing of files in Zsh is an essential skill for efficiently handling large volumes of data or executing repetitive tasks with minimal user intervention. Unlike interactive data manipulation, batch processing allows scripts to operate on multiple files simultaneously, saving both time and reducing human error. This capability becomes invaluable when managing extensive datasets, performing system maintenance, or deploying applications across various environments.

A cornerstone of batch file processing in Zsh is the use of shell scripting. At its core, this type of processing leverages loops and pattern matching to apply commands to any number of files, automating operations such as renaming, moving, modifying content, and more.

Looping Constructs for File Processing

Within Zsh, the for loop is a primary tool for iterating over files. It sequentially processes each file matched by a given pattern, executing specified commands on them. A typical use case involves renaming files with a set prefix:

```
for file in *.txt; do
  mv "$file" "processed_$file"
done
```

The script renames each file with a .txt extension by adding a pro-cessed_ prefix. Zsh's loop syntax is straightforward and efficient, capable of matching multiple files using globbing patterns (e.g., *.txt), and encourages flexibility in tailoring operations to match file patterns dynamically.

In data preprocessing tasks, such as converting formats or extracting relevant lines from logs, batch processing shines. Consider this script that normalizes text files to lowercase using the tr command:

```
for file in data_*.log; do
  tr '[:upper:]' '[:lower:]' < "$file" > "processed_$file"
done
```

Here, each log file prefixed with data_ is converted to lowercase, ensuring uniformity—a criterion critical in data analysis tasks where case consistency improves reliability in parsing.

Advanced Pattern Matching with Globs

Zsh extends typical wildcard capabilities with advanced globbing features, complementing batch file processing with flexibility. Extended globbing allows for matching files against multiple complex patterns, beyond the traditional *, ?, and []. This can be activated within user scripts or interactively as:

```
setopt extended_glob
```

Utilizing extended globbing, users can execute targeted operations with pattern exclusion or inclusion, such as processing only images not in .jpg format:

```
for img in *.(#i)!(jpg); do
  convert "$img" "${img%.*}.jpg"
done
```

This script iterates through all image files not in .jpg format, using Im-ageMagick's convert command to reformat them to jpg, highlighting

145

Zsh's proficiency in handling filename manipulations through parameter expansions like %.* which strips file extensions.

Parallel Processing for Efficiency

To further increase efficiency in batch processing, particularly across multiple cores on modern hardware, Zsh supports tools like xargs with the -P flag for parallel execution:

```
find . -name "*.bak" | xargs -P 4 rm
```

The command above finds files ending with .bak and removes them using rm, distributing tasks across four processes. It demonstrates a paradigm shift from serial to parallel execution in batch processing, significantly reducing time for compute-intensive operations.

For more complex scenarios, GNU parallel facilitates distributed processing:

```
ls *.csv | parallel gzip
```

This command compresses all .csv files using gzip, executing compression in parallel which leverages multi-core processors effectively.

Conditional Operations in Batch Processing

Zsh empowers scripts to include conditional logic within batch processed loops, enabling sophisticated workflows contingent on file states or content. Consider this snippet, where a backup operation only occurs if changes are detected:

```
for file in *.cfg; do
  if [ "$(grep -c 'changed' "$file")" -gt 0 ]; then
    cp "$file" /backup/
  fi
done
```

It checks each .cfg file for any lines containing the word changed. If found, the file is copied to a backup directory—a proactive measure often integrated into maintenance tasks to ensure file versions are preserved and easily restored if modifications lead to errors.

Environment Adjustments for Batch Processing

Zsh scripts can incorporate environment adjustments that enhance the functionality and reliability of batch processing. A common example involves adjusting umask to control default file permissions for new files:

```
umask 077
for file in *.sh; do
  chmod +x "$file"
done
```

Setting umask to 077 ensures new files are created with restrictive permissions, protecting them from unauthorized access. Moreover, every shell script in the directory receives executable privileges, signifying a preparatory step for batch execution.

To further optimize batch processes, Zsh scripts often define functions for reusability and encapsulation of repeated logic:

```
process_file() {
  # Placeholder for processing logic
  echo "Processing $1"
}

for f in documents/*.docx; do
  process_file "$f"
done
```

Here, the process_file function centralizes processing logic, enabling modifications in a single location, an approach that enhances readability, maintainability, and minimizes potential for coding errors.

Error Handling and Logging in Batch Scripts

Reliable batch processes incorporate error handling and logging to diagnose issues post-execution. Zsh can redirect standard output and errors to log files, preserving execution traces for monitoring or audit purposes:

```
exec > batch_process.log 2>&1
for file in *.md; do
  pandoc "$file" -o "${file%.md}.pdf"
done
```

This configuration saves all command output to batch_process.log for review, imperative when processing fails or yields unexpected results, emphasizing transparency and traceability in file transformations.

Error handling strategies often embed traps that capture exits or specific error signals, allowing cleanup or notification routines before a script terminates:

147

```
trap 'echo "Error on line $LINENO"; exit 1' ERR
for img in gallery/*; do
  [ -f "$img" ] && convert "$img" -resize 800x600 "resized/$img"
done
```

Studies illustrate the reduction in manual intervention and error rates when robust handling and logging mechanisms are employed, enhancing both operational integrity and end-user trust in the output.

Security Considerations in Batch File Processing

Batch file processing introduces security concerns, particularly regarding inadvertent exposure of sensitive information or excessive permissions. Scripts should always validate and sanitize inputs prior to execution and employ principle of least privilege in handling files:

```
for report in /reports/*.log; do
  if [[ ! "$report" =~ [^a-zA-Z0-9._/-] ]]; then
    grep "ERROR" "$report" > error_summaries/"$(basename "$report")"
  fi
done
```

Ensuring filenames match allowed patterns mitigates risks from path traversal or command injection attacks. Moreover, designated log output directories should maintain secure access controls, curtailing unauthorized reads.

Targeted permissions, combined with cryptographic verification methods, ensures that processed data is both trustworthy and secure—a necessity in protecting operational confidentiality and compliance with organizational or regulatory standards.

Automating Batch Processing with Cron and Systemd

For ongoing tasks, batch processing scripts benefit from automation using cron jobs or systemd timers, offloading routine executions to the system scheduler:

```
# Example cron entry
0 2 * * * /usr/local/bin/daily_cleanup.sh
```

This entry schedules daily_cleanup.sh to run daily at 2 AM, standardizing workflows and freeing user resources for other projects.

Alternatively, system packages like systemd offer granular control over task execution environments, including dependencies and path isolation:

```
# Sample unit file for a systemd timer
[Timer]
OnCalendar=daily
Unit=batch-process.service
```

These facilitate integration into more comprehensive, resilient service architectures, demonstrating the versatility and scalability of batch processing in systems administration.

Batch processing of files in Zsh transcends basic script execution, emphasizing automation, efficiency, and robustness. Through understanding loops, advanced globbing, parallelization, and integrating security and error handling strategies, users are poised to harness the full potential of Zsh in handling significant data volumes with precision and confidence.

From preparing deployment assets, data conversions, to maintaining extensive document archives, batch processing stands as an indispensable tool in a programmer's arsenal—a testament to the elegance and power of Unix-inspired shells. Such mastery not only augments individual productivity but propels organizational capabilities in computational data handling and transformations into advanced, scalable dimensions.

6.5 Symlinks and Hardlinks

Links in Unix-like systems, such as those managed through Zsh, provide powerful methods for accessing files or directories without duplicating their contents. Two primary types of links are symbolic links (symlinks or soft links) and hard links. While both serve to streamline file manipulation and access, they operate under different principles and use-cases, which directly affects their management and implications on system resources.

Symlinks are particularly useful for creating shortcuts or aliases for files across different parts of the file system, whereas hard links offer a more direct reference to the physical data content within the same file system. Understanding the differences between these links, alongside their operational intricacies, is crucial for leveraging their benefits in efficient file system management.

Understanding Symbolic Links

Symbolic links, created using the ln -s command, are essentially pointers to the target file or directory. Unlike hard links, symbolic links can span across different file systems and reference directories, offering greater flexibility in linking strategies. Here is a basic example of creating a symbolic link:

```
ln -s /path/to/originalfile symlinkfile
```

In this command, symlinkfile is created as a pointer to /path/to/originalfile. This allows users to interact with originalfile through symlinkfile as if it were the file itself, though any operations executed through the symlink are transparently redirected to the original file.

A key aspect of symbolic links is their relative path referencing abilities. If intended for redistribution along with the linked file, relative paths preserve linkage integrity when both elements are relocated jointly. This characteristic is facilitated by:

```
ln -s relative/path/originalfile symlinkfile
```

Symbolic links also allow chaining, wherein a symlink itself references another symlink. While this permits construction of complex directory architectures, circular references should be avoided owing to potential infinite loop resolutions during traversal and access.

Symlinks Behavior with Files and Directories

Directory linking facilitates applications like software development where dependency directories or shared resources are accessed through common names:

```
ln -s /usr/local/lib/foo /home/user/project/libfoo
```

By linking /usr/local/lib/foo into a project's directory structure as libfoo, developers maintain a uniform interface to shared resources while minimizing disruptions from path changes.

However, symlinks come with vulnerabilities, such as "dangling symlinks," where the referenced target is deleted or moved. Attempts to access such links result in errors:

```
$ cat symlinkfile
cat: symlinkfile: No such file or directory
```

Precautionary validations, through scripts or manual checks, ensure symlink integrity by verifying existence:

```
if [ -h "symlinkfile" ] && [ ! -e "symlinkfile" ]; then
    echo "Warning: symlink points to non-existent target."
fi
```

Hard Links: Direct Data Access

Hard links differ from symlinks by pointing directly to the inode of the target file, rather than a file path:

```
ln /path/to/originalfile hardlinkfile
```

Executing the above creates hardlinkfile, an alias that functions as another name for originalfile. Conversely, any changes to the file through either reference are mirrored; this can be attributed to them being indistinguishably recognized by the system.

An important limitation is that hard links only function within the same filesystem. This restriction stems from reliance on inodes, which are unique to a filesystem but not necessarily across filesystems.

Relative Advantages and Limitations

Hard links have several advantages, such as robustness against target deletion. If originalfile is deleted, hardlinkfile remains intact, as actual data isn't removed until all references are dropped. Nonetheless, it is impossible to distinguish which was created first:

```
$ stat originalfile
$ stat hardlinkfile
```

Both commands return identical inode and size information, attesting to their equality in data representation.

On the other hand, hard links cannot reference directories due to recursive loops potentially ensuing in directory structures. System tools detect and prevent such creation attempts:

```
$ ln /path/to/directory hardlinkdir
ln: '/path/to/directory': hard link not allowed for directory
```

Practical Applications and Use-Cases

Symbolic links excel where flexibility is paramount—rapidly redirecting program executables or scripting configurations for user space adaptations. Applications include:

- Backup Systems: Organizing directories while minimizing physical storage requires symlinks to configure backup paths dynamically.

- Development Environments: Environmental set-up scripts use symlinks to represent versioned dependencies (e.g., Java SDK links) across diverse directories, simplifying project configurations.

- User Personalization: Dotfiles, widely used in configuring shells, editors, or version control systems, employ symlinks to import authoritative preference files universally.

Hard links find valuable applications in scenarios demanding data redundancy without storage duplication:

- File Versioning: In systems tracking file versions, hard links ensure older versions remain accessible, preserving modifications historically.

- Data Integrity: Ensures that multiple users/programs modifying a dataset maintain consistent views and share inode-level access.

Maintenance, Monitoring, and Scripting with Links

System administrators often incorporate link management in their scripts, ensuring linked structures maintain functional accuracy. Situational checks and link adjustments are conducted, especially during migrations or organizational transitions:

```
for link in /some/dir/*; do
    if [ -L "$link" ] && [ ! -e "$link" ]; then
        echo "$link is a broken symlink."
        # optional: remove or recreate link
    fi
done
```

The script above identifies broken symlinks within a directory, facilitating manual or automated remediation.

Understanding link counts offers insights into hard links' presence:

```
ls -l
```

The link count (second column) indicates the number of hard links associated, aiding administrators or users in capacity planning and structural assessments.

Security Considerations and Best Practices

Managing links securely necessitates vigilance. Symbolic links, susceptible to exploitation if improperly managed, require careful handling, particularly in ensuring administrative scripts respect link destinations fully verified as legitimate or anticipated.

Implementation of link permissions and ownerships under secure contexts discourages exploitation avenues, such as file system attacks where symlink traversal may redirect unintended writes to critical locations. Fastidious attention to user privileges and access rights fortifies security postures:

```
chmod -h o-w symlinkfile
```

Directing permissions on symlinks—or their targets—ensures that link modification remains under careful administrative control.

Symbolic and hard links in Zsh represent methodologies for file and directory referencing that optimize storage while enhancing accessibility and flexibility. Mastery of these links broadens user capabilities, promoting effective organisational frameworks that adapt to evolving system requirements and enterprise needs.

The decision between symbolic and hard links effectively balances between traversal flexibility and data redundancy, each approach nurturing distinct operational paradigms. As administrators and users develop complex infrastructures, integrating these principles into system designs secures and streamlines file access, achieving robust, scalable, and manageable solutions in Unix-like environments. Through informed use, links transform from simple pointers into powerful tools for configuring, maintaining, and securing sophisticated systems.

6.6 Zsh and File Compression

File compression is a critical component of data management, optimizing storage use and enabling swift file transfers across networks. In the Zsh environment, file compression and decompression are efficiently managed through a suite of powerful command-line tools, including tar, gzip, bzip2, and zip. Mastering these tools within Zsh provides users with the ability to manipulate large volumes of data with speed and reliability, crucial across diverse scenarios from backups to deployment systems.

Understanding Basic Compression Concepts

Compression reduces the size of files by eliminating redundancy, making it possible to store greater quantities of data in a limited space or transfer these files more efficiently over networks. Various algorithms achieve this—some preserving all original information without loss (lossless), while others might sacrifice some data for greater size reduction (lossy). Zsh primarily facilitates lossless compression using utilities like gzip and bzip2, where the integrity of original data upon decompression is maintained.

GNU Tar for Archive Management

The tar utility (**tape ar**chiver) stands central in the Unix family for file archiving. Although not inherently a compression tool, tar consolidates multiple files or directory structures into a single archive. This operation is preliminary for activities like backup creation or distribution of encapsulated components across systems:

```
tar -cf archive.tar directory/
```

This command generates an archive named archive.tar from directory/. The -c option specifies **c**reate, while -f designates the **f**ile name output.

To list contents within the archive, necessary for validation before extraction:

```
tar -tf archive.tar
```

The -t option instructs tar to **t**able the archive contents, providing insights into its composition. Extraction follows the principle of e**x**traction:

```
tar -xf archive.tar
```

With tar, the procedure preserves file attributes and directory structures, vital characteristics that sustain original storage formats post-
compression processes.

Integrating Compression with Tar

Frequently, tar is used conjointly with compression algorithms to create Tarballs, compressed archives denoted typically by extensions like
.tar.gz or .tar.bz2. Combining tar with gzip, an industry-standard, expedites archive processes:

```
tar -czf archive.tar.gz directory/
```

Arranged here, -z specifies gzip compression, establishing an efficient
pipeline from archival to compression operations. Decompressing and
extracting in tandem requires:

```
tar -xzf archive.tar.gz
```

Users should recognize that whereas gzip boasts speed in compression
and decompression, bzip2, accessed respectively through adding -j in
place of -z, offers superior compression rates at a computational cost:

```
tar -cjf archive.tar.bz2 directory/
```

Awareness of application contexts—from system-level backups impli-
cating quick restore points to data transfers where bandwidth constraints prioritize reduced sizes—guides the choice of compression
strategy.

Using Gzip and Bzip2 Directly

Often specific files require individual compression/decompression
without amalgamation into bigger archives. For these instances, gzip
and bzip2 are employed directly. Here, gzip compresses a file in place,
replacing the input file with a .gz form:

```
gzip myfile.txt
```

Upon completion, the original myfile.txt is deleted, substituted with
myfile.txt.gz. Decompression is straightforward:

155

```
gzip -d myfile.txt.gz
```

Conversely, bzip2 processes files analogously, with extensions reflecting the .bz2 suffix:

```
bzip2 myfile.txt
bzip2 -d myfile.txt.bz2
```

Each utility supports verbosity flags (-v) to convey operational progression for long-running compressions, instilling user confidence in operational status without constant manual intervention.

File Compression with Zip and Unzip

Unlike the previously mentioned tools, zip amalgamates and compresses simultaneously, forming zipped files individually or collectively. For compressing a directory, including subfolders, -r (recursive) becomes central:

```
zip -r archive.zip foldername/
```

Even though zip lacks certain Unix-centric chops, its cross-platform compatibility makes it a go-to in environments mixing different system paradigms. Extracting a zip archive is a direct process:

```
unzip archive.zip
```

Before applying unzip, scanning file lists ensures destination integrity without unwarranted overwriting:

```
unzip -l archive.zip
```

Files named similarly within the extract directory can be less than desirable; hence, opt for listing contents as a safeguard, especially where archives interface with shared directories.

Scripting File Compression in Zsh

Zsh supports scripting these compression tools, enhancing automation where repetitive, predefined compression routines dominate. An example illustrating a backup script is depicted below:

```
#!/bin/zsh

backup_directory="/backups"
source_directory="$HOME/documents"
```

```
timestamp=$(date +%Y%m%d_%H%M%S)
archive_name="docs_backup_$timestamp.tar.gz"

tar -czf "$backup_directory/$archive_name" -C "$source_directory" .

echo "Backup completed: $archive_name"
```

This script encapsulates the documents folder into a timestamped tar.gz archive, demonstrating automation simplicity. Logs or status messages appended to operations provide further user insight.

Additionally, setting up automated cron jobs for routine file compressions as an integral part of administrative maintenance perpetuates operational fluidity:

```
0 2 * * * /path/to/backup_script.zsh
```

This entry activates nightly backup executions, diminishing manual administrative burdens while perpetuating robust data protection mechanisms.

Performance Considerations and Optimizations

Performance concerns guide decision-making on when and how to implement compression. gzip offers swifter operations suitable for time-sensitive tasks or server environments with multi-threaded capabilities (using pigz, a parallel variant):

```
pigz mylargefile
```

For processor-heavy efforts on single cores or systems where CPU overhead is less a concern, bzip2's compactness excels. Besides, attention to environment-specific factors, such as:

- Disk I/O: Ensure sufficient throughput to prevent compression from becoming a bottleneck.

- Memory Utilization: Buffer sizes during compression impact both performance and memory footprints, with parameters like bzip2's -s option constricting resource utility.

- Space Efficiently Caches: Temporarily suspend disk-intensive processes incompatible with concurrent compressions to heighten I/O delivery for prioritized processes.

157

Security Implications and Best Practices

Despite utility benefits, compression operations entail security implications demanding rigorous evaluations:

- Encryption Considerations: Neither gzip nor bzip2 inherently encrypts; avid practitioners incorporate encryption in post-compression steps using utilities like gpg.

- Exclusion Lists: Scripting routines require exclusion file lists for files with volatile security considerations, reducing inadvertent exposures.

- Validation of Compressed Packages: Using Integrity Checkers (hash validations) is standard to ascertain archive legitimacy before trustful deployment. Utilizing sha256sum or similar utilities checksums archives pre/post transfers, thus signifying authenticity and reliability.

Enabling signatures on critical archives safeguards home kits or customer-oriented packages against tampering risks.

Zsh's interplay with file compression mechanisms facilitates development of efficient, secure, and versatile solutions, reshaping mundane data transports into streamlined conduits of information flow across networks or systems. Whether harnessing the scalability of tar, the adeptness of gzip, or the universality of zip, users hone comprehensive technical acumen, charting sophisticated approaches that enhance operational efficiencies and enrich systemic resources management.

Advanced comprehension of these tools, marshalling automated sequences within Zsh, enables practitioners to maximize potential and affect impactful outcomes—ensuring not just the transmission of contents, but secure, agile, and systemic-scale proficiency.

Chapter 7

Zsh and Workflow Automation

This chapter explores how Zsh can be leveraged for workflow automation, highlighting the creation and utilization of scripts to automate repetitive tasks. It discusses scheduling with cron jobs, background execution, and seamless integration with other tools. The chapter also covers advanced parameter expansion techniques and the use of functions to streamline workflows, providing users with efficient strategies to enhance productivity through automation.

7.1 Automating Tasks with Scripts

The use of Zsh for task automation significantly enhances scripting capabilities, offering users a range of functionalities to streamline repetitive tasks effectively. Automating tasks through scripts saves time and reduces the potential for human error in everyday operations. The essence of scripting lies in its ability to abstract complex, repetitive sequences of commands into streamlined, reusable scripts that can execute with minimal user intervention.

Creating a script in Zsh begins with understanding the basic structure of a script file. A typical script is a plain text file that includes a series of commands to be executed and is usually saved with a '.zsh' extension to denote its association with the Zsh environment.

Every script starts with a shebang (" '#!' ") line that specifies the interpreter to be used for executing the script. For Zsh scripts, this line appears as:

```
#!/bin/zsh
```

The presence of the shebang line ensures that the execution environment recognizes the script is intended for interpretation by Zsh, distinguishing it from scripts intended for other shells such as Bash or Sh.

After defining the script file and including the shebang, the script is made executable. This often involves modifying the script's file permissions using the chmod command:

```
chmod +x script_name.zsh
```

This command changes the script to be executable, a necessary step before running the script directly.

Once the script is prepared, it can be executed from the command line by prefixing the script path with ./, as shown below:

```
./script_name.zsh
```

Automating tasks requires comprehension of several key scripting concepts, including variables, loops, conditionals, functions, and command substitution. Mastery of these concepts allows for the creation of versatile and efficient scripts.

- **Variables:** Variables in Zsh scripts are used to store and manipulate data. Variables are typically assigned without a preceding $, and they are referenced with a $.

  ```
  #!/bin/zsh

  # Variable assignment
  file_name="example.txt"

  # Using a variable
  echo "The file name is $file_name"
  ```

Variables can hold strings, integers, or the results of command executions, providing flexibility to scripts.

- **Loops:** Loops facilitate the repeated execution of a set of operations. Zsh supports several types of loops, including for, while, and until loops. Employing loops reduces code redundancy and enhances readability.

An example of a for loop in Zsh:

```
#!/bin/zsh

# Iterate over a list of numbers
for i in {1..5}
do
    echo "Iteration $i"
done
```

The 1..5 syntax utilizes brace expansion, a feature in Zsh that extends a set of elements within a specific range automatically.

- **Conditionals:** Conditionals guide the script's flow based on specified criteria. The primary conditional statements include if, elif, else, and fi. By incorporating conditionals, scripts can make decisions at runtime, increasing their adaptability.

Example of an if statement:

```
#!/bin/zsh

read -p "Enter your age: " age

# Conditional execution
if [ "$age" -ge 18 ]; then
    echo "You are eligible to vote."
else
    echo "You are not eligible to vote."
fi
```

- **Functions:** Functions encapsulate reusable blocks of code, promoting modularity and simplifying maintenance. Functions are defined once and invoked multiple times throughout the script.

Example of a function:

```
#!/bin/zsh

# Function definition
greet_user() {
    echo "Hello, $1!"
```

```
}

# Function invocation
greet_user "Alice"
greet_user "Bob"
```

In this script, greet_user is a function that accepts an argument and prints a greeting message.

- **Command Substitution:** Command substitution captures the output of a command for use within another command. Enclosed within backticks ` or $(...), the command output is substituted into the larger command structure.

  Example of command substitution:

```
#!/bin/zsh

# Command substitution
current_date=$(date)
echo "Today's date is: $current_date"
```

  Remarkably, Zsh enhances command substitution with improved syntax and efficiency.

Applying these fundamental concepts empowers users to automate diverse tasks. Consider automating file management operations, such as backing up files, renaming files, or organizing directories by file type.

- **File Backup Script:** A script to back up important files involves copying specified files to a backup directory. The following illustrates a basic backup script:

```
#!/bin/zsh

# Source and backup directories
source_dir="$HOME/documents"
backup_dir="$HOME/backup"

# Create backup directory if it does not exist
mkdir -p "$backup_dir"

# Copy files to backup directory
cp "$source_dir"/* "$backup_dir"

echo "Backup completed successfully."
```

This script ensures that the specified files from source_dir are copied to backup_dir, creating the backup directory if it does not yet exist.

- **Directory Organization Script:** Scripts can also automate the organization of files into directories based on extensions:

```zsh
#!/bin/zsh

# Target directory
target_dir="$HOME/downloads"

# Iterate over files in the target directory
for file in "$target_dir"/*
do
    # Extract file extension
    extension="${file##*.}"

    # Create a directory for the extension
    mkdir -p "$target_dir/$extension"

    # Move file into the corresponding directory
    mv "$file" "$target_dir/$extension/"
done

echo "Files organized by extension."
```

This approach dynamically moves files into directories corresponding to their file types based on extensions, reducing manual oversight.

Diving deeper, Zsh scripts can incorporate arrays, associative arrays, and an extensive set of available plugins. These advanced features expand script functionality and adaptability, proving invaluable for more complex automation tasks.

- **Using Arrays:** Arrays manage lists of elements efficiently. In Zsh, arrays are defined using parentheses and accessed with indices.

```zsh
#!/bin/zsh

# Array of filenames
file_list=("file1.txt" "file2.txt" "file3.txt")

# Iterate over array elements
for file in "${file_list[@]}"
do
    echo "Processing $file"
done
```

- **Associative Arrays:** Associative arrays provide key-value pair storage, allowing data to be indexed by named keys.

```zsh
#!/bin/zsh

# Declare an associative array
declare -A user_details

# Assign key-value pairs
user_details[name]="Alice"
user_details[age]=30

# Accessing associative array elements
echo "Name: ${user_details[name]}"
echo "Age: ${user_details[age]}"
```

Associative arrays are ideal for situations where relational data is necessary within scripts, such as tracking configuration settings or complex data.

- **Plugins and External Tools:** Zsh's community provides a wide range of plugins, such as oh-my-zsh, to augment script abilities with additional functions, themes, and tools. Integrating external commands and programs within a script can further enhance its capabilities.

The application of these techniques converts Zsh from a mere interactive shell into a powerful automation framework, giving users a means to continuously enhance productivity by minimizing repetitive manual tasks and focusing on processes that enhance creativity and decision-making.

Automating tasks with Zsh scripts requires a foundational understanding of scripting constructs, including variables, loops, and conditionals, enriched by utilizing advanced features such as arrays and functions. By leveraging these tools and techniques, tasks that once took considerable time and effort can now be executed efficiently and effortlessly. This foundational knowledge of Zsh scripting lays the groundwork for subsequent discussions on advanced automation strategies, including cron jobs, background execution, and seamless integration with other tools, further enhancing the potency of Zsh in workflow automation.

7.2 Using Cron Jobs for Scheduling

In workflow automation, the ability to execute scripts at specified times is a fundamental capability. This is managed in Unix-like systems through cron jobs, a built-in utility that schedules tasks to run at regular intervals. Understanding and using cron jobs effectively can significantly enhance automation processes, enabling scripts to execute unattended according to predefined schedules. This section delves into the configuration and management of cron jobs, illustrating their potential in automating processes at scale.

Basic Concepts and Setup

The cron daemon is a time-based job scheduler that runs in the background, constantly checking for tasks that need execution. These tasks, known as cron jobs, are specified in a file called the crontab.

The syntax of crontab is simple but powerful, enabling the expression of complex timing schedules in just a few lines. Each line in a crontab file represents a single job and consists of six fields:

- **Minute** (0 - 59)

- **Hour** (0 - 23)

- **Day of the month** (1 - 31)

- **Month** (1 - 12)

- **Day of the week** (0 - 7, where both 0 and 7 represent Sunday)

- **Command** to execute

The fields for time can contain numbers or special characters like '*', which represents every possible value in that position; ',', which separates multiple values; '-', which defines a range of values; and '/', which specifies step values.

Setting Up a Cron Job

To create a new cron job, users must access the crontab editor. This can be accomplished using the following command:

```
crontab -e
```

This opens the crontab file in the default text editor, allowing the definition of new cron jobs or modification of existing ones.

Example: Running a Script Daily at Midnight

Consider a task that needs to be executed every day at midnight. The crontab entry would appear as follows:

```
0 0 * * * /path/to/script.sh
```

Breaking this line down:

- 'o' specifies the minute, meaning the job runs when the minute is 'o' (on the hour).

- 'o' specifies the hour, meaning the job runs at 'o' hours, or midnight.

- The '*' for the day of the month, month, and day of the week indicates the job will run every day, every month, regardless of weekday.

- '/path/to/script.sh' is the path to the script that must execute.

Example: Running a Script Every Monday at 8:00 AM

For a script that should run at 8:00 AM every Monday, enter the following:

```
0 8 * * 1 /path/to/weekly_script.sh
```

Here:

- 'o' indicates the start of the hour.

- '8' signifies 8 AM.

- The third and fourth '*' represent every day of the month and every month, while '1' specifies Monday for the day of the week.

Special Macros and Syntax

Cron also supports several shorthand macros that simplify setting up frequent schedules:

- '@reboot' - Runs once at startup.

- '@yearly' or '@annually' - Runs once a year ('0 0 1 1 *').

- '@monthly' - Runs once a month ('0 0 1 * *').

- '@weekly' - Runs once a week ('0 0 * * 0').

- '@daily' or '@midnight' - Runs once a day ('0 0 * * *').

- '@hourly' - Runs once an hour ('0 * * * *').

Using these macros can significantly reduce the complexity of cron job entries and improve readability.

Managing Cron Jobs

The 'crontab' command provides several options for managing cron jobs. Users can list existing cron jobs using the following command:

```
crontab -l
```

If users need to remove all scheduled cron jobs, they can use:

```
crontab -r
```

Note: This will remove all cron jobs for the user, so it should be used with caution.

Advanced Patterns and Techniques

Cron jobs support advanced patterns that allow for more complex scheduling needs. For example, running a job every 15 minutes can be scheduled with:

```
*/15 * * * * /path/to/frequent_script.sh
```

In this entry, the '*/15' syntax in the minute field specifies that the job should execute every 15 minutes, akin to adding '0,15,30,45'.

Running a script on weekdays at 6 PM can be specified with:

167

```
0 18 * * 1-5 /path/to/weekday_script.sh
```

Here, '1-5' in the day of the week field restricts execution to Monday through Friday.

Error Handling and Notifications

One challenge with unattended script executions is error handling and monitoring. By default, cron jobs produce no output unless there is an error detected by the mail system. To ensure awareness of failures, users can direct output to log files or email notifications.

Redirecting output can be implemented by amending the cron job:

```
0 0 * * * /path/to/script.sh >> /var/log/myscript.log 2>&1
```

In this example, '» /var/log/myscript.log' appends standard output to a log file, whereas '2>&1' combines standard error with standard output, ensuring all output is captured.

Alternatively, users may configure email notifications by defining the 'MAILTO' environment variable at the top of their crontab file:

```
MAILTO="user@example.com"
```

This sends the output of the cron job to a specified email address, providing a mechanism to alert users to any issues requiring attention.

Integrating Cron with Zsh Scripts

Zsh scripts scheduled through cron can take advantage of Zsh-specific features to create sophisticated automation solutions. Consider using parameter expansion and command substitution to enhance the real-time adaptability of scripts executed by cron.

Moreover, combining cron jobs with system utilities akin to 'rsync', 'tar', or 'curl' can further extend automation capabilities for complex workflow needs, such as scheduled backups, data synchronization, or periodic API calls.

Example: Automated Backup with Zsh

Consider the following script designed to back up the user's documents directory daily at midnight:

```
#!/bin/zsh
```

```
# Backup source and destination
source_dir="$HOME/documents"
backup_dir="/backup/$(date +\%Y-\%m-\%d)"

# Create backup directory if it doesn't exist
mkdir -p "$backup_dir"

# Perform backup using rsync
rsync -av --delete "$source_dir/" "$backup_dir/"
```

In this script, parameter expansion is used to dynamically create a dated directory for organized backups, leveraging the power of rsync for efficient data transfer.

Configuring the Cron Job

The corresponding cron job entry looks as follows:

```
0 0 * * * /path/to/backup_script.zsh
```

Setting up cron jobs requires foresight and planning to align schedule parameters with task requirements effectively. Users should ensure that all paths, permissions, and variables are meticulously verified to mitigate errors from inadequate preparation.

Best Practices for Robust Cron Job Management

Ensuring reliability and effectiveness in using cron jobs involves adopting several best practices:

- **Testing:** Rigorously test scripts in an isolated environment before deploying them in production. This can prevent syntactic errors and incorrect logic that may go unnoticed until production.

- **Documentation:** Maintain comprehensive documentation within the script and crontab entries. This allows for ease of maintenance and transferability if handed off to different users or teams.

- **Resource Estimation:** Carefully estimate the resource consumption of scheduled scripts, especially during peak system usage, to avoid any disruption of crucial services.

- **Monitoring:** Implement robust monitoring solutions for cron jobs using log files or third-party monitoring tools. This ensures prompt detection of failures and a swift response.

- **Environment Variables:** Explicitly define any necessary environment variables within the script to avoid dependency on shell-specific defaults, which may differ under cron.

Understanding and leveraging cron jobs equips users with a formidable toolset for automating and scheduling tasks. When used effectively, cron jobs transform the prospects of workflow automation, freeing users from the constraints of manual task management and facilitating the scaling of repetitive processes across varied environments.

As part of a comprehensive automation strategy, cron jobs synergize with Zsh scripting to automate standard tasks and unlock capabilities for intricate, long-term scheduling requirements. This integration allows not only the execution of foundational scripts but the realization of sophisticated, enduring automation workflows that cater to diverse operational needs.

7.3   Background and Scheduled Execution

The efficacy of automating workflows significantly hinges on the seamless execution of tasks in both background and scheduled environments. This section explores techniques and mechanisms involved in executing commands and scripts without user intervention, focusing on background execution and advanced scheduling methods. Mastering these concepts is crucial for optimizing resource utilization, reducing foreground latency, and ensuring that tasks are executed at the most opportune times.

- **Understanding Background Execution:** Background execution enables commands and processes to run without blocking the terminal. This allows users to initiate long-running tasks and continue working, improving multitasking efficiency. Background execution in Zsh and other Unix-like shells involves utilizing the & operator.

170

Initiating Processes in the Background

The simplest way to start a command in the background is to append an & at the end of the command:

```
long_running_command &
```

Once executed, the shell returns control to the user immediately, displaying the job ID and process ID (PID).

Example:

```
sleep 60 &
[1] 1234
```

In this example, the sleep command is set to pause for 60 seconds in the background. The job ID is [1], and the process ID is 1234.

Managing Background Jobs

Zsh provides several built-in utilities to manage background jobs.

The jobs command lists all current background jobs and their statuses:

```
jobs
```

Foregrounding a background job utilizes the fg command:

```
fg %1
```

This brings job number 1 to the foreground. Conversely, the bg command resumes suspended jobs in the background:

```
bg %1
```

Killing Background Jobs

To terminate a background job, the kill command, followed by either the job percentage number:

```
kill %1
```

or the process ID can be used:

```
kill 1234
```

Forcible termination is accomplished with the -9 option:

```
kill -9 1234
```

Understanding the management of background jobs not only enhances workflow fluidity but also prevents inadvertent resource drains from unmonitored scripts.

- **Complex Background Tasks Using Subshells:** While simple background execution is useful, more complex tasks may require subshell environments to manage isolated processes. A subshell inherits environment variables of the parent shell but does not alter them upon exit, offering a controlled environment for discrete operations.

Launching a subshell with a command:

```
(ls -l; echo "Done") &
```

Both ls -l and echo "Done" run in a subshell separated from the interactive shell. Output and error messages remain bound to this block, which can be essential for tasks needing environmental isolation.

- **Scheduled Execution through the** at **Command:** While cron jobs are optimal for regular execution, the at command facilitates the execution of jobs once at a specific future time. This feature is particularly useful for one-time tasks that don't require the repetitive schedule that cron affords.

Configuring at Tasks

The at command uses a queue system to store jobs for future execution. To schedule a job, specify the execution time and then provide the commands:

```
echo "echo 'Task executed'" | at 15:00
```

This schedules the echo command to run at 3:00 PM, yielding flexible timing with natural language input.

Specifying Times and Dates

The at command accepts numerous time formats, including:

172

- Precise time: at 10am or at 23:30

- Relative time: at now + 1 hour

- Specific day: at 11:00 AM tomorrow or at 2:00 PM next week

Managing at Jobs

Pending at jobs can be viewed using:

```
atq
```

Cancel an upcoming job with atrm:

```
atrm 5
```

Where 5 is the job number in the queue.

Advanced Use Cases

Integrations of at with Zsh allow running Zsh scripts at designated times without manual scheduling in the crontab, offering flexibility for less frequent actions requiring automation.

- **Advanced Scheduling Techniques:** For complex scenarios where cron and at scheduling do not suffice, users may need to explore advanced schedulers like systemd timers or custom scheduling scripts that provide more powerful control over execution parameters and dependencies.

Using Systemd Timers

systemd is a system and service manager available on many Linux distributions. Systemd timers can replace cron for newer systems, considering dependencies and failures more robustly.

Creating a Timer

Set up a timer involves creating two files: a service unit describing the task and a timer unit describing the schedule.

Example service file /etc/systemd/system/mytask.service:

```
[Unit]
Description=My Scheduled Task
```

```
[Service]
Type=oneshot
ExecStart=/usr/bin/mytask.sh
```

Corresponding timer file /etc/systemd/system/mytask.timer:

```
[Unit]
Description=Run My Task Daily

[Timer]
OnCalendar=*-*-* 06:00:00

[Install]
WantedBy=timers.target
```

To initiate the timer:

```
systemctl start mytask.timer
systemctl enable mytask.timer
```

Leveraging Custom Scripts

Where native tools fall short, scripts combining logic, file states, or network dependencies can augment scheduling capabilities on unique environments. For example, a custom script that checks server availability could wrap task execution within conditional logic predicated on successful pings.

```
#!/bin/zsh

# Check server availability
if ping -c 1 server.example.com &> /dev/null; then
    /path/to/network_task.sh &
else
    echo "Server not reachable at $(date)" >> /var/log/task_errors.log
fi
```

Here, task execution is contingent upon successful communication with a designated server, demonstrating conditional task management.

- **Utilizing** screen **and** tmux **for Enhanced Session Management:** Persistent background task execution can benefit from using terminal multiplexers such as screen or tmux. These tools allow users to manage multiple shell sessions persistently, which remain running across network disconnections or terminal closures.

Screen Basics

174

screen creates a virtual session that can be detached and resumed later.
Start a new screen session:

```
screen
```

Detach from a session with Ctrl-a d, resulting in continued background
execution.

List active sessions:

```
screen -ls
```

Resume a session:

```
screen -r <session_id>
```

Tmux Fundamentals

tmux offers more features and customization than screen.

Start:

```
tmux
```

Detach from a session: Ctrl-b d

List sessions:

```
tmux ls
```

Resume:

```
tmux attach-session -t <session_name>
```

Both tools enhance task management by ensuring that commands initiated in virtual sessions persist through unexpected SSH termination
or user logout, vital for maintaining long-running processes without
direct supervision.

- **Best Practices for Execution Management:** The intent behind executing tasks deliberately impacts system reliability and
  performance; hence, best practices emphasize:

- Resource Monitoring: Deploy resource-monitoring tools to evaluate CPU, memory, and IO usage for background tasks. This

175

ensures long-running processes do not over-consume system resources, leading to potential bottlenecks.

- Error Handling: Incorporate comprehensive error-handling routines to anticipate failures, enabling alert mechanisms for swift diagnoses.

- Environment Configuration: Confirm scripts are executed with a consistent environment, explicitly setting necessary variables and paths, mitigating assumptions inherent in shell defaults.

- Security Considerations: Appropriately restrict available commands and files for scripts, applying principles of least privilege to safeguard against exploitation.

- Documentation and Auditing: Maintain detailed records and documentation of scheduling setups for auditing and continuity, ensuring task criteria and objectives are transparent.

Through the synchronized utilization of background and scheduled execution, productivity surges and manual dependencies decrease, allowing system processes to occur autonomously and predictably. Users familiar with these technical strategies can design execution environments that respond agilely to changing requirements, equipping themselves with the knowledge to cultivate innovative, resilient workflow solutions.

7.4   Integrating Zsh with Other Tools

The Zsh shell, known for its flexibility and interactive features, becomes extraordinarily powerful when integrated with various command-line tools and applications. Such integrations extend the capabilities of Zsh, enabling users to create efficient, interconnected workflows and automate complex tasks seamlessly. This section explores various methodologies and practices for integrating Zsh with other tools, highlighting the benefits and providing practical coding examples to illustrate how these combinations can enhance productivity and efficiency.

Utilizing Command-Line Tools

Command-line tools are the backbone of many automation processes. Integration of these tools with Zsh allows users to create sophisticated scripts that leverage the strengths of each application. Popular command-line utilities such as awk, sed, grep, and find are extensively used in scripting with Zsh.

Integration with grep

grep is an essential tool for pattern matching and text searching within files. Leveraging its power within Zsh scripts can elevate data manipulation capacities.

Example of a grep integration in a Zsh script:

```zsh
#!/bin/zsh

log_file="/var/log/system.log"

# Search for error occurrences in the log file
grep -i "error" "$log_file" > /tmp/error_summary.txt

echo "Error summary saved to /tmp/error_summary.txt."
```

This script searches for case-insensitive instances of "error" within a system log and outputs them to a summary file, automating a routine log-checking task.

Integration with awk

awk excels at text processing, with particular strengths in structure-based data manipulation. Its integration with Zsh can be potent for extracting and summarizing data from structured text files.

Example with awk:

```zsh
#!/bin/zsh

data_file="data.csv"

# Calculate and print the total of the second column
awk -F"," '{sum += $2} END {print "Total:", sum}' "$data_file"
```

This script uses awk to sum values in the second column of a CSV file, demonstrating how structured data can be processed efficiently.

Combining Multiple Tools in a Pipeline

Pipelines are a distinctive feature in Unix-like systems that facilitate the transfer of data between the output of one command to the input of another. Zsh scripts benefit immensely from this approach, allowing integration of multiple tools to perform complex data manipulations in a single pipeline.

Example of a data processing pipeline:

```zsh
#!/bin/zsh

# Define file names
input_file="data.log"
output_file="summary.txt"

# Process the data pipeline
grep "INFO" "$input_file" |
awk '{print $3,$4}' |
sort |
uniq -c > "$output_file"

echo "Log summary generated in $output_file."
```

This Zsh pipeline first filters log entries with "INFO," extracts the third and fourth fields, sorts, and provides a unique count of occurrences, outputting the results to a summary file.

Integrating Zsh with Version Control Systems

Version control systems, particularly Git, are integral to modern development workflows. They provide change-tracking and collaborative features that are essential for any scripting or software project.

Interactive Git Prompt

Zsh can enhance Git usage with custom prompts that provide situational awareness regarding repository status. Using third-party plugins such as oh-my-zsh, customization is straightforward.

Example configuration using .zshrc:

```
# Enable plugins
plugins=(git)

# Customize the prompt to show Git status
PROMPT='%n@%m:%c$(git_prompt_info)%# '

# Function to display the git info
git_prompt_info() {
    branch=$(git symbolic-ref HEAD 2>/dev/null | sed -e 's/^refs\/heads\///')
    [ -n "$branch" ] && echo " ($branch)"
}
```

The prompt dynamically displays the current Git branch, integrating Git awareness directly into the terminal interaction.

Automating Git Workflows

Zsh scripts can automate repetitive Git tasks, ensuring consistent and efficient operation of version control tasks.

Example of a simple Git automation script:

```zsh
#!/bin/zsh

# Automate the commit process
git_add_commit() {
    git add .
    git commit -m "$1"
    git push
}

message="Automated commit at $(date)"
git_add_commit "$message"
```

This function automates the process of adding, committing, and pushing changes with a timestamped message, streamlining routine update workflows.

Integrating Zsh with Task Management Tools

Task management tools, such as taskwarrior, offer enhanced task tracking capabilities. Integrating these with Zsh helps users maintain effective productivity by interfacing with task databases directly from the shell.

Task Management with Taskwarrior

taskwarrior is a command-line task management application that integrates seamlessly with Zsh, enabling task list manipulation directly.

Example Zsh alias for task management:

```zsh
# Alias to list incomplete tasks
alias tasklist='task status:pending'

# Function to add new tasks
add_task() {
    task add "$1" +$2
}

# Usage: add_task "Buy milk" home
# This adds a new home-related task "Buy milk"
```

179

Here, the alias quickly lists pending tasks while the function adds new tasks under specified categories, illustrating task management efficiency.

Aliases and Functions for Enhanced Productivity

Aliases and functions in Zsh provide shortcuts and expanded functionality for integrated tool management.

```
# Alias and function examples
alias ll='ls -lah'
alias gs='git status'

backup_data() {
    rsync -av --progress ~/data/ /backup/data/
    echo "Backup completed."
}
```

These aliases (ll and gs) and functions (like backup_data) simplify complex workflows, enabling efficient command execution and integration.

Integrating Zsh with Text Editors

Text editors such as vim or nano are frequently used for script editing. Integrating these editors with Zsh enhances the scripting workflow through faster file access and simplified editing commands.

Vim Integration for Programming in Zsh

Enable Vim for rapid editing and syntax highlighting in the Zsh environment using configuration files.

Example .vimrc setup:

```
" Enable syntax highlighting
syntax on

" Set line numbers
set number

" Customize tab settings for scripting
set tabstop=4
set shiftwidth=4
set expandtab
```

This configuration improves code readability and consistency while scripting in Zsh.

Leveraging Plugins for Enhanced Editor Capabilities

Install and configure plugins within Vim to extend its capabilities in Zsh, such as GitGutter or NerdTree, accessed directly from Git repositories.

Install a plugin using Vim-Plug:

```
call plug#begin('~/.vim/plugged')

" Example plugins
Plug 'airblade/vim-gitgutter'
Plug 'preservim/nerdtree'

call plug#end()
```

These plugins incorporate functionalities directly into the editing workflow, improving efficiency and reducing context switching between applications.

Leveraging External Scripting Languages

Zsh scripts can integrate external scripting languages like Python or Ruby, adding higher-level functionality and custom libraries to shell automation tasks.

Python Integration in Zsh Scripts

Embedding Python within Zsh scripts leverages advanced data processing libraries (e.g., pandas), making complex operations more accessible.

Example of Python integration:

```
#!/bin/zsh

# Execute Python code from within a Zsh script
result=$(python3 <<END
import math
print(math.factorial(5))
END
)

echo "The factorial of 5 is $result."
```

This integration runs Python code directly, using its computational power within a Zsh script.

Integrating API Interactions using curl

curl is a versatile command-line tool for data transfer. It integrates with Zsh to perform API calls, enhancing automation capabilities

181

through services interaction.

API Request with curl

Perform HTTP requests via curl from a Zsh script, utilizing it for applications ranging from web scraping to remote data fetching.

Example API interaction:

```
#!/bin/zsh

# Fetch data from a public API
api_url="https://api.example.com/data"
response=$(curl -s "$api_url")

# Process the JSON response
echo "Data obtained from API: $response"
```

This simple request model can scale with authentication and complex parameters, forming the basis for comprehensive API-driven tasks.

Combining jq **for JSON Processing**

jq is used in conjunction with curl to parse JSON data, transforming API interactions into data-aware scripts.

Example with JSON processing:

```
#!/bin/zsh

api_url="https://api.example.com/data"
response=$(curl -s "$api_url")

# Use jq to parse and extract data
name=$(echo $response | jq -r '.name')
echo "Fetched user name: $name"
```

By using jq, this example efficiently extracts information from JSON data, highlighting the synergetic power of integrating multiple tools in Zsh scripts.

The integration of Zsh with other command-line tools creates a cohesive environment where shell efficiency meets specialized utility functionality. This symbiotic relationship underpins advanced, automated workflows capable of handling varied and intricate tasks with finesse.

Extending these integrations, users can optimize their workflows by identifying repetitive actions, converting them into automated scripts, and applying them within broader, strategic processes, ultimately driving enhancements in productivity and operational precision across technical domains.

7.5 Parameter Expansion for Efficiency

Parameter expansion in Zsh encompasses a wealth of features that provide efficient data manipulation and subprocess management, well beyond the capabilities typically associated with shell scripting. Through
a series of syntactic constructs, parameter expansion allows script authors to dynamically manipulate variable values, construct filenames,
and modify strings on the fly, optimizing both the efficiency and readability of scripts. This section delves deeply into the concepts, advanced techniques, and practical applications of parameter expansion
in Zsh, equipping users with a powerful toolset for attaining automation efficiency.

At its core, parameter expansion in Zsh involves the evaluation and
modification of parameters, producing more versatile and context-
sensitive scripts. Basic parameter expansion involves addressing a
variable with expansions that introduce dynamic content into a script.

Basic Use Cases

The simplest example of parameter expansion is represented by retrieving the value of a variable:

```
#!/bin/zsh

name="Alice"
echo "Hello, $name"
```

Here, '$name' is replaced by the value 'Alice', expressing how the shell
evaluates parameter names by substituting their values.

Beyond straightforward substitutions, Zsh's parameter expansion features a variety of advanced operations:

Default Values and Assignments

One of the most powerful uses of parameter expansion is handling variables with defaults or conditional assignment:

```
#!/bin/zsh

# Assign a default value if variable is unset
```

```
greeting=${name:-"Hello World"}
echo $greeting
```

In this example, if 'name' is unset or null, 'greeting' defaults to "Hello World." This functionality keeps scripts robust against undefined variables.

Assigning a default value:

```
#!/bin/zsh

# Assign 'User' to name if it is unset, set name to its current value otherwise
name=${name:="User"}
echo $name
```

Here, 'name' is permanently initialized to "User" if not already assigned.

String Manipulation

Zsh provides mechanisms for manipulating strings directly through parameter expansion:

```
#!/bin/zsh

filename="data_file.txt"

# Remove suffix
echo ${filename%.txt} # Output: data_file

# Remove prefix
echo ${filename#data_} # Output: file.txt
```

In these examples, '$filename%.txt' trims the '.txt' suffix, while '$filename#data_' strips away the 'data_' prefix using pattern matches, exhibiting Zsh's built-in string-editing capabilities without auxiliary commands like 'sed'.

Substring Extraction

Understanding how to extract substrings is vital for efficient data handling:

```
#!/bin/zsh

string="Zsh scripting language"

# Extract substring starting at position 4 with length 9
part=${string:4:9}
echo $part # Output: scripting
```

184

In this scenario, the substring "scripting" is derived from position 4 to length 9, catering to cases demanding segment isolation.

Arrays, a crucial data structure in scripting, are well-supported by Zsh for complex data aggregation:

Basic Array Operations

Defining and accessing arrays showcases Zsh's parameter expansion within indexed collections:

```zsh
#!/bin/zsh

# Define an array
colors=("red" "green" "blue")

# Access first element
echo ${colors[0]} # Output: red

# Length of array
echo ${#colors[@]} # Output: 3
```

In these examples, individual array elements are accessed using '$colors[index]', while '$#colors[@]' calculates the array's length, fundamental for programmatically traversing data sequences.

Slicing Arrays

Expanding on array manipulation involves slicing for sublists:

```zsh
#!/bin/zsh

fruits=("apple" "banana" "cherry" "date")

# Slice array from index 1 to 2
subset=(${fruits[@]:1:2})
echo ${subset[@]} # Output: banana cherry
```

This constructs an array subset from elements at indices 1 and 2, demonstrating the potential of collating partial array data seamlessly through parameter expansion.

Parameter expansion is indispensable for sophisticated substitutions where transformations on a variable's content become necessary:

Search and Replace

Perform substitutions within strings directly:

```zsh
#!/bin/zsh
```

185

```
path="/var/log/system.log"

# Replace .log with .bak
backup_path=${path/.log/.bak}
echo $backup_path # Output: /var/log/system.bak
```

Basic substitutions replace '.log' extensions with '.bak', imparting flexibility for output file management and real-time adjustments within paths or filenames.

Case Modifications

Manipulations involving capitalization changes are simple yet impactful:

```
#!/bin/zsh

original="zsh is fun"

# Capitalize each word
capitalize=${(C)original}
echo $capitalize # Output: Zsh Is Fun

# Entire string to uppercase
uppercase=${(U)original}
echo $uppercase # Output: ZSH IS FUN
```

Through the application of modifiers such as '(C)' for capitalizing initials and '(U)' for full uppercase conversions, Zsh facilitates case management, crucial for standardizing outputs across diverse contexts.

Using parameter expansion efficiently requires understanding how to merge the features with proper scripting practices, ensuring smooth and expected script behavior.

Environment Configuration Check

Confident script execution often relies on verifying environmental parameters, achieved with default value expansions:

```
#!/bin/zsh

# Verify environment variables
proj_path=${PROJECT_PATH:?"Project path not set"}
db_conn=${DB_CONNECTION:?"Database connection string not set"}

echo "Project path is $proj_path"
echo "Database connection string is $db_conn"
```

The ':¿ operator halts the script if environment variables remain unset, providing error validation out-of-the-box.

Real-World Application: File Processing

Consider dynamic log file generation, where efficiency is paramount for daily administrative or processing tasks:

```
#!/bin/zsh

# Dynamic file creation based on current date
logdir="/var/logs"
logfile="access_$(date +%Y-%m-%d).log"

fullpath="$logdir/$logfile"

# Touch the logfile
touch ${fullpath}

echo "Log file created: ${fullpath}"
```

Here, parameter expansion intertwines with 'date' command substitution to ensure log filenames are dynamically adjusted for daily processing, thus demonstrating effective automation.

When parameter expansion operates in tandem, emphasizing readability without sacrificing performance becomes essential:

Leveraging Escape Sequences

It is crucial to safely expand variables without mishandling special characters, achieved through rigorous escaping:

```
#!/bin/zsh

user_input="User said: \"Use Zsh!\""

# Safely handle special characters
echo "${user_input}"
```

Consistency in message output management necessitates careful encoding during variable expansion, especially when containing special characters like quotes, ensuring predictability and accuracy.

Explicit Naming Conventions

Naming variables descriptively can further facilitate a coherent scripting narrative:

```
#!/bin/zsh

# Descriptive variable naming
```

187

```
config_directory="/etc/myapp/configs"
current_user=$(whoami)

echo "Current user ${current_user} is accessing ${config_directory}"
```

Descriptive naming converges logic and narrative, making the script more intuitive for maintainers and reducing the ambiguity often encountered in rapid automation development.

Harnessing the capabilities of parameter expansion in Zsh contributes profoundly to script efficiency, enabling data preprocessing directly in the shell without external utilities. These expansions refine scripts, economizing on resources and accelerating execution, especially within high-demand environments.

When integrated with best practices for readability, script authors can attain a balance that encapsulates robust functioning with clean, communicative logic. This potent fusion of expansion constructs with procedural clarity constitutes a vital asset for any developer pursuing automation excellence within the dynamic realm of Zsh scripting. The adaptability and versatility offered by these expansions extend beyond mere substitution, anchoring a foundation that supports a wide breadth of practical automation needs, consistently across diverse domains and environments.

7.6 Streamlining Workflows with Functions

Functions are integral components of programming that enhance modularity, reusability, and clarity in scripts. This is especially true in Zsh, where functions allow users to encapsulate blocks of code for repeated use across scripts, leading to more structured and maintainable automation workflows. This section elaborates on the role of functions in optimizing workflows and explores best practices and advanced techniques for leveraging functions effectively in Zsh scripting.

Fundamentals of Function Definition and Usage

Functions in Zsh, much like other programming languages, are defined using a specific structure that includes a name and a block of code to execute. This basic form includes the following elements:

```zsh
#!/bin/zsh

# Define a function
greet() {
    echo "Hello, World!"
}

# Call the function
greet
```

This example introduces a simple function 'greet', which, when invoked, outputs a greeting. Functions are reusable units in a script, reducing redundancy and enhancing organization.

Passing Arguments to Functions

Functions gain versatility when they can accept parameters, allowing the implementation of dynamic logic by operating with different inputs:

```zsh
#!/bin/zsh

# Function with parameters
display_info() {
    echo "Name: $1"
    echo "Age: $2"
}

# Call the function with arguments
display_info "Alice" 30
```

In this case, 'display_info' accepts two arguments, 'name' and 'age', demonstrating parameterization. '$1' and '$2' represent positional parameters, which make functions adaptable to varying data.

Return Values and Exit Status

Functions can return values through explicit output, and their execution status is indicated by an exit status, following the conventions of command execution:

```
#!/bin/zsh

# Function returning value
multiply() {
    echo $(($1 * $2))
}

# Capture the return value
result=$(multiply 6 7)
echo "Product is: $result"

# Function exit status
check_file() {
    [ -f "$1" ]
}

check_file "/etc/passwd"
echo "Exists: $?"
```

Here, 'multiply' returns a value via standard output, captured and stored in 'result'. The 'check_file' function returns an exit status, '0' for a success or '1' for a failure, based on a file's existence check.

Variable Scoping in Functions

Scoping is a vital consideration when defining functions to prevent conflicts and ensure that variables are isolated unless explicitly intended for global scope:

```
#!/bin/zsh

# Function illustrating variable scope
calculate() {
    local sum=$(( $1 + $2 ))
    echo $sum
}

calculate 5 10 # Output: 15
echo $sum # Output: nothing, as 'sum' is local
```

Variables declared as local within a function, using the 'local' keyword, limit their visibility and lifecycle to the function's execution scope, ensuring each function operates independently.

190

Advanced Features and Techniques with Functions

Beyond elementary functionality, Zsh functions incorporate advanced features that drastically broaden their application in automation scripts:

Using Option Flags Functions can parse command-line-like option flags, similar to standalone executables, using internal argument parsing:

```
#!/bin/zsh

# Function utilizing option flags
process_data() {
    while getopts "f:v" opt; do
        case $opt in
            f) file="$OPTARG" ;;
            v) verbose="true" ;;
            *) echo "Usage: process_data [-f file] [-v]" ;;
        esac
    done
    shift $((OPTIND -1))

    if [ "$verbose" = "true" ]; then
        echo "Processing file: $file in verbose mode"
    fi
}

process_data -f "data.txt" -v
```

This flexible approach allows functions to emulate executable behavior, increasing their usability in versatile scenarios.

Recursive Functions Zsh accommodates recursive function designs, enabling complex operations such as directory traversal or iterative calculations:

```
#!/bin/zsh

# Example recursive function
factorial() {
    if [ "$1" -le 1 ]; then
        echo 1
    else
        echo $(( $1 * $(factorial $(( $1 - 1 ))) ))
    fi
}
```

```
factorial 5 # Output: 120
```

The recursive 'factorial' function calculates a number's factorial, demonstrating how recursion resolves complex computational problems within scripts.

Modular Design and Code Organization

Effective workflow management through Zsh functions necessitates modular design principles, advocating for smaller, purposeful functions combined to perform comprehensive tasks. This decomposes monolithic scripts into more manageable components:

Modularity through Library Functions A library of functions encapsulates standard tasks, allowing reuse across multiple scripts or projects. This strategy enhances maintainability and promotes DRY (Don't Repeat Yourself) practice:

```
#!/bin/zsh

# Math library file, mathlib.sh
add() {
    echo $(($1 + $2))
}

subtract() {
    echo $(($1 - $2))
}

# Include this library in other scripts
```

Including 'mathlib.sh' within a Zsh script adopts these math operations throughout a suite of scripts without repetitively redefining them:

```
#!/bin/zsh

# Source the library
source "./mathlib.sh"

# Utilize the library functions
result=$(add 10 20)
echo "Result: $result"
```

Best Practices for Robust Functions

Functions are instrumental in constructing resilient automation frameworks in Zsh. Adapting design conventions and strategic practices ensures their effectiveness:

Documentation and Comments Document functions thoroughly to clarify their purpose, parameters, and usage. Comments improve comprehendibility and collaborative development:

```zsh
#!/bin/zsh

# Function to calculate area of a rectangle
# Parameters:
# $1 - Length of the rectangle
# $2 - Width of the rectangle
calculate_area() {
    local length=$1
    local width=$2
    echo "Area: $(( length * width ))"
}
```

By clearly documenting each element within functions, the same clarity translates to comprehensive understanding and ease of updates.

Consistent Naming Conventions Adopt consistent and descriptive naming for functions, enhancing recognition and usability:

```zsh
#!/bin/zsh

# Consistent function naming
backup_database() {
    echo "Database backed up."
}

optimize_images() {
    echo "Images optimized."
}
```

The above conventions ensure immediate insight into a function's action based purely on consistent naming schemes.

Error Handling and Debugging Craft functions to include error handling, preventing unexpected failures from propagating in automation processes:

193

```zsh
#!/bin/zsh

# Function with error handling
copy_file() {
    local src=$1
    local dest=$2
    if cp "$src" "$dest"; then
        echo "File copied successfully."
    else
        echo "Error: Failed to copy." >&2
        return 1
    fi
}
```

The inclusion of explicit error messages and non-zero return statuses bolsters error recovery strategies and minimizes operational disruptions.

Parallel Execution with Functions

Leveraging Zsh's ability to run functions concurrently taps into naturally parallelizable domains:

```zsh
#!/bin/zsh

# Parallel execution of functions
download_data() {
    curl -O "http://example.com/data.csv"
}

process_images() {
    mogrify -resize 800x600 *.jpg
}

# Execute functions in parallel
download_data &
process_images &
wait # Wait for all background jobs
echo "All tasks completed."
```

Executing functions in the background minimizes wall-clock time while maximizing resource utilization, effectively streamlining workflow pipelining.

Building Complex Automation Solutions

As a culmination of function capabilities, build automated pipelines encapsulating the entire scope of desired operations:

Example: Automated Deployments Implement automated environments where Zsh functions govern all phases of deploying software, from fetching the latest code base to performing sanity checks:

```zsh
#!/bin/zsh

# Pull the latest code from version control
fetch_code() {
    git pull origin main
}

# Build the software
build_software() {
    make
}

# Deploy the software
deploy_software() {
    ./deploy.sh
}

# Orchestrate deployment
deploy() {
    fetch_code
    build_software && deploy_software
}

# Execute the deployment function
deploy
```

The resulting script defines a clear sequence, utilizing functions to compartmentalize and safeguard each stage of the deployment process.

Mastering functions within Zsh scripting propagates a paradigm of refined organization, flexibility, and efficiency across automation workflows. By adopting a structured, modular approach, scripts become more manageable and scalable, capable of addressing both simple tasks and complex, multi-phase operations with equal ease.

This depth in function utilization anchors scripts not merely as executive command sequences but as cohesive automation ecosystems, facilitating maintenance, adaptation, and expansion in evolving operational landscapes. Proficiency with functions, therefore, underscores the ability to streamline and innovate workflows, significantly enhancing productivity and precision within the domain of shell scripting.

Chapter 8

Error Handling and Debugging in Zsh Scripts

This chapter focuses on techniques for effective error handling and debugging in Zsh scripts. It covers the interpretation and use of exit statuses, the application of debugging options, and implementing strategies for graceful error management. Additionally, it discusses the use of traps for exception handling, logging practices, and validation processes to ensure script reliability, equipping users with essential skills to create robust and error-resistant scripts.

8.1 Understanding Exit Status and Codes

In any programming or scripting environment, understanding exit statuses and codes is crucial for effective error handling and debugging. In Zsh scripting, this is no different. An exit status, also known as an exit code, is an integer that a process returns to its parent process when it terminates. It serves the primary purpose of indicating the success or failure of the script or command that was executed. Understanding how these work within Zsh scripts can empower you to manage and handle errors gracefully.

Every command executed within a shell script is assigned an exit status, a numeric code used by the shell to determine whether the command completed successfully or failed. In conventional use, an exit status of '0' signifies success. Non-zero values represent various types of errors or conditions that indicate the command did not execute as intended.

A command's exit status can be accessed immediately after its execution by examining the special variable $?. This variable holds the exit status of the last command that was executed. Knowing how to check this variable is essential for scripting tasks that rely on conditional logic for error handling.

The following is an example where a simple command's execution status is evaluated:

```zsh
#!/bin/zsh

# Run a simple command
ls /some/nonexistent/directory

# Capture the exit status
status=$?
echo "The exit status of 'ls' was $status"
```

In this example, if the directory does not exist, the 'ls' command will fail, and the script will output a non-zero exit status. If 'status' equals '0', the command executed successfully. Otherwise, the error code provides insight into what might have gone wrong.

The exit status mechanism is integral to writing scripts that can handle a wide range of conditions. Consider a script meant to process files. By using exit codes, the script can distinguish between a successful operation and one that failed due to reasons such as a file not existing or a process being unable to allocate required resources.

- 0: Success – The command executed successfully without any errors.

- 1: General Error – Catchall for general errors.

- 2: Misuse of Shell Builtins – Indicates a misuse of shell builtins or syntax errors.

- 126: Command Invoked Cannot Execute – Permission problem or command is not an executable.

- 127: Command Not Found – The command was not found.

- 128: Invalid Argument to Exit – Exit with a status outside the expected range.

- 130: Script Terminated by Ctrl+C – Indicates the script was terminated manually.

- 255: Exit Status Out of Range – Often occurs when an exit status exceeds 255 or no argument is given with different return possibilities.

Using these codes enhances the script's ability to communicate the reason for failure clearly. Consider a scenario where differentiated actions are desired based on the type of failure encountered. Tailoring responses based on exit codes can streamline troubleshooting and recovery actions.

To effectively use exit codes in Zsh scripts, it is common to employ conditional statements. The 'if' statement is frequently used to alter script behavior depending on a command's exit status.

```zsh
#!/bin/zsh

# Function to check existence of a directory
check_directory() {
  if [ -d "$1" ]; then
    echo "Directory exists."
    return 0
  else
    echo "Directory does not exist."
    return 1
  fi
}

# Use the function
check_directory "/some/nonexistent/directory"
status=$?

if [ $status -eq 0 ]; then
  echo "Proceeding with the operation..."
else
  echo "Operation aborted."
fi
```

In this example, 'status' is checked after calling 'check_directory'. Depending on the exit code, the script branches into different operational paths. This paradigm results in more robust scripts, capable of adapting to various situations by integrating logic based on exit statuses.

In certain contexts, relying solely on predefined exit codes may not provide sufficient granularity for error reporting. Zsh scripts often benefit from custom exit codes that allow scripts to define their own meaningful statuses. This can be particularly useful in larger scripts where tracking a wider range of specific conditions and failures is necessary.

Defining custom exit codes is straightforward. You choose a series of integers not likely to be confused with standard exit codes and use them consistently throughout your script. Here's an example:

```zsh
#!/bin/zsh

# Define custom exit codes
SUCCESS=0
ERROR_NO_FILE=101
ERROR_NOT_ROOT=102

# Function to check root privileges
check_root() {
  if [ "$EUID" -ne 0 ]; then
    echo "You need to run this script as root."
    return $ERROR_NOT_ROOT
  fi
  return $SUCCESS
}

# Function to process a file
process_file() {
  if [ ! -f "$1" ]; then
    echo "Required file not found!"
    return $ERROR_NO_FILE
  fi
  echo "Processing file..."
  # Simulate file processing
  return $SUCCESS
}

# Main script logic
check_root || exit $ERROR_NOT_ROOT
process_file "data.txt" || exit $ERROR_NO_FILE

echo "Script executed successfully."
exit $SUCCESS
```

In this example, the script defines custom exit codes 101 and 102 for specific errors such as a missing file and lack of root privileges. Using these specific exit codes makes debugging more precise, as you can quickly discern which part of the script encountered a problem.

Often, a script will run multiple sequential commands, each dependent on the previous command's success. In these situations, the '&&' and '||' operators are useful in creating a command chain that halts on error or continues upon success.

- && – Execute the subsequent command only if the preceding command was successful (exit status 0).

- || – Execute the subsequent command only if the preceding command failed (non-zero exit status).

The use of these logical operators can result in compact scripts where error handling is both intuitive and efficient.

```
#!/bin/zsh

# Check if directory exists, create if not
mkdir -p /some/directory && echo "Directory is ready."

# Attempt to copy a file, exit on failure
cp source.txt /some/directory/ || { echo "Failed to copy file."; exit 1; }

echo "File copied successfully."
```

In this case, the script creates a directory if it does not already exist. If the 'mkdir' command fails, the functioning halts without attempting to copy the file, thereby preventing errors related to missing directories. Similarly, failure in the 'cp' command results in an immediate exit with an error message.

In complex scripts, iterative structures such as loops frequently account for scenarios where commands may fail within the loop body. Handling exit statuses within loops requires careful attention to ensure that errors are correctly captured and do not disrupt subsequent iterations unless intended.

```
#!/bin/zsh

# Array of files to process
files=("file1.txt" "file2.txt" "file3.txt")

for file in "${files[@]}"; do
  if cat "$file"; then
    echo "$file processed successfully."
```

```
  else
    echo "Error processing $file."
  fi
done
```

In this loop, each file's processing status is checked individually, allowing the script to log successes and errors. Such handling ensures that a failure in processing a single file does not prevent the script from attempting to process additional files.

There are rare instances when the exit status should deliberately be ignored. This is typically feasible with commands whose failure under certain conditions is acceptable or expected.

Using the 'true' command or appending '|| true' to an otherwise failing command achieves this purpose, allowing the script to continue executing.

```
#!/bin/zsh

# Attempt to remove a non-existing directory, ignore failure
rmdir /some/nonexistent/directory || true

echo "Continuing script execution."
```

Here, the script ignores a potential error from 'rmdir', as the non-existence of the directory is not critical to subsequent operations. This practice should be used sparingly, as it could neutralize important errors if applied indiscriminately.

In Zsh, functions can use exit codes similarly to scripts. Specifying a return value within a function using the 'return' statement provides an exit code that can be evaluated by the calling context.

```
#!/bin/zsh

# Function: Divide two numbers
divide() {
  if [ "$2" -eq 0 ]; then
    echo "Division by zero error."
    return 1
  fi
  echo $(($1 / $2))
  return 0
}

# Call the function and check the status
divide 10 2
status=$?
```

```
if [ $status -eq 0 ]; then
  echo "Division successful."
else
  echo "Failed to execute division."
fi
```

In this script, the 'divide' function checks for an error condition before attempting division, reflecting the exit status through the 'return' command. Handling function exit statuses in this manner underscores the modular approach to scripting with granulated error checks.

Exit statuses and codes are instrumental in enabling robust error handling within Zsh scripts. Whether using standard codes for generic errors or defining custom codes for specific conditions, understanding and effectively leveraging these can lead to more resilient and maintainable script development. As scripts grow in complexity, embedding logic based on exit statuses becomes an indispensable practice for ensuring reliability and efficiency.

8.2 Debugging Techniques with set Options

Debugging is an essential skill when it comes to developing robust Zsh scripts. One of the most powerful features in Zsh for debugging purposes is the use of 'set' options. These options allow the script writer to control the behavior of the shell environment by specifying how commands and edge cases should be managed. This aspect of Zsh can significantly enhance a developer's ability to debug scripts effectively.

Zsh provides several options that can be set to modify the shell's behavior. Among these, the use of 'set -x' is particularly pivotal for debugging. This option enables the debugging mode, printing each command to the standard error output with expanded arguments, which is invaluable for tracing script execution.

To activate these options within a script, the 'set' command is used followed by the desired option letter prefixed by a hyphen. Options can be turned off using a '+' sign instead of a '-'. Using these options can help script developers identify where errors occur and understand the flow of data and execution within the script.

- **Using set -x for Tracing Execution**

'set -x' is perhaps the most utilized option for debugging. When enabled, it provides a detailed trace of commands and their arguments as they are executed. This is crucial for identifying unexpected behavior in scripts, especially when dealing with complex logic or when integrating multiple commands that rely on specific outputs.

Consider the following example script, where 'set -x' is used to demonstrate the benefit of command tracing:

```zsh
#!/bin/zsh

set -x # Enable command tracing

# Basic operations
echo "This is a script for demonstration."
x=5
y=10
echo "x=$x, y=$y"
result=$((x * y))
echo "Result: $result"

set +x # Disable command tracing
```

When this script is run, the output will include each command preceded by a '+' sign. This output helps the developer to verify the values being processed and the sequence of command executions. It provides an immediate visual cue of the operations occurring within the script.

- **Applying set on Conditional Constructs**

Another area where 'set -x' proves useful is in conditional constructs. For instance, debugging complex 'if' statements or 'case' structures can be daunting without visibility into evaluated expressions and path navigation.

```zsh
#!/bin/zsh

# Enable debug mode
set -x

# Conditional checks
number=15

if ((number > 10)); then
  echo "Number is greater than 10."
else
```

```
    echo "Number is 10 or less."
fi

# Disable debug mode
set +x
```

By enabling 'set -x', developers can observe how expressions within conditionals are interpreted and executed in real time. This insight is invaluable when trying to uncover logical errors or unexpected conditional evaluations.

- **Debugging Loops with set -x**

Loops are fundamental constructs in scripting, often subject to errors due to incorrect iteration, infinite loops, or unexpected exits. Using 'set -x' within loops can help debug these issues by illuminating each iteration and command execution in detail.

```
#!/bin/zsh

numbers=(1 2 3 4 5)

set -x # Start debugging

# Loop through numbers
for num in "${numbers[@]}"; do
  square=$((num * num))
  echo "Square of $num is $square"
done

set +x # Stop debugging
```

The trace output from this script shows the evaluation and computation for each value in the array, assisting the developer in confirming correct behavior or identifying any discrepancies.

- **Debugging Functions with set -x**

When scripts are divided into functions, debugging can become more challenging due to the encapsulation of commands and local variables. Using 'set -x' within function definitions or calls can provide the needed transparency.

```
#!/bin/zsh

# Function to calculate factorial
```

205

```
factorial() {
  local n=$1
  local result=1
  while ((n > 1)); do
    result=$((result * n))
    ((n--))
  done
  echo $result
}

set -x # Enable debugging

# Call the factorial function
factorial 5

set +x # Disable debugging
```

By encapsulating 'set -x' in functions, every action within the function is logged, allowing the developer to verify each step of the process. This can quickly reveal unexpected behaviors, such as incorrect initializations or omitted commands.

- **The Importance of set -e, set -u, and set -o pipefail**

While 'set -x' focuses on tracing executions, other 'set' options like '-e', '-u', and '-o pipefail' are crucial for enforcing strict error checking and control flow management. These options enhance script reliability by imposing stricter conditions on error handling and variable usage.

- 'set -e': This option causes a script to immediately exit when any command with a non-zero exit status is encountered. This is particularly useful for stopping a script when an unrecoverable error occurs, minimizing the potential for the script to continue executing flawed or incomplete logic.

- 'set -u': By enabling this, the script will exit with an error if an undefined variable is referenced. This promotes early detection of typographic errors and reduces the risk of relying on uninitialized or incorrect variables.

- 'set -o pipefail': This option ensures that a pipeline's exit status is the last non-zero exit status of any command within the pipeline. This is vital in scenarios where a series of piped commands are used, preventing silent failures in upstream commands.

206

Here is a script employing these options:

```
#!/bin/zsh

set -euo pipefail # Enable strict mode

# Function to read from a file
read_file() {
  local filename=$1
  cat "$filename" | grep "important"
}

# Main logic
filename="data.txt"
read_file "$filename"
```

In this example, the script will terminate if any of the commands within the pipeline fail. This pattern is often used to create more robust scripts that are less susceptible to subtle errors propagated through command sequences.

- **Combining Debugging Options**

Combining 'set -x' with other options like '-e', '-u', and '-o pipefail' can provide comprehensive debugging and safety measures within scripts. The balance achieved between visibility and error-resilient scripting is a hallmark of well-constructed scripts.

```
#!/bin/zsh

set -xeuo pipefail # Enable all relevant debugging and safety options

# Function demonstrating loop and conditions
check_even() {
  local nums=("$@")
  for num in "${nums[@]}"; do
    if ((num % 2 == 0)); then
      echo "$num is even."
    else
      echo "$num is odd."
    fi
  done
}

# Call function with an array of numbers
check_even 1 2 3 4 5

set +x # Disable debugging trace
```

This script executes with debug traces and maintains robustness through strict failure and variable checks. This approach empowers developers by providing detailed diagnostics while ensuring the script does not proceed with erroneous states.

- **Practical Considerations in Debugging with set Options**

While 'set' options are indispensable, it's fundamental to consider the practical implications of their use within production scripts. Debugging output can be verbose, potentially overwhelming for large scripts, so debug traces are often used during development and disabled in final iterations.

Additionally, excessive or inappropriate use of shell options can introduce performance penalties and clutter output logs, detracting from script readability. Thus, developers should exercise discernment by enabling these features during controlled development and testing phases.

Scripts that rely heavily on external resource manipulation or third-party binary execution should integrate these debugging options to preempt effective troubleshooting. When debugging interactive scripts or those involving dynamic input/output operations, understanding Zsh's additional options for debugging can further enhance script reliability.

In scenarios where additional debugging capabilities are required beyond 'set' options, developers might consider incorporating trace files or detailed logging to external resources. This approach can complement shell options, ensuring that diagnostic data is available to developers for post-execution analysis.

Lastly, developers should tailor their use of debugging techniques to match the script's complexity and the execution environment— balancing visibility with operational efficiency to deliver scripts that are not only functionally correct but also resilient to operational errors.

By mastering these options, developers can greatly enhance their debugging workflow in Zsh scripts, facilitating quicker identification of issues and enabling the crafting of high-quality, dependable scripts.

8.3 Handling Errors Gracefully

In Zsh scripting, error handling is a crucial aspect that distinguishes a robust script from a fragile one. By designing scripts that handle errors gracefully, script developers can ensure that their code behaves predictably and reports meaningful information to end-users even when something goes wrong. This section delves into the methodologies and constructs available in Zsh for managing errors effectively and responsibly.

The ability to handle errors with elegance is predicated on anticipating potential points of failure and embedding logic to manage these occurrences without halting script execution unexpectedly. This is particularly important in environments where scripts are part of automated workflows or interact with other systems and processes.

Fundamental Principles of Error Handling

Before exploring the specifics of handling errors in Zsh scripts, it is vital to understand the key principles underlying robust error management:

- **Detection**: An error cannot be handled if it is not detected. This necessitates methods for recognizing when things do not go according to plan.

- **Diagnosis**: Proper error handling involves understanding the cause of the failure or problem.

- **Recovery**: After detecting and diagnosing the error, the script must be able to take appropriate actions to recover gracefully.

- **Notification**: Finally, users or systems executing the script should be informed about the nature of errors, allowing them to respond accordingly.

These principles guide the techniques and tools used for error management, which are contextually applied based on the nature of the script and its operational environment.

Use of Exit Status in Error Handling

As discussed previously, exit statuses provide initial insights into whether a command succeeded or encountered an issue. By examining

209

exit statuses, scripts can branch into different paths of execution, enabling them to adapt to unexpected scenarios gracefully.

A quintessential pattern in scripting involves using conditional statements to assess exit statuses and handle errors. Here's an example where exit statuses guide the error management flow:

```zsh
#!/bin/zsh

# Function to demonstrate error handling
process_file() {
  local file="$1"

  if [ ! -f "$file" ]; then
    echo "Error: File '$file' not found."
    return 1
  fi

  # Process the file (dummy command)
  cat "$file" | grep "Sample" > /dev/null

  if [ $? -ne 0 ]; then
    echo "Error: Failed to find sample text in '$file'."
    return 1
  fi

  echo "File '$file' processed successfully."
  return 0
}

# Script execution
filename="example.txt"
process_file "$filename"

if [ $? -ne 0 ]; then
  echo "An error occurred during file processing."
else
  echo "File was processed without errors."
fi
```

In this script, error handling relies on checking the results of file existence and content processing, with meaningful error messages returned to the user.

Using Conditional Logic for Error Handling

When working with Zsh scripts, conditionals such as 'if', 'case', and logical operators are indispensable for handling errors gracefully. They allow developers to create branches that can adequately manage and respond to varying scenarios:

```zsh
#!/bin/zsh
```

```
# Function to calculate division
divide_numbers() {
  local num1=$1
  local num2=$2

  if [[ $num2 -eq 0 ]]; then
    echo "Error: Division by zero is undefined."
    return 1
  fi

  echo "Result: $((num1 / num2))"
  return 0
}

# Invoking the divide function
divide_numbers 20 4 # Proper division
divide_numbers 10 0 # Division by zero
```

This script demonstrates using 'if' conditionals to avoid division by zero, a common source of errors in numerical scripts. In such scenarios, providing a specific error message and exiting gracefully with an appropriate exit status is crucial for informing the user about the error's nature.

Implementing Trap for Exceptional Situations

Zsh provides a 'trap' mechanism to specify commands that should be executed when the script encounters specific signals or exits in particular manners. This capability extends error handling by allowing developers to clean up resources or modify the program flow when an error condition arises. 'trap' is especially powerful in handling unanticipated interruptions.

```
#!/bin/zsh

# Function to handle interruptions
cleanup() {
  echo "Cleaning up resources..."
}

# Setup the trap for signals
trap cleanup EXIT INT TERM

# Script operations
echo "Executing script operations..."
sleep 10

echo "Script completed."
```

In this script, regardless of how it terminates (whether naturally through completion or due to external interruption such as a Ctrl+C),

211

the 'cleanup' function is invoked to ensure that resources are released and the environment is left in a consistent state. This exemplifies preparing scripts for exceptional conditions by anticipating potential disruptions.

Error Logging and Notification

Handling errors effectively requires not just detecting and responding to them, but also communicating them to users or logging systems for analysis. Providing clear error messages and logs helps track down issues in real-time and is indispensable in complex environments where scripts form part of larger systems.

Consider redirecting error messages to a log file for diagnostic purposes:

```
#!/bin/zsh

log_file="error.log"

execute_command() {
  echo "Executing command..."

  # Attempt a faulty command
  bogus_command 2>> $log_file

  if [ $? -ne 0 ]; then
    echo "An error occurred, check $log_file for details."
    return 1
  fi

  return 0
}

execute_command
```

Here, any error output generated by 'bogus_command' is redirected to an error log file. This strategy ensures that users are alerted to check the log file while retaining the error details for troubleshooting.

Using Exit on Error Mode

Enabling 'set -e' causes the script to immediately terminate when a command fails (i.e., when a command returns a non-zero exit status). While 'set -e' can prevent scripts from continuing in an erroneous state, it needs careful management to ensure it does not prematurely exit scripts when failures are acceptable:

```
#!/bin/zsh
```

```
set -e

run_task() {
  echo "Starting task..."

  # Simulate a command that might fail
  false command || { echo "Handled error, continuing..."; }

  echo "Task completed."
}

run_task
```

In the above example, the use of '||' to handle the error tactically allows subsequent lines to execute without invoking automatic exit by 'set - e'. This combination empowers scripts to terminate effectively on non-recoverable errors while permitting continued execution when failures have back-up handling strategies.

Examples of Graceful Degradation

Graceful degradation involves adapting functionalities in case scenarios when errors disrupt standard script operations. For instance, when attempting network operations, if network connectivity is unavailable, scripts should handle these errors by either retrying, waiting, or switching to alternative processes:

```
#!/bin/zsh

# Function to download a file
fetch_file() {
  local url="$1"
  local retries=3

  while [ $retries -ge 0 ]; do
    wget "$url" && return 0
    echo "Download failed, retrying..."
    ((retries--))
    sleep 2
  done

  echo "Failed to download after multiple attempts."
  return 1
}

# Try to download a file
fetch_file "http://example.com/sample.txt"
```

The script retries downloading a file multiple times upon failure, subsequently signalling an error if all attempts fail. This handling exemplifies graceful degradation by maximizing chances of success without

213

generating outright failures.

Custom Errors and Exception Handling

In Zsh scripts, defining custom error messages or handling bespoke exceptions allows developers to offer context-driven insights that align with domain-specific needs. This often involves augmenting state checks with custom messages:

```zsh
#!/bin/zsh

# Function to check user privilege
ensure_root() {
  if [ "$(id -u)" -ne 0 ]; then
    echo "Error: This script must be run as root."
    return 1
  fi
  return 0
}

# Integrate error messaging
ensure_root || { echo "Exiting due to insufficient privileges."; exit 1; }

echo "Running privileged actions..."
```

This illustrates how scripts using user-centric messages improve readability and facilitate troubleshooting by explaining failure reasons without needless ambiguity.

Managing errors gracefully in Zsh scripts is integral to developing reliable and user-friendly scripting solutions. By using a combination of exit status checks, conditionals, traps, logging mechanisms, robust defaults, and retry logic, scripts can anticipate and recover from errors effectively. Thereby, scripts become not only more durable but also facilitate smoother experiences when executed in the often-uncertain conditions of automated and interconnected systems. These strategies support developers in anticipating potential pitfalls and equipping scripts with layers of resilience against them, promoting stability integral to both automated and interactive scripting environments.

8.4 Using Traps for Exception Handling

In scripting, especially within environments like Zsh, it is vital to manage exceptions to ensure that scripts can handle unexpected conditions with resilience. The 'trap' mechanism in Zsh offers a powerful way to capture and handle signals or exceptions, allowing scripts to respond to critical events, perform clean-ups, or exit gracefully under anomalous situations.

The use of 'trap' is an essential aspect of error management and process control. It allows script authors to specify commands that should be automatically executed when the script receives particular signals, such as terminal interrupts, or upon exit. This capability extends the robustness of error handling strategies by providing hooks into the otherwise abrupt processes of termination and interruption.

- Understanding Signals and Traps

Signals are notifications sent to a process to indicate events such as interrupts or exceptions. In Unix-like systems, signals are used for various purposes, e.g., terminating processes, pausing execution, or triggering specific actions. Each signal is signified by an integer or a name, such as 'SIGINT' for interrupts ('Ctrl+C') or 'SIGTERM' for termination.

A 'trap' in Zsh is configured by invoking the 'trap' command followed by a list of actions and the signals or situations that should trigger these actions. Signals can be designated by number or by their standard name.

Here is a foundational usage of the 'trap' command:

```
#!/bin/zsh

# Define a function to execute on interrupt
handle_interrupt() {
  echo "Script execution was interrupted."
  # Clean-up actions go here
}

# Set a trap on SIGINT
trap handle_interrupt INT

echo "Running script. Press Ctrl+C to interrupt."
sleep 30

echo "Script completed successfully."
```

In this example, pressing 'Ctrl+C' during the script execution will invoke the 'handle_interrupt' function, providing an opportunity to manage what occurs upon interruption, such as logging the event or per-

215

forming resource clean-up.

- Commonly Used Signals

When working with 'trap's, it is helpful to understand some common signals one might handle in a script:

- 'SIGINT' (2): Interrupt signal, typically generated by pressing 'Ctrl+C'.

- 'SIGTERM' (15): Termination signal used to request program termination.

- 'SIGKILL' (9): Forceful termination signal; cannot be caught or ignored.

- 'SIGHUP' (1): Hang up signal sent when terminal disconnects.

- 'EXIT': Pseudo-signal triggered when the script exits for any reason.

- Implementing Exit Clean-ups

One of the primary uses of 'trap' is performing clean-up operations before a script exits. This ensures resources such as temporary files, locks, or network connections are properly released, maintaining system integrity and preventing resource leakage.

```zsh
#!/bin/zsh

# Function to perform clean-up
cleanup() {
  echo "Performing clean-up..."
  # Example: Removing temporary files
  rm -f /tmp/mytempfile.txt
}

# Trigger clean-up function on script exit
trap cleanup EXIT

# Script body
echo "Creating temporary file..."
touch /tmp/mytempfile.txt

echo "Performing operations..."
# Simulated operations
```

```
sleep 10
echo "Operations complete."
```

In this script, the 'cleanup' function is defined to remove a temporary file when the script exits. By using the 'EXIT' trap, it's guaranteed that clean-up actions will run whether the script completes normally or is interrupted.

- Handling Multiple Signals in a Trap

Scripts often need to respond to various signals simultaneously. 'trap' allows setting up a single command or function to be invoked when any of several signals are received. This is useful for unifying response strategies across different signal types and ensuring consistent clean-up or logging processes.

```
#!/bin/zsh

# Define a comprehensive handler
handle_signal() {
    echo "Caught a signal, performing actions..."
    # Actions common for multiple signals
}

# Set traps for several signals
trap handle_signal INT TERM EXIT

echo "Script is running. Send signals to test trapping."
sleep 45

echo "Script completed."
```

By setting traps for 'INT', 'TERM', and 'EXIT', this script ensures consistency in the handling process, making it easier to implement broad strategies or policies for signal management.

- Analyzing Signal Contexts

Trap handlers can analyze the context in which a signal is received, adapting their behavior based on what triggered the signal. For example, scripts might distinguish between different termination types to adjust their clean-up priorities or logging verbosity.

In Zsh, you can use the $? variable to get the exit status of the last executed command and respond within a trap action:

```zsh
#!/bin/zsh

# Define an exit handler to evaluate context
exit_handler() {
  exit_code=$?
  echo "Script exited with status $exit_code."

  if [ $exit_code -eq 0 ]; then
    echo "Normal completion."
  else
    echo "Exited with errors."
  fi
}

# Trap on exit
trap exit_handler EXIT

# Normal execution
echo "Performing some task..."
# Simulate a failure
false

echo "Script reached the end."
```

This handler checks the exit status and provides context-specific messages, reinforcing the utility of traps for sophisticated exception handling.

- Balancing Complexity with Trap Functions

As trap logic grows, organizing it into dedicated functions can encapsulate complexity and promote reusability. This enhances script maintainability, particularly when dealing with intricate signal management policies.

```zsh
#!/bin/zsh

# Define a detailed clean-up function
perform_cleanup() {
  exit_code=$?
  echo "Cleaning up resources for exit code: $exit_code."
  # Resource management logic
}

# Define a function to handle signals
handle_termination() {
  echo "Termination signal received. Initiating clean-up."
  perform_cleanup
}

# Trap configuration
trap handle_termination INT TERM
```

```
# Simulate work
echo "Script is running. Use 'kill' command to send signals."
sleep 60

echo "Script ending."
```

In this script, clean-up and termination-handling tasks are organized within separate functions, enabling greater control over the signal management logic.

- Using Conditional Traps for Granular Control

Conditionally setting traps allows scripts to adapt their signal handling based on the execution environment or specific criteria, delivering more refined exception management strategies.

```
#!/bin/zsh

# Function to conditionally trap based on environment variable
conditional_trap() {
  echo "In trap - environment: $ENV_TYPE"
}

# Set trap only if in specific environment
if [[ "$ENV_TYPE" == "production" ]]; then
  trap conditional_trap EXIT
fi

echo "Script running in $ENV_TYPE environment."
sleep 20

echo "Script finished."
```

This example demonstrates conditional traps that activate based on specific criteria, like environment type, allowing for tailored responses in different deployment contexts.

- Restoring Default Behavior

After trapping a signal, scripts might need to restore the default handling behavior, such as when exiting gracefully disregarding ongoing traps or when conditions change during script execution. This is handled by assigning an empty string to the trap command for specific signals.

```
#!/bin/zsh

# Function for handling interruptions
interrupt_handler() {
  echo "Interrupted - executing handler."
}

# Set and later restore
trap interrupt_handler INT

echo "Press Ctrl+C to trigger an interrupt."
sleep 5

echo "Restoring default signal handlers."
trap - INT

echo "Interrupt handling is back to default."
sleep 10
```

In this script, temporarily set traps are cleared, illustrating how to adapt to different phases within a script when maintaining signal control.

- Challenges and Best Practices

While traps provide powerful exception handling, they also introduce complexity. Certain signals like 'SIGKILL' and 'SIGSTOP' cannot be trapped, so additional mechanisms may be required to handle such conditions externally. Users should be wary of over-complicating scripts with excessively intricate trap logic, which could lead to maintenance challenges and obscure testability.

To maximize the effectiveness of traps in Zsh:

- Document each trap's purpose, capturing the logic in comments.

- Maintain modularity by encapsulating logic within functions.

- Model consistent response patterns that align with system and user expectations.

- Regularly test traps under realistic conditions to confirm they behave as expected.

The judicious and careful employment of traps in Zsh scripts can transform error handling into a robust and reliable feature. By integrating

traps effectively, developers can enhance script resilience and responsiveness, ensuring that scripts handle both anticipated and unexpected
events with finesse and clarity. This level of control is indispensable
for producing stable and user-friendly automation scripts that operate
within diverse and dynamic environments.

8.5 Logging and Output Redirection

In the sophisticated realm of Zsh scripting, logging and output redirection stand as pillars for monitoring and debugging. By directing script
output—from standard messages to error diagnostics—into structured
logs, developers facilitate real-time monitoring, analysis, and troubleshooting. Effective logging not only boosts script maintainability
but also enhances transparency in automated workflows. Moreover,
output redirection helps manage script output by directing it away
from the standard terminal and into files, other commands, or even
null outputs.

The Fundamentals of Output Redirection

Output redirection involves channeling the standard and error outputs
of commands to different destinations. By grasping this fundamental
capability, developers can refine script outputs, manage clutter on the
terminal, and store records for post-execution analysis.

In Zsh, the primary forms of output include:

- **Standard Output (stdout):** Typically displays command results.

- **Standard Error (stderr):** Commonly used for error messages
  and diagnostics.

These outputs are characterized by file descriptors:

- 1: stdout

- 2: stderr

The basic redirection operator in Zsh is >, which is used for redirecting stdout. For redirecting stderr, 2> is used. To capture both stdout and stderr into a single file, &> or 2>&1 can be employed.

A simple demonstration of redirecting stdout and stderr:

```zsh
#!/bin/zsh

# Redirect stdout to a file
echo "This is standard output." > output.log

# Redirect stderr to the same file
ls non_existent_file 2>> output.log
```

In this example, the echo command redirects its output to output.log, while any error from the ls command is appended to the same log file using 2».

Advanced Output Redirection Techniques

Combining redirection techniques allows for more sophisticated control over outputs:

- **Appending Output:** Using » appends rather than overwrites, preserving existing log content.

- **Combining Outputs:** Redirecting both stdout and stderr to the same target for consolidated logging.

- **Null Redirection:** Redirects unnecessary output into /dev/null, effectively silencing it.

Here's how these methods can be applied:

```zsh
#!/bin/zsh

# Append stdout and stderr to a single log file
execute_task() {
  echo "Starting task..." >> task.log
  echo "This performs some operations."
  invalid_command 2>&1 >> task.log
  echo "Task completed." >> task.log
}

execute_task
```

In this script, all output (normal and error messages) from invalid_command is appended to task.log, thus maintaining a comprehensive record of task activity.

Centralized Logging Strategies

Centralized logging involves directing outputs from multiple script components or related scripts to a unified log destination. This approach aids in assembling comprehensive records of application behavior, particularly valuable in complex multi-component systems.

Centralized logging benefits range from simplified log parsing and analysis to being able to correlate logs within a single timeline. Naming conventions and timestamps enhance log entries, providing further clarity:

```zsh
#!/bin/zsh

LOG_FILE="/var/log/script.log"

# Log function with timestamp and script name
log() {
    echo "$(date +'%Y-%m-%d %H:%M:%S') [$0] $1" >> $LOG_FILE
}

log "Script started."

# Simulate various operations with logging
{
    echo "Operation 1 executing..."
    false_command
    echo "Operation 2 completed."
} &>> $LOG_FILE

log "Script completed."
```

This script demonstrates centralized logging, organizing entries with timestamps to facilitate sequence tracking while encapsulating errors from false_command.

Leveraging syslog for Enhanced Logging

Beyond file-based logging, Zsh scripts can send logs to the system logger, syslog. This practice aligns script output with centralized system logging mechanisms, enhancing oversight facilities, particularly in server environments where consolidated log management is crucial.

To interface with syslog, the logger command is used:

```zsh
#!/bin/zsh

# Log a message to syslog
logger "Script execution started via Zsh script."

# Simulated script logic
```

```
echo "Working with files..."
if ! cp source.txt destination.txt; then
   logger -p user.err "Error: Failed to copy file from source.txt to destination.txt"
fi

logger "Script execution completed."
```

This script sends messages to syslog, distinguishing different log priorities with the -p flag, allowing for the error message to be easily filtered and acted upon by system administrators.

Rotating and Archiving Logs

Keeping log files manageable involves strategies for rotating and archiving log content, especially to prevent uncontrolled disk usage. This strategy involves moving log files to archive storage and starting fresh logs—often through tools like logrotate.

Scripts can integrate basic log rotation logic or rely on external tools like logrotate:

```
# Basic log rotation example
MAX_LOG_SIZE=100000 # 100 KB

rotate_log() {
   local log_file="$1"
   if [[ $(stat -c%s "$log_file") -ge $MAX_LOG_SIZE ]]; then
      mv "$log_file" "${log_file}.old"
      touch "$log_file"
      echo "Log file rotated."
   fi
}

LOG_FILE="application.log"

rotate_log $LOG_FILE
echo "New log entry" >> $LOG_FILE
```

This example shows checking if application.log exceeds a specified size and rotating the log file. This script provides the foundational logic that, when scaled with system tools, helps manage logs effectively.

Analyzing Log Content

Logging serves little purpose if not intelligently analyzed. Logs can be parsed with scripts to extract value, identify patterns, diagnose issues, and visualize performance metrics.

Consider using awk, grep, or custom scripts:

```zsh
#!/bin/zsh

# Function to parse error logs
analyze_errors() {
  log_file=$1
  echo "== Error Analysis Report =="
  error_count=$(grep -c "error" $log_file)
  echo "Total errors found: $error_count"

  echo "Top errors:"
  grep "error" $log_file | sort | uniq -c | sort -nr | head
}

# Usage
LOG_FILE="application.log"
analyze_errors $LOG_FILE
```

Here, the application error log is analyzed for frequency and distribution of errors, showcasing how basic log analysis offers immediate insights into operative issues.

Integrating Output Redirection with Units

For modular script architectures using functions and components, uniform output redirection strategies ensure that logging remains coherent and interpreted correctly across all levels of execution. By setting consistent redirection logic at a central script level, modular code enforcement maintains a streamlined logging practice:

```zsh
#!/bin/zsh

# Redirect function output coherently
process_job() {
  exec > job_output.log 2>&1
  echo "Processing job..."
  false_command
}

# Centralized output logic
exec > script_output.log 2> script_errors.log

echo "Starting script."
process_job
echo "Script completed."
```

In this script, the exec command at the script and function levels designates consistent output management and maintains logical separation between regular and error outputs.

Logging and output redirection in Zsh scripts systematically organize and manage script output, enhancing clarity in execution, simplifying

225

diagnostics, and supporting maintainable scripting practices. By leveraging diverse techniques—from basic redirection and centralized logging to system log integration and intelligent analysis—developers ensure their scripts operate transparently, communicate effectively, and comply with broader system management policies. This foundational access to accrued information supports efficient incident handling, resource management, and system integrity, ultimately maximizing both the robustness and reliability of script-based solutions.

8.6 Testing and Validation of Scripts

Ensuring the reliability and correctness of Zsh scripts hinges on thorough testing and validation. Testing serves to identify defects and validate that the script behaves as expected across diverse scenarios, while validation ensures that the script meets the intended user requirements and execution conditions. Given the critical roles these scripts often play in larger systems—ranging from automation and deployment to data processing—effective testing and validation practices are essential to maintain system integrity and performance.

Unit Testing in Script Development

Unit testing involves isolating the core components or functions of a script and testing them individually. This practice ensures that each segment of the code performs as expected before it's integrated into the broader logic. By subjecting discrete units to rigorous testing, developers can identify and resolve issues early in the development cycle.

Although unit testing is more prevalent in traditional software development, it is equally beneficial in script development. Here is an example of how a function can be tested within a script:

```
#!/bin/zsh

# Function to add two numbers
add_numbers() {
  echo $(($1 + $2))
}

# Unit test for add_numbers
test_add_numbers() {
  local result
  result=$(add_numbers 2 3)
```

226

```
if [[ "$result" -ne 5 ]]; then
    echo "Test failed: Expected 5, got $result"
    return 1
fi
echo "Test passed."
}

# Run the test
test_add_numbers
```

This script demonstrates a basic structure for testing the add_numbers function. It defines a test function that captures the output, verifies the expected value, and returns an indicative message and exit status.

Automated Testing Frameworks

To automate the process of testing scripts, various frameworks and tools can be integrated into the development workflow. Tools such as 'bats' (Bash Automated Testing System) extend the capability of shell scripting by adding features to script tests in a more structured and reusable manner.

Using 'bats' for example:

```
#!/usr/bin/env bats

# Test the addition functionality
@test "add_numbers should return the correct sum" {
    run bash -c 'source myscript.sh && add_numbers 10 20'
    [ "$status" -eq 0 ]
    [ "$output" -eq 30 ]
}
```

In such frameworks, developers can construct a suite of tests covering multiple functionalities, ensuring comprehensive coverage and facilitating recurrent tests across various development stages.

Integration Testing and Coordination

Whereas unit testing focuses on isolated components, integration testing assesses the interaction between units and the overall functionality within a system. Effective integration testing in the context of Zsh scripts often involves simulating the script's real operating environment to uncover interface issues or operational limitations.

The following represents an integration testing scenario involving file operations:

```
#!/bin/zsh
```

```
# Prepare environment for integration test
setup_integration_test() {
  # Create test directory and files
  mkdir -p test_env
  touch test_env/testfile1.txt test_env/testfile2.txt
}

# Run the script and verify integration
run_integration_test() {
  local output
  cd test_env
  output=$(bash ../myscript.sh)

  # Validate successful execution
  if [[ "$output" == *"Operation successful"* ]]; then
    echo "Integration test passed."
  else
    echo "Integration test failed."
  fi
  cd ..
}

# Cleanup environment
teardown_integration_test() {
  rm -rf test_env
}

# Execute tests
setup_integration_test
run_integration_test
teardown_integration_test
```

This script dynamically construes a testing environment, invokes the target script under test conditions, and validates its behavior, thus verifying proper integration.

Functional Testing and End-User Simulations

Functional testing focuses on testing the script against business or user requirements to ensure that it accomplishes its intended tasks. It bridges the gap between technical specifications and practical implementation by erecting tests around defined use cases and scenarios, reflecting real-world usage conditions.

Functional testing involves simulating these conditions as closely as possible and can be conducted using mock data and environmental elements. For example, a functional test might verify that a script correctly processes a set of input files, updating data according to user-defined rules:

```
#!/bin/zsh
```

```
# Mock environment setup
setup_functional_test() {
  echo "Mock data" > mock_input.txt
}

# Run functional test
test_functionality() {
  bash myscript.sh mock_input.txt processed_output.txt

  if grep -q "Expected Result" processed_output.txt; then
    echo "Functional test passed."
  else
    echo "Functional test failed."
  fi
}

# Cleanup after testing
cleanup_functional_test() {
  rm -f mock_input.txt processed_output.txt
}

# Execute functional testing
setup_functional_test
test_functionality
cleanup_functional_test
```

In this example, the script is tested on its ability to produce an expected output given a mock file input, directly aligning test outputs with desired outcomes.

Exploratory Testing and Ad Hoc Approaches

While structured approaches are fundamental, exploratory testing plays a critical role by leveraging human intuition and spontaneity to uncover edge cases and unexpected script behavior. This approach resists rigid testing scripts in favor of adaptable and intuitive interaction, often leading to invaluable insights which rigid tests previously omitted.

Exploratory testing could involve:

- Randomizing input parameters to discover failures.

- Subjecting scripts to varying environment conditions such as different user permissions.

- Twisting typical use cases slightly to test robustness.

Although less formal, async testing encounters can effectively complement formal testing strategies, reducing unforeseen cases in production. A journal or markdown log can maintain notes and observations, retaining insights for implementation adjustments.

Validation within Real-World Deployment

Validation extends the reach of testing by extending trials into real-world operations. This involves confirming that scripts satisfy user and business needs and continue to function as expected under production loads or conditions.

In real-world validation, executing a pilot deployment may be achieved:

```zsh
#!/bin/zsh

# Deploy script in a controlled real-world setting
deploy_pilot_test() {
  echo "Deploying to staging environment..."
  scp myscript.sh user@staging-server:/path/to/deploy
  ssh user@staging-server 'zsh /path/to/deploy/myscript.sh'
}

# Monitor output and confirm alignment to expectations
validate_staging_output() {
  scp user@staging-server:/path/to/outputs/output.log ./staging_output.log
  if grep -q "Expected Result" staging_output.log; then
    echo "Validation succeeded on staging environment."
  else
    echo "Validation failed on staging environment."
  fi
}

deploy_pilot_test
validate_staging_output
```

This example deploys the script to a staged setting, confirming that output matches expectations before full-scale production application, thus mitigating risk.

Testing Challenges and Mitigation Strategies

Various challenges accompany script testing and validation, including complexity, evolving requirements, constrained resources, and environmental differences. Addressing these proactively sustains testing postures capable of dynamic adaptation:

- **Complexity**: Modularize scripts to simplify unit tests and maintenance. - **Evolution**: Employ version control systems to manage iterative changes and enable regression testing. - **Deployment Con-

straints: Utilize containers for isolated, reproducible environments. - **Environmental Variability**: Implement configurable parameters and environment checks to accommodate multiple operating conditions.

A well-grounded approach in strategy, systems, and tools enhances effective script testing efforts, ensuring robust, predictable, and dependable Zsh scripts complement longer system architectures as intended.

Leveraging Continuous Integration and Testing

Incorporating script testing within a Continuous Integration/Continuous Deployment (CI/CD) framework substantially amplifies its value by embedding automated test execution within the broader development lifecycle, catching defects before deployment beyond the integration environment.

Utilizing popular CI systems like Jenkins or GitHub Actions allows scripts to be tested upon each commit automatically:

```
name: Run Tests

on: [push, pull_request]

jobs:
  zsh-tests:
    runs-on: ubuntu-latest

    steps:
    - uses: actions/checkout@v2
    - name: Set up BATS
      run: |
        sudo apt-get install bats
    - name: Run Tests
      run: bats tests
```

This configuration tells GitHub Actions to execute shell tests using 'bats' upon each push or pull request, keeping the codebase consistently vetted.

Testing and validation form the backbone of reliable, efficient Zsh script development; through systematic exploration and analysis of script behaviors against benchmarks and expectations, reliability and integrity are achieved. By balancing structural and intuitive approaches, integrating them within broader development frameworks, and adapting to changing circumstances and messages, developers cultivate script systems built just as much with scrutiny in

231

development as excellence in execution.

Chapter 9

Enhancing Productivity with Zsh Plugins

This chapter examines the use of Zsh plugins to enhance productivity and workflow efficiency. It provides an overview of the plugin ecosystem and offers guidance on installation and management through Oh My Zsh. Essential productivity plugins are identified, alongside strategies for customization and configuration. The chapter also explores developing custom plugins and troubleshooting common issues, enabling users to fully leverage Zsh's extensibility.

9.1 Overview of Zsh Plugin Ecosystem

The Z shell, or Zsh, has gained widespread popularity among developers and system administrators due to its interactive features and user flexibility. One of the powerful aspects of Zsh is its plugin ecosystem, which greatly enhances functionality and productivity by allowing users to customize their shell experience beyond the standard capabilities. This section provides an extensive exploration of the Zsh plugin ecosystem, illustrating the diversity and utility of available plugins.

Zsh benefits from a vibrant community contributing a wide array of plugins, which range from simple scripts and aliases to complex functions that significantly extend the shell's capabilities. The Zsh plugin ecosystem is not bound by a centralized repository, allowing developers to distribute and share their plugins freely. This decentralization has led to a large assortment of plugins available through different platforms, such as GitHub and other Git-based repositories, providing various enhancements for Zsh users.

A notable framework that enhances the use of Zsh plugins is *Oh My Zsh*. It serves as a community-driven tool for managing Zsh configurations and plugins, easing the process of configuring and maintaining a personalized and efficient shell environment. The framework simplifies the integration of a vast number of plugins through a systematic installation and configuration process.

Let us delve deeper into the types and categories of plugins available within this ecosystem, examining various functionalities and their contributions to workflow enhancement.

```
# Edit the ~/.zshrc file to include plugins
plugins=(
    git
    zsh-syntax-highlighting
    zsh-autosuggestions
)
# Then run this command to apply changes
source ~/.zshrc
```

The code snippet provided above demonstrates how to enable plugins in the Oh My Zsh framework. By specifying desired plugins within the 'plugins' array in the '.zshrc' configuration file, users can easily activate additional functionalities.

Categories of Zsh Plugins

The Zsh plugin ecosystem comprises several categories of plugins, each serving distinct purposes and user needs. Here, we discuss several prominent categories along with exemplary plugins that typify the functionalities they provide:

- *Productivity Enhancements:* For users who prioritize efficiency and speed, productivity plugins streamline tasks such as command execution, history search, and tab completion.

234

- *Zsh Syntax Highlighting:* Enhances readability by color-coding command syntax in real-time.

- *Zsh Autosuggestions:* Offers command suggestions based on historical entries, allowing swift command entry.

- *Git Integration:* For developers using Git, dedicated plugins provide shortcuts, prompt customization, and visual aids.

  - *git:* A widely-used plugin that provides Git related aliases and functions.

  - *Git Prompt:* Customizes the prompt to display Git branch and status information, promoting awareness of repository state.

- *Navigation and File Management:* These plugins assist in managing and navigating the file system more effectively.

  - *autojump:* Facilitates quick navigation to frequently accessed directories using a learning-based jump location feature.

  - *fasd:* Combines 'cd', 'pushd', and 'popd' functionality for efficiently accessing recent directories and files.

- *Appearance and Theming:* Aesthetic enhancements focus on improving the visual aspects of the terminal.

  - *Powerlevel10k:* A theme that modifies the appearance of the Zsh prompt, supporting extensive customization options.

  - *spaceship-prompt:* Offers a rich, minimalist aesthetic with status indicators for various tools and applications.

- *System Information and Performance:* Several plugins exist to monitor system performance metrics or hardware status, aiding in system administration tasks.

  - *zsh-system-plugins:* A collection of plugins for monitoring CPU, memory, and network statistics.

  - *diskutils:* Provides utilities for disk usage and partition management.

Insights into the Zsh Plugin Ecosystem

The diversity of the Zsh plugin ecosystem exemplifies the adaptability of Zsh in meeting varied user requirements. Plugins can convert Zsh into a powerful IDE-like environment, automate repetitive tasks, or simply provide aesthetic enhancements to make daily interaction more enjoyable and visually engaging.

Zsh plugins contribute to an improved user experience by promoting customization. Users can tailor the functionality of their shell environment to perfectly match their development and operational needs. This customization reduces the cognitive load associated with managing complex command-line operations and allows for a more seamless workflow.

Moreover, the modular nature of Zsh plugins encourages incremental improvement. Users can introduce or remove plugins without significantly altering their existing setup, leveraging new plugins to address specific needs as they arise. This extensibility contributes to Zsh's appeal as a dynamic and evolutionary shell environment.

Ethical Considerations and Best Practices

While leveraging the Zsh plugin ecosystem, ethical considerations and best practices should be maintained to ensure system reliability and performance:

- *Verify Provenance:* Ensure that plugins originate from credible and trusted sources. Unverified plugins might introduce vulnerabilities or exhibit malicious behavior.

- *Minimalism in Configuration:* Avoid loading excessive plugins simultaneously. Each plugin contributes to the loading time and resource usage of the shell. It is advisable to only include necessary plugins for specific tasks to maintain optimal performance.

- *Update Regularly:* Periodically update plugins to receive bug fixes, security patches, and improvements offered by the community.

- *Community Engagement:* Engage with the Zsh community to share insights, report issues, or contribute to plugin develop-

236

ment. This promotes a sustainable ecosystem where improvements benefit all users.

The Zsh plugin ecosystem represents a vast landscape of opportunities for enhancing and personalizing users' command-line environments. Through the strategic selection and configuration of plugins, users can significantly boost productivity, streamline workflows, and innovate in system navigation and appearance. Understanding and exploring the plugin ecosystem is fundamental for maximizing the potential of Zsh as a versatile and highly configurable shell, supporting diverse user needs from basic command execution to sophisticated system and development tasks.

9.2 Installing and Managing Plugins with Oh My Zsh

The process of installing and managing plugins in Zsh is substantially facilitated by the *Oh My Zsh* framework. Oh My Zsh is a robust, open-source, community-driven framework designed to simplify the management of Zsh configurations, plugins, and themes. It acts as a manager for shell customizations, offering a wealth of resources and functionalities that enhance user productivity and shell capabilities. Here, we delve into the details of installing and managing plugins within the Oh My Zsh framework, providing comprehensive instructions along with in-depth insights into its mechanisms.

The first critical step in leveraging the Oh My Zsh framework is its installation. Oh My Zsh is supported on UNIX-like systems, making it a suitable choice for macOS and Linux users.

```
# Use curl to install Oh My Zsh
sh -c "$(curl -fsSL https://raw.github.com/ohmyzsh/ohmyzsh/master/tools/install.sh)"

# Alternatively, use wget
sh -c "$(wget https://raw.github.com/ohmyzsh/ohmyzsh/master/tools/install.sh -O -)"
```

The above commands download and execute a script from the official Oh My Zsh GitHub repository, installing the framework on your system. Before proceeding with installation, ensure that necessary tools like curl or wget are installed, as they facilitate the retrieval of the installation script.

Once Oh My Zsh is successfully installed, the next step is to manage the plugins that enhance Zsh's functionality. The Oh My Zsh framework boasts a modular structure with a standardized location for its core files, themes, and, most importantly, plugins. Plugins are stored in the directory $ZSH/plugins, where each subdirectory within this location represents a distinct plugin.

To enable a specific plugin, users must declare it within the Zsh configuration file, typically located at /.zshrc. This configuration file orchestrates the behavior of the shell upon startup.

```
# Open the .zshrc file using a text editor like nano or vim
nano ~/.zshrc

# Edit the plugins line to include desired plugins
plugins=(
  git
  z
  zsh-autosuggestions
  zsh-syntax-highlighting
)
```

In the example above, the plugins git, z, zsh-autosuggestions, and zsh-syntax-highlighting are enabled by specifying them in the configuration's 'plugins' array. Upon making these modifications, one should apply the changes by sourcing the configuration file as follows:

```
# Source the updated .zshrc file
source ~/.zshrc
```

The source command re-evaluates the new configuration, applying the changes immediately without necessitating a terminal restart.

Oh My Zsh Core Plugin Paradigm

Oh My Zsh includes a variety of core and community-contributed plugins, each with specific utilities and functionalities. Core plugins are readily available post-installation within the $ZSH/plugins directory, saving users from manual plugin retrieval. A focus on some frequently utilized core plugins helps comprehend their abilities and integration simplicity.

- *git:* Provides a suite of shortcuts and aliases for efficient Git com-

238

mand operations, enhancing command-line interaction with Git repositories.

- *z:* Facilitates directory navigation based on frequency and recency of access, allowing quicker file system exploration.

- *zsh-autosuggestions:* Introduces command auto-completion suggestions based on historical data, sharpening efficiency in command recall and execution.

- *zsh-syntax-highlighting:* Implements real-time syntax highlighting, preventing typographical errors by distinguishing between valid commands and erroneous inputs.

Community Plugins and Manual Installation

In addition to core plugins, the Oh My Zsh framework also supports the integration of community-contributed plugins. These plugins must be downloaded and placed manually within the $ZSH_CUSTOM/plugins directory to retain core Oh My Zsh updates seamlessly.

```
# Create a custom plugins directory if not existent
mkdir -p $ZSH_CUSTOM/plugins

# Navigate to the custom plugin directory
cd $ZSH_CUSTOM/plugins

# Clone the desired repository, e.g., zsh-nvm
git clone https://github.com/lukechilds/zsh-nvm.git

# Enable the plugin in .zshrc as previously demonstrated
plugins=(... zsh-nvm ...)
```

The git clone command retrieves a community plugin from its remote repository, placing it within the designated $ZSH_CUSTOM/plugins directory. Enabling the plugin follows the standard protocol of including its identifier within the 'plugins' array in .zshrc.

Plugin Management and Updates

Oh My Zsh further supports efficient management of plugins through version control paradigms harnessed by Git. Users can seamlessly update their plugin suite using predefined functions integral to the Oh My Zsh framework.

To stay abreast of new functionality or security updates, the command upgrade_oh_my_zsh can be executed. This command initiates a series of Git commands that update the core Oh My Zsh framework along with its resident plugins and themes, ensuring the user is leveraging the latest iteration of their installed components.

For custom plugins, the process involves navigating to each plugin's directory and manually pulling updates through git pull. This conventional approach ensures that the integrated customizations align with old configurations while availing of new features.

Best Practices and Recommendations

While using Oh My Zsh for plugin management, several best practices warrant consideration to maintain a robust, efficient, and secure Zsh environment:

- *Backup Configuration:* Regularly backup the .zshrc file and related configurations, enabling quick rollback in the event of erroneous modifications.

- *Manage Load:* Limit the number of concurrently active plugins to avoid significant increases in resource consumption, impacting shell performance adversely.

- *Testing:* Testing new plugins in isolated shell instances or separate system environments minimizes risks associated with instability or incompatible configurations.

- *Community Engagement:* Engage with online communities for recommendations, troubleshooting tips, and newer plugin discoveries.

The Oh My Zsh framework stands as a versatile and powerful tool for managing Zsh plugins. Its modularity and user-friendly features simplify the installation, configuration, and updating of plugins, thus empowering users to customize and optimize their shell experience effectively. By following structured procedures and best practices, users can ensure a productive and personalized environment that meets their diverse and evolving computing needs.

9.3 Essential Productivity Plugins

Within the Zsh plugin ecosystem, several plugins stand out due to their capability to significantly enhance productivity for command-line users. These plugins streamline tasks, reduce keystrokes, and enrich the interactive experience, all of which are crucial for efficient workflows in software development and system administration. This section explores a selection of widely-regarded productivity plugins, providing insights into their functionalities, benefits, and usage through illustrative examples.

Productivity-focused plugins aim to optimize common command-line tasks, allowing users to automate repetitive actions and access complex commands with ease. The discussed plugins not only augment the Zsh shell with advanced functionalities but also contribute to a more enjoyable user experience by circumventing mundane command-line operations.

1. Zsh Syntax Highlighting

One of the most popular productivity plugins is *zsh-syntax-highlighting*, renowned for its ability to color-code command input in-real-time, thus elevating command-line readability and reducing errors. By distinguishing valid commands and arguments with differing colors, users are alerted to typos or invalid commands before execution.

```
# Clone the repository if not available in default Oh My Zsh plugins
git clone https://github.com/zsh-users/zsh-syntax-highlighting.git \\
   ${ZSH_CUSTOM:-~/.oh-my-zsh/custom}/plugins/zsh-syntax-highlighting

# Enable the plugin
plugins=(... zsh-syntax-highlighting ...)
```

Upon inclusion in the Zsh configuration, this plugin enhances productivity by mitigating errors, thus saving time otherwise spent on troubleshooting and debugging.

2. Zsh Autosuggestions

The *zsh-autosuggestions* plugin further expedites command entry through its predictive suggestion feature. By leveraging one's command history, it presents likely command completions,

241

decreasing the need for typing repetitive commands in their entirety.

```
# Install the plugin
git clone https://github.com/zsh-users/zsh-autosuggestions.git \\
  ${ZSH_CUSTOM:-~/.oh-my-zsh/custom}/plugins/zsh-autosuggestions

# Add to .zshrc plugin list
plugins=(... zsh-autosuggestions ...)
```

By presenting these historical suggestions in a dimmed text format on the right, users can confirm or override suggestions, contributing to quicker command entry and enhanced efficiency.

3. Autojump

Effective navigation within the file system is critical for workflow efficiency. *Autjump* is a productivity plugin that utilizes a heuristics-based learning system to accelerate directory navigation by remembering previously accessed directories and allowing users to quickly "jump" to them using a short form.

```
# Install autojump
sudo apt install autojump

# Enable the plugin
plugins=(... autojump ...)
```

By using the command j followed by a substring of the desired directory, users can reduce directory navigation time exponentially compared to traditional cd commands.

4. Fzf and Enhanced Search

Fzf is an interactive command-line fuzzy finder that transforms traditional search and navigation commands by providing dynamic, real-time search capabilities. With its broad applicability across command history, file searching, and Git operations, *fzf* embeds sophisticated search paradigms into the command-line experience.

To integrate *fzf* as a Zsh plugin and enjoy its productivity benefits:

```
# Install using a package manager
brew install fzf

# Set interactive key bindings and completion
$(brew --prefix)/opt/fzf/install

# Add as a Zsh plugin
plugins=(... fzf ...)
```

By integrating *fzf*, users exploit interactive previews and fuzzy matching, expediting complex queries and data retrieval endeavors.

5. Git Plugin

For developers using Git, the *git* plugin for Zsh defines aliases and functions that streamline version control operations, saving substantial time on common Git tasks such as commits, push, and branch navigation.

```
# Enable the git plugin
plugins=(... git ...)
```

Key productivity-enhancing aliases include: - gco: Short for git checkout, allows quick branch navigation. - gaa: Abbreviates git add all, staging all changes rapidly. - gc: Represents git commit with associated flags for message attachment.

These shorthands transform Git operations into concise, efficient workflows, crucial for fast-paced development environments.

6. UrlTools Plugin

The *urltools* plugin is an exceptional tool for managing URL encodings and related operations directly from the command line. It offers commands for encoding, decoding, and handling HTTP parameters without resorting to web-based tools.

```
# Activate the plugin
plugins=(... urltools ...)

# Usage examples
urlencode "My URL"
urldecode "My%20URL"
```

By decoupling browser dependency for these tasks, this plugin facilitates an efficient workflow for developers and system administrators frequently engaged in web-related URL manipulations.

7. Docker Plugin

Managing Docker containers efficiently is enhanced by the *docker* plugin, which introduces helpful aliases for managing Docker images, containers, and networks without typing verbose command strings.

```
# Enable the docker plugin
plugins=(... docker ...)
```

Aliases such as dps for docker ps and dcu for docker-compose up compress routine Docker commands into efficient sequences, reducing command complexity and aiding developers in managing containers with improved speed and effectiveness.

8. Fasd

Fasd extends the navigational capabilities of Zsh by tracking file and directory usage frequency, prioritizing frequently used files for quick access in a directory stack.

```
# Install fasd
brew install fasd

# Add to plugin configuration
plugins=(... fasd ...)
```

Commands such as f or d can be used to "frecall," showing a list of frequently accessed files and directories respectively, adding a substantial layer of efficiency to file system management.

Conclusion and Best Practices

Optimizing productivity through plugins requires judicious selection to ensure minimal disruption to system resources while maximizing the benefits of advanced features. When managing plugins, attention to update cycles, compatibility considerations, and cross-dependencies ensures seamless operation and integration. Furthermore, consistent engagement with the community and exploring plugin configurations can yield further customizations tailored to specific workflow prerequisites.

By harnessing these essential productivity plugins, Zsh users are equipped with tools to streamline operations, save time, and foster a more interactive and engaging command-line environment. These enhancements substantiate Zsh as a powerful, flexible shell, accommodating both routine and complex computational needs with finesse and dispatch.

9.4 Customizing Plugin Configuration

Customizing the configuration of Zsh plugins provides users with the opportunity to tailor their shell environment precisely to their needs. This flexibility ensures not only that each plugin operates optimally within the context of the user's workflows but also that the overall shell performance and aesthetics align with personal preferences. This section delves into the methods of customizing plugin configurations in Zsh, highlighting various approaches and examining examples that illustrate the potential for fine-tuning plugin behaviors and functionalities.

The customization of plugin configurations typically occurs within the .zshrc configuration file. This file is critical as it orchestrates the initialization of Zsh and controls the loading and configuration of plugins upon the shell's startup. By editing this file, users can specify plugin-specific options, set environment variables, and define functions or aliases that modify plugin behaviors.

Understanding Zsh Configuration and Initialization

Before customizing plugins, a solid understanding of the Zsh initialization process is beneficial. Zsh reads various startup files leading to the completion of its initialization, with the .zshrc being the most relevant for customizations. This file resides in the user's home directory and acts as a primary configuration script where users declare which plugins to load, set theme preferences, and modify shell options.

The typical format for customizing a plugin involves modifying existing options or adding new ones that either augment or redefine default plugin behavior. It often involves an interplay of variables, functions, and aliases specific to each plugin.

Custom Plugin Configurations: Illustrated Examples

To illustrate customizing plugin configurations, consider the following examples of popular Zsh plugins and their configurable parameters.

1. Zsh Syntax Highlighting Configuration

The *zsh-syntax-highlighting* plugin offers parameters that control how different syntax elements appear within the terminal. Users may customize colors used for syntax elements like commands, strings, and

245

options.

```
# Define colors for error and command elements
ZSH_HIGHLIGHT_STYLES[command]='fg=cyan,bold'
ZSH_HIGHLIGHT_STYLES[error]='fg=red,bold,underline'

# Source the plugin file in .zshrc
source ${(q-)PWD}/zsh-syntax-highlighting/zsh-syntax-highlighting.zsh
```

This customization results in highlighted commands appearing in cyan, while errors are easily discernible in bold red, enhancing the readability and learnability of command-line inputs.

2. Configuring Zsh Autosuggestions

The *zsh-autosuggestions* plugin significantly benefits from adjustable configuration variables that modify suggestion behavior and appearance. Users can control suggestion display style and the timing of suggestions.

```
# Set suggestion color to a subtle shade
ZSH_AUTOSUGGEST_HIGHLIGHT_STYLE='fg=8'

# Adjust delay for suggestion appearance
ZSH_AUTOSUGGEST_REDAWN_INTERVAL=0.5
```

These alterations ensure that suggestions do not overpower the terminal's visual environment while appearing promptly, promoting a smoother user interaction.

3. Personalizing Git Plugin Aliases

For the *git* plugin, custom aliases allow finer control and personalization of git commands to streamline development workflows. Users may define shortcuts unique to their preferences.

```
# Custom git aliases in .zshrc
alias gcob='git checkout -b' # Create and checkout new branch
alias gundo='git reset --soft HEAD~1' # Undo last commit
```

These customized aliases can transform complex command sequences into simple, memorable calls, significantly boosting productivity in version control tasks.

Utilizing Environment Variables for Customization

Environment variables within Zsh provide another layer of customization by controlling plugin settings at a broader system level. Many plugins expose parameters that can be adjusted globally through environment settings.

4. Configuring Environment Variables for Powerlevel10k

The *Powerlevel10k* theme, which functions via a plugin, enables users to customize prompt content extensively through environment variables.

```
# Customize prompt style
export POWERLEVEL9K_PROMPT_ON_NEWLINE=true
export POWERLEVEL9K_RIGHT_PROMPT_ELEMENTS=(status time)

# Load Powerlevel10k theme
source /path/to/powerlevel10k/powerlevel10k.zsh-theme
```

Adjusting these environment variables modifies the prompt's content layout and placement, tailoring the prompt interface to user-specific aesthetic and informational preferences.

Integrating External Scripts and Functions

Beyond internal adjustments, users can extend plugin functionality by defining external scripts or functions that integrate with the Zsh architecture. This openness fosters creativity and adaptability in customizing how plugins interact with the rest of the shell environment.

```
# Define a function to wrap git status with additional checks
gitstatus() {
  echo "Checking Directory: $(pwd)"
  git status
}
```

Adding custom functions like gitstatus refines how existing commands operate, introducing enhanced capabilities such as additional checks or preprocessing, without modifying the core plugin.

Best Practices in Plugin Customization

When custom tailoring plugin configurations, adhering to best practices ensures efficient performance and consistent operation across different environments:

- *Backup Configuration Files:* Regular backups of .zshrc and related files sustain rapid recovery and configuration continuity, reducing risks from experimental changes.

247

- *Modularize Settings:* Decouple complex configurations into separate files or sections within .zshrc to maintain an organized and comprehensible structure.

- *Test in Isolated Environments:* Local testing of custom configurations prevents broader system disruptions. Test changes in isolated shells or temporary profiles to examine behavior before major deployment.

- *Documentation and Comments:* Thorough annotation of configuration changes with comments aids in understanding and maintaining setup rationale over time, benefiting both individual users and collaborative settings.

Migration and Maintenance of Customized Configurations

Maintaining and migrating customizations across upgrades and system changes is integral to keeping configurations in sync with the underlying plugin advancements and shell compatibility. A regimented approach ensures configurations evolve alongside progressive functionalities introduced by plugins.

- *Regular Synchronization:* Consistently synchronize custom settings with updates in plugin repositories to incorporate the latest fixes and features while maintaining retained custom functionality.

- *Version Control Adoption:* Utilize version control systems like Git for configuration management, enabling rollback capabilities and change tracking that supports iterative development of custom settings.

- *Community Collaboration:* Engage with plugin-specific forums and user communities to exchange insights, challenges, and solutions, bolstering collective knowledge on advanced customization scenarios.

Through these approaches, users can exploit the full potential of plugin configurations to shape a Zsh environment that optimally supports their technical and operational requirements, embedding productivity and customization at the core of their computational experience.

9.5 Creating Your Own Zsh Plugins

The extensibility of Zsh through plugins offers a robust platform for customization and enhancement of user workflows. While numerous plugins are available within the community to address various needs, creating custom Zsh plugins allows users to tailor functionalities towards specific tasks or preferences, thereby maximizing productivity and efficiency. This section provides a comprehensive guide on developing your own Zsh plugins, from conceptualization to implementation, detailing best practices and insightful techniques for effectively expanding Zsh's capabilities.

Zsh plugins are essentially scripts or collections of scripts that add new functions, aliases, or customizations to the Zsh shell. They encapsulate functionalities that are automatically loaded and executed when the shell starts, providing new commands or altering existing ones to improve user interaction.

Understanding the Foundation of a Zsh Plugin

Before embarking on plugin creation, it is vital to understand the basic structure and functionality of a Zsh plugin. At its core, a Zsh plugin is a directory containing:

- Source files, typically written in shell script.

- A README.md offering details about the plugin's purpose and usage.

- Possible auxiliary files or resources required for the plugin's execution.

The following example illustrates the basic directory structure of a Zsh plugin:

```
my-zsh-plugin/
  my-zsh-plugin.plugin.zsh
  README.md
  functions/
    helper_function.sh
```

In this example, the main plugin logic resides in my-zsh-plugin.plugin.zsh, while additional functionality can be modularized

249

in separate scripts stored within a functions directory.

Step-by-Step Guide to Developing a Zsh Plugin

The process of developing a Zsh plugin starts with identifying the functionality or task that the plugin will address. With an idea in mind, follow these steps:

Initialize and set up your plugin:

Begin by creating a directory to hold all related files for your plugin within the $ZSH_CUSTOM/plugins (if using Oh My Zsh) or your preferred directory.

```
# Navigate to custom plugins directory
mkdir -p ${ZSH_CUSTOM:-~/.oh-my-zsh/custom}/plugins/my-zsh-plugin

cd ${ZSH_CUSTOM:-~/.oh-my-zsh/custom}/plugins/my-zsh-plugin
```

Craft the plugin script:

The main plugin script, often following the naming convention plugin-name.plugin.zsh, contains the core logic of your plugin. For example, creating a plugin to wrap common system checks:

```
# my-zsh-plugin.plugin.zsh

# Define a function for disk usage
check_disk_usage() {
  df -h
}

# Define a function for monitoring memory
check_memory() {
  free -m
}

# Aliases for quick access
alias cdisk="check_disk_usage"
alias cmemory="check_memory"
```

The above script adds two functions, check_disk_usage and check_memory, with respective aliases for ease of access, serving as a simple monitoring plugin.

Add documentation and resources:

A comprehensive README.md file becomes an essential component of your plugin, especially for sharing it with others or even for personal reference in future use:

```
# My Zsh Plugin

## Overview
This plugin provides quick access to basic system monitoring functions,
including disk usage and memory checks.

## Usage
- 'cdisk': Check disk usage.
- 'cmemory': Check current memory usage.

To install, copy the plugin directory into your '$ZSH_CUSTOM/plugins' and
add 'my-zsh-plugin' to the 'plugins' array in your '.zshrc' file.
```

Test and debug your plugin:

Test the plugin thoroughly in a separate shell session. Debug issues by leveraging Zsh's verbosity, which can be increased for debugging purposes:

```
# Enable verbose debugging
set -x
```

Here, set -x enables verbose mode, displaying command expansion, which aids in troubleshooting.

Enhancing Your Plugin with Advanced Features

To take your plugin beyond basic functionalities, consider integrating more sophisticated features:

- *Parameterization and Custom User Settings:* Allow users to modify default behaviors through environment variables or configuration files.

- *Integration with Existing Tools:* Leverage existing command-line tools and APIs, creating a higher level of abstraction and seamless interaction.

- *Error Handling and Logging:* Implement robust error handling and detailed logging to improve user feedback and plugin reliability.

Example with parameterized configuration:

```
# my-zsh-plugin.plugin.zsh

# Check custom threshold for disk usage
```

251

```
check_disk_usage() {
  local threshold=${DISK_WARNING_THRESHOLD:-90}
  df -h | awk -v threshold=$threshold '
    $5+0 > threshold {print "Warning: "$1" usage is at "$5}'
}

alias cdisk="check_disk_usage"
```

In this example, users can set a custom warning threshold through the DISK_WARNING_THRESHOLD environment variable, enhancing the plugin's flexibility and user interaction.

Sharing and Distribution of Your Plugin

Once development is complete, sharing the plugin with the community or specific user groups encourages feedback and collaboration. Host your plugin on platforms such as GitHub for visibility and collaborative opportunities.

Recommended practices for sharing include:

- Clear documentation with installation instructions and usage details.

- Examples of typical handling, configurations, and expected outputs.

- A changelog to track the history of updates and improvements.

Conclusion and Best Practices

Creating custom Zsh plugins allows users to address precise needs unfulfilled by existing plugins, personalizing their shell environment to better support their workflows. Essential best practices for effective plugin development include:

- *Modular Design:* Separate complex logic into distinct, reusable functions or files to enhance maintainability.

- *Consistent Formatting and Naming Conventions:* Ensure that code follows consistent styling and clear naming conventions to aid readability.

- *Community Integration:* Share your plugin with user communities, engaging in dialogues and contributions that enhance broader ecosystem advancements.

- *Regular Maintenance:* Regularly update based on user feedback and evolving shell requirements, ensuring your plugin remains useful and relevant over time.

By following these guidelines, developers can craft effective Zsh plugins that refine and extend shell interactions, driving efficiencies across technical tasks and operational processes.

9.6 Troubleshooting Common Plugin Issues

As with any software enhancements, the integration and use of plugins in Zsh can occasionally lead to issues that affect shell performance or behavior. Understanding how to troubleshoot these common problems is essential for maintaining a smooth and efficient command-line environment. This section covers typical challenges and provides detailed strategies for diagnosing and resolving them, ensuring that Zsh plugins function correctly and beneficially within user-specific setups.

Identifying Common Plugin Issues

Common issues stemming from Zsh plugins generally fall into several categories, including:

- *Installation and Activation Failures:* Problems arising from incorrect setup or activation, leading to unavailable or partially functioning plugins.

- *Compatibility Conflicts:* Conflicts between plugins or between plugins and the Zsh configuration, resulting in unexpected behaviors or errors.

- *Performance Degradation:* Plugins that introduce significant latency, slow shell start times, or affect the performance of other shell processes.

- *Unexpected Behaviors and Errors:* Incorrect plugin logic causing errors during execution or undesired command output.

By systematically categorizing issues, users can apply targeted troubleshooting strategies, streamlining the resolution process and minimizing disruption to their workflows.

Strategies for Troubleshooting Plugin Issues

Addressing plugin issues effectively involves a combination of diagnostic tools, methodical testing, and iterative adjustments. Below are strategies to troubleshoot and overcome common plugin issues:

1. Verifying Installation and Plugin Activation

The first step in troubleshooting plugins involves confirming correct installation and activation within the Zsh environment. Key actions include:

- *Check Installation Paths:* Ensure plugins are located in recognized directories, typically $ZSH_CUSTOM/plugins for non-core plugins and $ZSH/plugins for Oh My Zsh defaults.

- *Confirm Activation in .zshrc:* Verify the correct inclusion of plugins in the plugins array within the .zshrc file, as shown below:

```
# Check for correct entry of problematic plugin
plugins=(
  git
  zsh-autosuggestions
  my-custom-plugin # Ensure this line is present and correct
)
```

- *Review Logs and Console Feedback:* Pay attention to console messages and logs upon starting Zsh, as these can indicate missing files or incorrect path specifications.

2. Addressing Compatibility Conflicts

Plugins may sometimes conflict with each other or with existing Zsh configurations. To diagnose and resolve compatibility issues:

- *Isolate and Test:* Disable suspected conflicting plugins or configurations temporarily to observe interaction changes. Use binary exclusion (i.e., enabling/disabling halves of the list) to isolate conflicts quickly.

- *Evaluate Configuration Consistency:* Ensure compatibility of shell options (setopt / unsetopt) and variables specified by plugins or shared environmental settings.

```
# Temporary exclusion of plugins for isolation
plugins=(
  git
  # temporarily disable the plugin suspected of causing issues
  # my-custom-plugin
)
```

3. Monitoring and Improving Performance

Performance issues often arise with plugin-induced delays or excessive resource demands on shell startup. Strategies to counter this include:

- *Profile Shell Initialization:* Utilize tools like zprof to profile startup times and resource usage attributed to specific plugins or functions:

```
# Add to .zshrc to enable profiling
zmodload zsh/zprof

# At the end of .zshrc, invoke profiling output
zprof
```

The resulting analysis highlights which parts of the initialization process consume the most time, guiding optimization efforts by pinpointing plugins that could be replaced, optimized, or deferred in loading.

- *Consider Asynchronous Operations:* Where possible, implementing asynchronous techniques for non-critical plugin functionalities can reduce immediate initialization load times.

4. Diagnosing Unexpected Behaviors and Errors

Unexpected plugin behaviors often originate from errors within plugin scripts or misconfigurations. Diagnostic measures include:

- *Enable Verbose Debugging:* Activate verbose mode using set -x in .zshrc to trace command execution and identify erroneous segments:

255

```
# Enable debugging to trace commands
set -x
```

- *Review Plugin Code and Logic:* Examine plugin scripts for potential logic errors, syntax issues, or improperly defined functions and variables.

Best Practices for Robust Plugin Management

Proactively employing best practices in plugin management not only resolves current issues but also prevents future complications:

- *Maintain Current Versions:* Regularly update plugins to their latest versions for bug fixes, optimizations, and new features benefits.

- *Documentation Review:* Thoroughly consult the documentation for each plugin to understand configurable parameters, requirements, and any special installation steps.

- *Environment Consistency Checks:* Ensure system environments match plugin prerequisites, including versions of Zsh, operating system specifications, and necessary dependencies.

- *Backup Consistent States:* Maintain backups of known-working .zshrc configurations and custom plugin directories to facilitate prompt recovery from problematic states.

By adopting these practices, users fortify their Zsh environments against disruptions while maximizing the intended benefits of integrated plugins.

Engaging with Community Resources

In situations where troubleshooting exhausts solitary efforts, engaging with community resources such as online forums, GitHub repositories, or mailing lists can provide additional insights and solutions. Interaction with developers or fellow users often unveils fresh perspectives or shared experiences pertinent to resolving complex issues.

Committing to knowledge-sharing and collaborative debugging bolsters both individual problem-solving capacities and the collective resilience of the Zsh user community.

Troubleshooting Zsh plugin issues involves a comprehensive understanding of shell configurations, coupled with methodical diagnostic strategies. Successfully addressing common issues ensures that plugins operate harmoniously within the shell environment, contributing to both efficient workflows and enhanced user experiences. Users who embrace systematic troubleshooting approaches and adopt preventive best practices not only resolve immediate concerns but also lay solid groundwork for continuously enriching and evolving their Zsh experience.

Chapter 10

Best Practices and Common Pitfalls in Zsh Scripting

This chapter addresses the best practices in Zsh scripting that ensure code is readable, maintainable, and efficient. It highlights the importance of optimizing performance, securing scripts, and avoiding common errors. Additionally, it underscores the role of version control systems and adherence to scripting standards. By focusing on these practices, users are equipped to write reliable scripts while minimizing potential pitfalls in their development process.

10.1 Writing Readable and Maintainable Scripts

In scripting, particularly with Zsh, the importance of writing readable and maintainable code cannot be overstated. Scripts serve as a crucial component of automation and efficiency in the computing environment. However, when scripts are unclear or haphazardly constructed, they become more of a liability than an asset. This section explores various techniques and strategies to ensure that your Zsh scripts remain an effective tool for yourself and others who may use or maintain them in the future.

Clarity and conciseness are key attributes of readable scripts. Achieving these attributes requires attention to code structure, naming conventions, and documentation. By implementing these best practices, you can make scripts not only functional but also understandable and maintainable.

To begin with, consider the structure of your script. A well-structured script follows a logical progression: initialization, main logic, and cleanup. This flow allows others to follow the script's operation and make modifications when necessary. Here's a simple example to illustrate this structure:

```
#!/bin/zsh

# Initialization
input_file="data.txt"
output_file="result.txt"

# Function definitions
process_data() {
   # process the data from the input file
}

# Main logic
if [[ -f $input_file ]]; then
   process_data < $input_file > $output_file
else
   echo "Error: input file not found."
   exit 1
fi

# Cleanup
echo "Processing complete. Output saved to $output_file."
```

The script begins with an initialization section where variables and functions are defined. This is a good practice as it sets the stage for the main operations of the script. In the example above, the input and output file names are defined as variables, making them easier to modify if needed.

Next, the script includes a conditional statement to check if the input file exists. This is a basic but crucial step to avoid errors during execution. By including this check, you ensure that the script behaves predictably even in unexpected conditions.

Another facet of making scripts readable is adopting clear and concise naming conventions for functions and variables. The choice of descriptive names is vital. Variables like 'input_file' and 'output_file' instantly convey their purpose. Similarly, the function 'process_data' succinctly describes its role in the script. Avoid using cryptic names that require additional comments to explain their functionality.

Comments are another essential component of writing maintainable scripts. They provide context and explanations for specific code segments that may not be immediately apparent to someone reading your script for the first time. However, comments should be used judiciously to avoid cluttering the code. Good commenting practices suggest explaining the "why" behind a block of code rather than the "what," which should be evident from the code itself. Here's an illustration:

```
#!/bin/zsh

# Generate a processed version of the input data
process_data() {
  local line
  # Read each line from the input
  while read -r line; do
    # Trim leading and trailing whitespace from the line
    echo "${line//^[[:space:]]+|[[:space:]]+$}"
  done
}

# Main processing logic
process_data < $input_file > $output_file
```

In this snippet, comments are used to explain the purpose of the 'process_data' function and how each line is processed. Notice that it focuses on providing essential understanding rather than describing every single line of code, which can make comments redundant or verbose.

The readability of scripts can also be enhanced by structuring them with whitespace and indentation. These visual elements guide the reader through the logical flow of the script and distinguish between different code blocks. It is a best practice to maintain consistent indentation and spacing throughout your script. A recommended convention is to use two or four spaces per indentation level and to separate logically distinct tasks with a blank line.

261

Modularization, or the breakdown of a script into smaller, manageable pieces, aids in both readability and maintainability. This involves writing functions or sourcing scripts to encapsulate specific tasks. By creating functions like 'process_data', you encapsulate behavior that can be tested independently and reused elsewhere in the script or other scripts.

Furthermore, error handling is an often-overlooked aspect of script writing that significantly contributes to maintainability. By carefully managing potential errors and unexpected inputs, you prevent the script from failing silently or producing undesired results. In Zsh, you can handle errors using exit statuses, 'trap' statements, or more advanced error recovery techniques. Consider this approach:

```zsh
#!/bin/zsh

# Define an error handler
error_handler() {
  echo "Error on line $1"
  exit 1
}

# Set trap for any command that returns a non-zero status
trap 'error_handler $LINENO' ERR

# Example function that may fail
modify_file() {
  # Simulate a command that might fail
  cp non_existent_file.txt /backup/
}

# Call the function
modify_file
```

Here, we define an 'error_handler' function and set a trap for any command that fails, using the 'trap' built-in. This not only provides feedback on where the error occurred but also gives users a chance to handle the situation gracefully.

Beyond the script's internal logic, explicit input and output formats contribute to maintenance and clarity. Establish a clear contract for what inputs the script expects and what outputs it provides. Clearly documenting this at the beginning or end of the script helps users understand exactly how to work with it. Consider using command-line option parsing to manage input arguments more flexibly.

Version control is another layer to consider for maintainability. By employing systems such as Git, you can track changes over time, collaborate with others, and revert to previous states as needed. This repository of past versions becomes invaluable when scripts evolve or when debugging complex problems. A good practice is to include a versioning comment header within each script:

```
# Script: data_processing.zsh
# Author: Your Name
# Version: 1.2
# Date: 2023-10-01
# Description: This script processes data stored in a text file.
```

Finally, thoughtful testing is integral to both readability and maintainability. Testing scripts rigorously ensures they perform correctly under various conditions. Write automated test cases where feasible to verify the script's functionality, particularly for more complex scripts. Unit tests can be created for individual functions, measuring their responses to expected and unexpected inputs.

Writing readable and maintainable scripts in Zsh requires deliberate effort in organizing code, naming conventions, commenting, and error handling. It also extends beyond the script itself to include practices like version control and testing. By integrating these practices, you can greatly improve the clarity and robustness of your scripts, facilitating easier problem-solving and collaboration.

10.2   Optimizing Script Performance

Optimizing the performance of Zsh scripts is a critical practice for harnessing the full potential of shell scripting, particularly when dealing with large volumes of data or complex operations. Performance optimization involves not only improving execution speed but also reducing resource consumption, ensuring smooth operation even in resource-constrained environments. This section delves into various strategies for enhancing script performance, covering both conceptual techniques and practical coding practices.

One fundamental aspect of optimizing performance in scripts is understanding the overhead associated with various shell operations and commands. For instance, external command calls are generally more costly in terms of time and system resources than built-in shell commands. Therefore, optimizing scripts can often involve replacing external commands with equivalent shell built-ins where possible. Consider the following example:

```
#!/bin/zsh

# Using an external command
line_count=$(wc -l < large_file.txt)

# Using a built-in command
line_count=0
while IFS= read -r; do
  ((line_count++))
done < large_file.txt
```

In this example, instead of using the 'wc' command, a loop iterates through the file to count the lines. Although this example's performance benefits may vary based on context and file size, choosing shell built-ins could potentially enhance performance due to reduced context-switching between the shell and external programs.

Another way to optimize Zsh script performance is to avoid unnecessary use of subshells and command substitutions. Subshells can be convenient but introduce additional overhead by creating new processes. For better performance, consolidate commands whenever feasible within the same execution environment. The following example demonstrates this approach:

```
#!/bin/zsh

# Using subshell
result_1=$(some_command | another_command)

# Avoiding subshell
some_command | {
  # Directly pipe to another command within the same shell
  result_2=$(another_command)
}
```

By reducing the use of subshells and instead using direct piping within the shell, scripts can circumvent the expensive process creation, thereby leading to performance gains.

When dealing with arrays and loops, a few optimizations can further enhance script execution speed. For instance, using 'for' instead of the more complex 'while' or 'until' loops, especially with known array

264

bounds, can reduce iteration time due to simpler loop mechanics. Furthermore, leveraging built-in array operations within Zsh, which supports array slicing and manipulation natively, can save on computation and parsing time compared to manual methods. Consider the following efficient handling of arrays:

```zsh
#!/bin/zsh

# Define an array
numbers=(1 2 3 4 5 6 7 8 9 10)

# Using for-loop for array iteration
for num in "${numbers[@]}"; do
  echo $num
done

# Performing operations on array slices
subarray=( "${numbers[@]:3:5}" ) # Extracts a subarray from index 3 to 7
```

Zsh provides robust array handling capabilities, allowing scripts to efficiently manage data sets and perform slice operations directly without accumulating significant overhead.

Loop unrolling is another advanced technique that can be employed when working with iterations. Although it may introduce complexity to script logic, unrolling loops can effectively reduce the overhead associated with loop control, especially in cases with a fine iteration grain:

```zsh
#!/bin/zsh

# Traditional loop
for ((i=0; i<1000; i++)); do
  process_item $i
done

# Loop unrolling
for ((i=0; i<1000; i+=4)); do
  process_item $i
  process_item $((i + 1))
  process_item $((i + 2))
  process_item $((i + 3))
done
```

In this case, loop unrolling processes four items per iteration instead of one, reducing the number of loop control evaluations and potentially improving performance for specific workloads.

Another important aspect of script performance is efficient file and input/output (I/O) handling. I/O operations are among the slowest

265

parts of script execution, often being a bottleneck. Therefore, minimizing the number of I/O operations or batch processing files can lead to significant performance improvements. Here's an example that illustrates buffering instead of line-by-line processing:

```zsh
#!/bin/zsh

# Process file line-by-line (slower)
while read -r line; do
  process_line "$line"
done < large_input.txt

# Process file in batches (faster)
chunk_size=100
buffer=()

while IFS= read -r line; do
  buffer+=("$line")

  # If buffer is full, process batch
  if (( ${#buffer[@]} == chunk_size )); then
    process_batch "${buffer[@]}"
    buffer=() # Clear buffer
  fi
done < large_input.txt

# Process any remaining lines in buffer
if (( ${#buffer[@]} > 0 )); then
  process_batch "${buffer[@]}"
fi
```

In this scenario, file processing is performed in chunks instead of line-by-line, decreasing the interaction frequency with the I/O system and thereby enhancing efficiency, particularly for large files.

Additionally, Zsh supports features such as lazy evaluation of commands and command pooling, which can contribute to performance optimization. Using these features appropriately can lead to less resource consumption and faster script execution.

On a broader perspective, considering parallel execution when applicable can tremendously enhance performance, especially on modern multi-core systems. By splitting tasks that do not depend on each other into separate processes or threads, you can leverage the full capabilities of CPU architectures. However, parallelization requires careful handling of shared resources and potential race conditions. The '&' operator can background tasks, and 'wait' commands can synchronize them:

```zsh
#!/bin/zsh

# Function to process a file in background
process_file() {
    local file=$1
    # Simulated processing
    sleep 2
    echo "Processed $file"
}

files=( "file1.txt" "file2.txt" "file3.txt" )

# Parallel processing
for file in "${files[@]}"; do
    process_file "$file" &
done

# Wait for all background processes to complete
wait
```

Here, each file is processed independently in the background, allowing simultaneous execution and reducing total processing time.

Lastly, optimization of script performance includes regular profiling and benchmarking to identify bottlenecks and inefficiencies. Tools like 'time', 'strace', and 'perf' can help assess the runtime performance and system calls of scripts. A typical routine involves measuring execution times, understanding system call frequency, and refining those parts of the script with the highest cost or longest time.

Optimizing the performance of Zsh scripts involves a comprehensive approach that considers command selection, script structure, I/O handling, parallel execution, and careful resource management. By integrating these optimization techniques, you can significantly increase the efficiency and robustness of your scripts. This allows for more effective automation solutions and can make a palpable difference in resource-constrained environments, providing faster and more reliable script executions.

10.3 Security Considerations in Scripting

Security in scripting languages, such as Zsh, is an essential aspect of development, particularly given the powerful capabilities of shell

267

scripts in manipulating files, executing commands, and automating tasks. Recognizing and addressing potential vulnerabilities in scripts is crucial to protect systems from unauthorized access, data theft, and other malicious activities. This section provides detailed insights into security considerations when writing shell scripts, offering strategies and practices to mitigate risks.

One of the primary security concerns in scripting is the handling of user inputs. Scripts that accept user inputs, for instance from command-line arguments or environment variables, should validate these inputs rigorously to prevent injection attacks. The risk arises because shell scripts often compose and execute dynamic commands based on user inputs, making them susceptible to shell command injection if not properly sanitized.

A common strategy to mitigate injection threats is input validation. This involves verifying that inputs adhere to expected constraints, such as character set and length, before processing them. Here's an example demonstrating safe handling of user inputs:

```zsh
#!/bin/zsh

# Safe input validation
expected_length=10

validate_input() {
  local input="$1"
  # Check for alphanumeric characters only
  if [[ ! "$input" =~ ^[a-zA-Z0-9]+$ ]]; then
    echo "Error: input contains invalid characters."
    return 1
  fi

  # Check if input length is acceptable
  if (( ${#input} > expected_length )); then
    echo "Error: input exceeds expected length."
    return 1
  fi
  return 0
}

# Read user input
read -p "Enter username: " username

# Validate user input
if validate_input "$username"; then
  echo "Validated input: $username"
else
  echo "Invalid input received. Exiting."
  exit 1
fi
```

In this example, the validate_input function ensures that the input is strictly alphanumeric and does not exceed a predefined length, mitigating the risk of injection attacks.

Environment variables, often used in scripts to pass configuration or state information, can also pose security risks if not carefully managed. Untrusted or inadequately sanitized environment variables can introduce vulnerabilities that attackers may exploit. Scripts should explicitly expect and validate required environment variables while rejecting or ignoring others.

In addition to input validation, safe execution of shell commands is another critical consideration. Using positional parameters ("$1", "$2", etc.) and avoiding command substitution whenever feasible can prevent unintended command executions. Moreover, it is good practice to use $(...) for command substitutions instead of backticks for improved readability and to eliminate ambiguity associated with varying character encodings.

For scripts that involve executing other commands or programs—particularly with elevated privileges—it is crucial to ensure that the executed commands are the intended ones. Specify absolute paths for commands instead of relying on the system PATH, which may be modified maliciously. Here's how specifying explicit paths enhances security:

```zsh
#!/bin/zsh

# Specify full paths for utilities
BIN_LS="/bin/ls"
BIN_RM="/bin/rm"

# Securely remove files
secure_remove() {
  local filepath="$1"
  if [ -e "$filepath" ]; then
    "$BIN_RM" -- "$filepath"
  else
    echo "File not found: $filepath"
  fi
}

# List contents of the directory
"$BIN_LS" -l
```

Explicit paths guarantee that only the intended binaries, not altered or malicious versions in the PATH, are executed, thereby enhancing

269

security.

File permissions play an equally vital part in script security. Scripts should ideally follow the principle of least privilege, where users are given only the minimum levels of access necessary. Adopt secure file permissions and ownership settings, avoiding the use of overly permissive 777 permissions or executing scripts as root unless absolutely necessary. Incorporate checks and establish correct permissions programmatically:

```zsh
#!/bin/zsh

# Check and set secure permissions
secure_file() {
  local file="$1"
  chmod 600 "$file" # Read/write for owner only
  chown "$(whoami)" "$file" # Ensure ownership
}

my_sec_file="secure_data.txt"
secure_file "$my_sec_file"
```

By using chmod and chown, scripts enforce strict file accessibility and ownership conventions, curbing unauthorized access and potential data tampering.

Proper error handling further strengthens script security. Use strategies like exit traps and explicit error messages to manage errors effectively, which reduces the risk of unintended script behavior that attackers could exploit. An example of robust error handling is as follows:

```zsh
#!/bin/zsh

# Setup an exit trap for cleanup
trap 'custom_cleanup' EXIT

custom_cleanup() {
  # Specify cleanup actions here
  echo "Cleaning up..."
  rm -f /tmp/secure_tempfile
}

main() {
  # Intentional error to trigger cleanup
  false # Simulate an error
}

main
```

Through the trap function, which registers custom_cleanup to execute

270

upon script termination, the script can reliably handle unexpected terminations and prevent leaving sensitive temporary files behind.

Minimizing the script's attack surface involves regularly reviewing and hardening the script by removing unnecessary functionality, debugging outputs, and verbose messages that might leak sensitive information. Additionally, keeping scripts updated and aligned with best practices in shell scripting helps close commonly exploited security holes.

Where feasible, auditing tools and static analysis tools tailored for scripts can automatically detect and highlight potential security issues, ensuring that scripts remain free from vulnerabilities as they evolve.

Security considerations in Zsh scripting encompass careful input handling, proper command execution, meticulous file permission management, comprehensive error handling, and regular audits. By following these guidelines, scriptwriters can safeguard their scripts against common vulnerabilities, ensuring robust protection of executing environments and data. This proactive approach is vital in an increasingly complex security landscape, where scripts are not isolated but integral components that drive broader computing architectures.

10.4 Avoiding Common Scripting Mistakes

Scripting, though powerful, is prone to various mistakes, especially when done without adherence to best practices. Such errors can lead to inefficient, unreliable, or insecure scripts. Understanding and avoiding common pitfalls is essential for anyone working with Zsh or any shell scripting language. This section explores typical scripting errors and offers detailed solutions to enhance script reliability and effectiveness.

A frequent mistake in scripting occurs with improper quotation handling, which can lead to issues such as unexpected splitting of variables, misinterpretation of special characters, and command injection vulnerabilities. A pivotal rule is to consistently quote variables, especially when they can contain spaces or special characters. Consider the following incorrect handling and subsequent correction:

```
#!/bin/zsh

# Incorrect: variable not quoted
filename_without_extension=input data.txt
echo $filename_without_extension # Outputs: input

# Correct: variable quoted
filename_with_spaces="input data.txt"
echo "$filename_with_spaces" # Outputs: input data.txt
```

In the first example, without quotes, the variable filename_without_extension is mishandled if it contains spaces. By quoting variables, scripts prevent unwanted word splitting and preserve the intended variable contents.

Another common oversight is the incorrect use of conditionals. Misusing condition checks and operators can lead to logical errors that affect script flow. Clearly understanding and using the appropriate syntax for conditionals is crucial:

```
#!/bin/zsh

# Incorrect: using single =
if [ "$VAR" = "value" ]; then
  echo "Value matches"
fi

# Correct: using ==
if [[ "$VAR" == "value" ]]; then
  echo "Value matches"
fi
```

In Zsh, the extended test [[ ]] allows for more robust condition checks. It is generally safer and more portable for complex condition evaluations compared to [ ].

Deadlocks and infinite loops also constitute a significant category of scripting errors, often caused by improper loop controls or missing termination conditions. To avoid such issues, scripts must ensure proper exit conditions are included within loops. Here's an example to illustrate:

```
#!/bin/zsh

# Incorrect: Potential infinite loop
while true; do
  echo "Press q to quit."
  read input
done
```

```
# Correct: Proper loop exit condition
while true; do
  echo "Press q to quit."
  read input
  [[ "$input" == "q" ]] && break # break out of loop
done
```

The correction incorporates a clear condition to terminate the loop, preventing it from running indefinitely, which could otherwise consume resources unnecessarily.

Environment management is another critical consideration; scripts can inadvertently rely on unexplained environment variables, leading to unpredictable behavior. Scripts should explicitly define necessary variables or expect them as input parameters to ensure a controlled environment. Here's a demonstration:

```
#!/bin/zsh

# Incorrect: assuming environment variable
echo "Processing file: $DATA_FILE"

# Correct: explicitly check and handle
if [[ -z "$DATA_FILE" ]]; then
  echo "Error: DATA_FILE environment variable is not set."
  exit 1
fi
echo "Processing file: $DATA_FILE"
```

By validating the presence of $DATA_FILE, scripts prevent runtime errors stemming from undefined variables, increasing reliability.

Variable name collisions are another prevalent mistake. Using global variables without consideration often leads to accidental overwrites or unexpected values. It is a best practice to localize variables within functions:

```
#!/bin/zsh

# Incorrect: global variable overwrite
my_function() {
  temp_file="output.txt"
  echo "Function uses $temp_file"
}

temp_file="data.txt"
my_function
echo "Outside function, temp_file is $temp_file"

# Correct: using local keyword
```

273

```
my_function() {
  local temp_file="output.txt"
  echo "Function uses $temp_file"
}

temp_file="data.txt"
my_function
echo "Outside function, temp_file is $temp_file"
```

Localizing variables avoids unintended side effects on global variables, maintaining script integrity and predictable outcomes.

Improper error handling is a recurrent weakness in scripts. A laissez-faire approach to errors can result in unnoticed failures leading to incorrect results or even system damage. Employing explicit error-handling strategies fosters robustness:

```
#!/bin/zsh

# Incorrect: No error handling
execute_command
echo "Command executed successfully."

# Correct: With error handling
if ! execute_command; then
  echo "Error: Command failed."
  exit 1
fi
echo "Command executed successfully."
```

Integrating error checks allows scripts to respond appropriately to failures, guiding the script along a secure, expected pathway and facilitating debugging.

Concurrency and parallel execution in scripts necessitate careful management of shared resources. Scripts often overlook potential race conditions. To avert inconsistencies from concurrent processes, use locking mechanisms:

```
#!/bin/zsh

# Use a lock file to prevent concurrent script execution
lockfile="/tmp/my_script.lock"

if [[ -e $lockfile ]]; then
  echo "Script is already running."
  exit 1
fi
touch $lockfile

# Simulated task
```

```
sleep 5

# Remove lock file after task completes
rm $lockfile
```

Lock files or semaphores ensure that script instances do not interfere with each other, restraining stability and correctness across execution.

Lastly, pay heed to resource management. Failure to release resources, such as file descriptors or memory, can exhaust system capacities, leading to script and system failures. Ensure all resources are correctly allocated and deallocated:

```
#!/bin/zsh

# Correct file handling
exec 3<> somefile.txt # Open file descriptor 3

# ... perform operations ...

exec 3<&- # Close file descriptor
```

By methodically closing file descriptors, you reclaim system resources, preventing gradual unaddressed consumption.

Many script errors stem from a lack of attention to best practices and conventions in the areas of variable handling, conditional checks, looping mechanisms, environment management, error handling, concurrency, and resource allocation. Addressing these issues head-on empowers script developers to write reliable, efficient, and secure scripts. Regularly revisiting these principles fosters a culture of continuous improvement in scriptwriting skills, enhancing overall resilience and functionality of shell scripts across diverse environments.

10.5 Version Control for Scripts

In the context of scripting, particularly within environments like Zsh, maintaining a clear and organized history of changes is imperative for efficient management and collaboration. Version control systems (VCS), such as Git, provide the framework necessary to capture the evolution of scripts, ensure code integrity, and facilitate teamwork. This section provides a comprehensive exploration of the principles of version control as they apply to script management, alongside practical guidance on effectively leveraging these tools.

Version control is the practice of tracking and managing changes to software code. In scripting, this means recording revisions of scripts, allowing developers to revert to previous versions, compare changes, and collaborate with others seamlessly. The utility of version control becomes particularly evident in complex environments where scripts need to be modified frequently or by multiple team members.

- **The Basics of Git for Script Version Control**

Git is a distributed version control system that has become the de facto standard in the industry. Its functionality supports not only small scripts but also large-scale projects. Understanding the fundamental Git workflows is essential:

- **Initialization**: Begin by initializing a Git repository in the directory where your scripts reside. This marks the root of your version-controlled source.

```
cd /path/to/your/scripts
git init
```

- **Committing Changes**: As you modify your scripts, you should commit changes at logical checkpoints. This may include bug fixes, new features, or configuration updates. Each commit should be descriptive to provide context for the changes.

```
git add script_name.zsh
git commit -m "Describe the changes made in this commit."
```

- **Branching and Merging**: Branching allows you to experiment or develop new features without disrupting the main codebase. Once changes are tested, they can be merged back into the main branch.

```
git checkout -b new-feature
# make and commit changes
git checkout main
git merge new-feature
```

Using branches can isolate work on specific features or issues until they are ready to be integrated. This also provides the flexibility of troubleshooting in parallel without service interruption.

- **Handling Conflicts and Collaboration**

When multiple developers contribute to the script repository, conflicting changes may occur. Git affords tools to resolve these conflicts without losing progress or overwriting changes inadvertently:

- **Understanding Diffs**: Before resolving conflicts, it's crucial to understand the differences that led to a conflict. The 'git diff' command helps visualize these differences.

```
git diff HEAD
```

- **Resolving Conflicts**: Use a text editor to manually resolve the conflicts highlighted by placeholders (e.g., '«««<', '=======', '»»»>') and commit the resolved changes.

```
# After resolving conflicts in the editor
git add resolved_script.zsh
git commit -m "Resolve merge conflicts in script"
```

Collaboration via Git also benefits from techniques such as pull requests, which prevent direct changes to the main codebase without review. Employing feature branches alongside review mechanisms ensures quality control and reduces the likelihood of introducing bugs.

- **Version Tags and Releases**

In scripts, tagging specific states of the repository can denote releases or important milestones. Releases can then be referenced in deployments, ensuring consistency across environments:

```
# Tagging a release version
git tag -a v1.0.0 -m "First release of the script"
git push origin v1.0.0
```

Tags are immutable once created, providing a reliable reference point for the state of the script repository at a particular time. When rolling out new versions of scripts, these tags can help quickly identify which scripts are in use across different systems.

- **Automating and Integrating Version Control**

Modern development practices emphasize automation to reduce manual errors and increase consistency. Git can be integrated with continuous integration/continuous deployment (CI/CD) pipelines for automation in script management:

- **Continuous Integration**: Automatically testing scripts when changes are pushed ensures that inadvertent changes don't introduce errors or regressions. Tools like Jenkins, Travis CI, or GitHub Actions can automate this process.

  ```
  # Example GitHub Actions Workflow for Zsh Scripts
  name: CI

  on:
    push:
      branches: [ main ]

  jobs:
    test:
      runs-on: ubuntu-latest

      steps:
        - uses: actions/checkout@v2
        - name: Run tests
          run: ./test-suite.zsh
  ```

- **Continuous Deployment**: Upon passing tests, scripts can automatically be deployed to production environments, ensuring that the latest stable versions are always in use.

- **Best Practices for Version Control in Scripting**

To maximize the efficacy of version control, consider the following best practices specific to scripting environments:

- **Descriptive Commit Messages**: Clearly describe what changes were made and why. This is even more important in scripts where changes might affect operational processes directly.

278

- **Atomic Commits**: Each commit should encapsulate a single logical change. This makes it easy to review changes and if necessary, revert specific changes without affecting others.

- **Regularly Synchronizing with Remote Repositories**: Push your local commits to a remote regularly to mitigate data loss and facilitate collaboration.

- **Backing Up and Secure Access**: Ensure that your repositories are properly backed up and employ secure protocols (SSH over HTTPS) to prevent unauthorized access.

- **Historical Analysis and Audit Trails**

Version control isn't only about managing current script versions but also about understanding the evolution of the scripts. Git provides powerful tools to conduct historical analysis:

- **Log Inspection**: Use 'git log' to view a history of commits. Flags like '–stat' and '–oneline' provide concise insights:

```
git log --oneline --graph --decorate
```

- **Blame and Annotate**: Determine who last edited particular lines in your code using 'git blame', which is invaluable for debugging and accountability.

```
git blame script_name.zsh
```

- **Employing Version Control Across Teams**

Introducing Git for version control enhances collaborative script development:

- **Conduct Code Reviews**: Code reviews using pull requests can expose potential script logic errors or inefficiencies, improving overall code quality.

- **Setup Integration Standards**: Develop clear guidelines or workflows for integrating changes to avoid conflict and maintain consistency.

279

- **Mentor Team Members**: Provide training and resources to ensure all team members are comfortable and proficient in using Git.

Version control provides a structured method for managing changes to scripts, promoting resilience against changes in team composition and the inevitable modifications over time.

Version control for scripts, through systems such as Git, provides indispensable capabilities for monitoring and managing script changes, fostering better collaboration, and enhancing code stability. By implementing version control best practices, script developers can ensure high-quality, maintainable code that adapts smoothly to technological and organizational shifts. Throughout the scripting lifecycle, employing a robust version control system not only augments operational efficiency but also cultivates a disciplined approach to coding that anchors long-term project success.

10.6   Adhering to Shell Script Standards

In the development of shell scripts, including those written for Zsh, adherence to standardized coding practices is crucial for ensuring consistency, maintainability, and compatibility across diverse environments. Shell script standards serve as guidelines that help developers create scripts that are robust, readable, and portable. This section explores the importance of adhering to these standards and provides comprehensive insights into best practices in shell scripting.

- **Importance of Shell Script Standards**

  Shell script standards are critical for several reasons. They ensure that scripts are:

  - **Readable**: Clear and consistent formatting enhances readability, enabling developers to quickly comprehend the logic and flow of a script.
  - **Maintainable**: Applying standards makes scripts easier to maintain and extend, reducing the effort required for updates and minimizing errors.

- **Compatible**: Standards help ensure that scripts are compatible with different shell environments and versions, promoting portability.

- **Secure**: By following defined standards, developers can avoid common pitfalls that lead to security vulnerabilities.

The benefits of standardization are compounded in collaborative settings, where multiple developers or teams might contribute to a codebase, each needing to understand and work with scripts efficiently.

- **Basic Style and Formatting Guidelines**

  A fundamental aspect of adhering to shell script standards is maintaining a consistent style and formatting throughout your scripts:

  - **Indentation and Spacing**: Use a consistent number of spaces (commonly two or four) for indentation. This helps to visually delineate blocks of code, such as loops or conditionals, enhancing readability.

    ```
    #!/bin/zsh

    for file in *.txt; do
      if [[ -f "$file" ]]; then
        echo "Processing $file..."
      fi
    done
    ```

  - **Line Length and Wrapping**: To enhance readability, maintain a reasonable line length, typically not exceeding 80 characters. Long lines should be wrapped following logical breaks.

    ```
    #!/bin/zsh

    long_command --option1 value1 --option2 value2 \
            --option3 value3 --option4 value4
    ```

  - **Naming Conventions**: Consistently use lowercase names for variables and functions with underscores to separate words for clarity. Constants are usually written in uppercase.

281

```
#!/bin/zsh

output_file="results.txt"
readonly MAX_ATTEMPTS=5

process_file() {
  local filepath="$1"
  cat "$filepath"
}
```

- **Commenting and Documentation**: Include meaningful comments to describe complex logic or assumptions in the script. Provide a header at the top of the script detailing its purpose, author, and date.

```
# Script: data_cleaner.zsh
# Author: Jane Doe
# Date: 2023-10-01
# Purpose: Clean and normalize data files for analysis.
```

- **Structuring Shell Scripts**

  Proper script structure promotes organization and clarity:

  - **Logical Sections**: Divide scripts into sections such as variable declarations, function definitions, main logic, and cleanup. Use comments to demarcate these sections.

```
#!/bin/zsh

# Variable declarations
input_file="data/input.txt"
output_file="data/cleaned.txt"

# Function definitions
clean_data() {
  # Function to clean and process data
}

# Main logic
if [[ -f "$input_file" ]]; then
  clean_data < "$input_file" > "$output_file"
fi

# Cleanup
echo "Script execution completed."
```

  - **Functions for Modularity**: Break down complex scripts into functions to promote reusability and simplify testing and debugging.

```
#!/bin/zsh

calculate_average() {
  local total_sum=0
  local count=0

  for number in "$@"; do
    (( total_sum += number ))
    (( count++ ))
  done

  echo $(( total_sum / count ))
}

# Usage
calculate_average 10 20 30 40 50
```

- **Error Handling and Reporting**

  Robust error handling is a hallmark of quality scripts. Scripts should anticipate and gracefully handle common errors:

  - **Exit Codes and Error Messages**: Verify exit codes of commands and provide meaningful error messages.

    ```
    #!/bin/zsh

    if ! cp source.txt destination.txt; then
      echo "Error: Failed to copy file." >&2
      exit 1
    fi
    ```

  - **Assertions and Validation**: Implement checks for script assumptions, such as valid input types and expected outcomes.

    ```
    #!/bin/zsh

    assert_file_exists() {
      local file="$1"
      if [[ ! -f "$file" ]]; then
        echo "Error: File $file does not exist."
        exit 1
      fi
    }

    assert_file_exists "data.txt"
    ```

  - **Use of 'trap'**: Utilize 'trap' to ensure that cleanup activities occur even if the script exits prematurely.

283

```
#!/bin/zsh

trap 'echo "An error occurred. Cleaning up..."; rm -f /tmp/tempfile'
     EXIT

process_data() {
  # Simulated error
  false
}

process_data
```

- **Portability and Cross-Shell Compatibility**

  One of the challenges in shell scripting is writing portable code that executes consistently across different environments:

  - **Avoid Shell-Specific Extensions**: Write POSIX-compatible code when aiming for portability, using standard shell constructs that are supported widely.

  ```
  #!/bin/sh

  # Portable loop construct
  for file in *.txt; do
    echo "Processing $file"
  done
  ```

  - **Specifying the Interpreter**: Use a shebang ('#') to explicitly define the interpreter used for executing the script, ensuring predictable behavior.

  ```
  #!/usr/bin/env zsh
  ```

  - **Environment Variables**: Use explicit paths for executables and protect scripts from differences in environment variables across systems.

  ```
  #!/bin/zsh

  PATH="/usr/bin:/bin"

  # Use absolute paths for executables
  /usr/bin/grep "pattern" file.txt
  ```

- **Secure Coding Practices**

  Adhering to security standards in script writing is vital to prevent vulnerabilities like injection attacks:

284

- **Input Sanitization**: Validate and sanitize all external inputs to avoid potential security threats.

```zsh
#!/bin/zsh

sanitize_input() {
  local input="$1"

  # Remove harmful characters
  echo "${input//[^a-zA-Z0-9]/}"
}

user_input="input with special chars!"
clean_input=$(sanitize_input "$user_input")
```

- **Permission Management**: Set appropriate file permissions and avoid executing scripts with elevated privileges unless necessary.

```zsh
#!/bin/zsh

# Secure permissions for temporary files
temp_file="/tmp/data.txt"
chmod 600 "$temp_file"
```

- **Testing and Deployment Practices**

Testing scripts before deploying them is a critical step in the development lifecycle to ensure accuracy and efficiency:

- **Unit Tests**: Develop test cases for functions in scripts to verify expected behavior.

```zsh
#!/bin/zsh

test_calculate_average() {
  local result expected

  result=$(calculate_average 10 20 30)
  expected=20

  if [[ "$result" -ne "$expected" ]]; then
    echo "Test failed: expected $expected but got $result."
  else
    echo "Test passed!"
  fi
}

# Run tests
test_calculate_average
```

- **Continuous Integration**: Employ CI tools to automate the testing of scripts, catching regressions early.

- **Documentation and Change Logs**

  Maintaining comprehensive documentation helps others (and yourself at a future time) understand and utilize scripts effectively:

  - **Inline Comments and Docstrings**: Clearly comment functions and logic to explain behavior and assumptions.

  - **Change Logs**: Log changes in the script to track modifications over time.

    ```
    # Change Log
    # 2023-10-01: Added logging functionality
    # 2023-09-25: Fixed input validation bug
    ```

By adhering to shell script standards, developers can enhance the readability, maintainability, security, and cross-platform compatibility of scripts. Through consistent application of these principles, scripts transform from ad-hoc solutions into reliable, professional-grade software capable of addressing complex tasks and processes within modern computational environments.

www.ingramcontent.com/pod-product-compliance
Lightning Source LLC
LaVergne TN
LVHW051436050326
832903LV00030BD/3118